PAPER
JUGGERNAUT

Walter Stewart

PAPER JUGGERNAUT

Big Government Gone Mad

McClelland and Stewart

Copyright © 1979 McClelland and Stewart

All rights reserved

The Canadian Publishers
McClelland and Stewart Limited
25 Hollinger Road, Toronto   M4B 3G2

Printed and bound in Canada
by John Deyell Company

Canadian Cataloguing in Publication Data

Stewart, Walter, 1931-
Paper juggernaut

ISBN 0-7710-8306-8

1. Airports – Ontario – Toronto metropolitan area.
2. Airports – Ontario – Pickering. I. Title.

HE9797.5.C22T68   387.7'36'0971354   C79-094520-7

Contents

Chapter 1

The Comfortable Wasteland

Isobel Thompson, activist:
"What this did socially will never be measured. The families that were broken up, the neighbours who turned against each other, the friends who fell out, the people who took to drink, the hearts that went, the way it affected people. How many moved, how many gave up, how many turned against government, any government? There was no humanity in them. Old people would call at eleven o'clock at night, frightened out of their wits, and we would have to go over and calm them. To the government, they were just so many bodies to be moved."

William Huck, former Administrator, Canadian Air Transportation Administration:
"It's unfortunate that things have to be built that hurt people, but what can you do?"

The place is a mess. The house, solid brick, constructed more than a century ago, built to last, looks battered and forlorn. Generations have been born here, grown up, married, moved away, died. Nothing is left but memories – and trash. The doors have been smashed away, the windows shattered, plaster is torn from pock-marked walls and old lathing shows through, except where it is hidden by ribbons of mildewed wallpaper. Everywhere there is rubbish, broken bottles, crumpled cans, piled-up newspapers, half-full cartons of miscellaneous junk. Weeds have taken over the lawns and gardens, the bushes are overgrown, the small pond is stinking and green with slime. Most of the siding is missing from the gap-toothed barn, and in the machine shed, a farmer from a couple of concessions over is pulling down boards that were hammered into place before he was born; he's going to use them to expand his pigpen. It sure is a mess around here, he says.

The people who lived in this house have gone, nobody knows where, and now the place is a shelter of sorts, for kids who come into the area to raise hell. They use the house to smoke pot in, he thinks, and they bring girls here. He wouldn't let his daughter come here. Five generations were raised here, but now it is not the kind of place you would let your daughter come to. Beyond the machine shed, which will soon be stripped to a torn roof and battered frame – the supporting beams aren't worth the trouble of taking down – the farmland slopes down to the 26-27 Sideroad of Pickering Township. It is lovely country, a land of rolling hills and magnificent maples, towering pines, lush cornfields and rows of apple trees. This is some of the richest, as well as some of the prettiest, farmland in Canada, just north and east of the fringe of Metropolitan Toronto. A few miles away, there are teeming streets, jammed apartments, people with nowhere comfortable to live; here there are empty houses, crumbling walls, deserted lanes. It is an eerie place.

At first, it is hard to say exactly what it is that marks the land, that makes it unnatural. The cornfields are well kept, the roads in good repair, the scenery quite lovely. But there is only a scattering of people here. Up and down the concession roads and township lines, houses stand empty and forlorn, their windows torn out, their doors awry, their contents looted, their barns stripped, their gardens rank and overgrown. Just south of here, along busy Highway 7, stands a superb old farmhouse, crumbling into the ground. All the windows are boarded up, and the place looks blind. The barn has been ravaged of its siding and the shed roof has collapsed on the corpse of a bright red sports car. Along the Ninth Concession, a row of houses stands, each more battered and desolate than the last. Here and there across the rolling hills are the blank spots, where houses have been torn out and moved away, their cellars filled in, and nothing left to mark the place where families grew but the gardens, gone to seed, around the scar where a house once stood. The lawns that were placed here with infinite toil and tended with loving care have grown to hay, have disappeared, melded into the surrounding tangle. Hydro lines have been ripped away, and the lanes that wind through alleys of trees to once-cozy homesteads are torn and ditched, all but impassable. Everywhere, the implacable signs bark out prohibitions: "PRIVATE PROPERTY," "DO NOT ENTER," and "NO TRESPASSING." Once, sturdy farm trucks rolled down these lanes and, before that, horse-drawn wagons and buggies. Now, there are only the ceremonial patrols of security guards, who park their station-wagons at the bottoms of the lanes, trudge around the decaying houses, and make solemn note of the latest damage before driving off again.

Behind the façade of neat roads and crowded fields, this place

8

has not been as deserted since white men first settled here, early in the last century. Ghost towns are not unusual, but this tract outside Toronto is a ghost countryside, a comfortable wasteland. Corn is still grown here, and carefully tended, because local farmers rent the land, cheaply, for cash crops. Each spring, they sow the soil with corn and lash it with pesticides; each fall, they take off the crop, and if the land suffers from intensive cultivation with nothing returned, well, that is not the concern of the farmers. This is not their land, it belongs to the government.

Once, four million gallons of milk were taken off this land every year, and every year the area poured out 200,000 eggs, over a million pounds of beef, 375,000 pounds of pork, 45,000 bushels of wheat, and 30,000 chickens. But these were the crops of people who grew up here; now, what the area grows mostly is a hell of a lot of corn. Corn and despair are the principal crops. Once, there were families up and down these roads, and dogs barking, kids hollering, men working, women hanging out the wash – it was a community and had been a community for over a century. Now there are renters, and a residue of the original families, and everywhere the dead and decaying houses and the dead and decaying dreams.

It was not a hurricane that devastated this area; neither flood nor fire nor famine wreaked this havoc. The destruction was entirely man-made, the by-product of misdirected memos. Pickering Township lay across the path of a paper juggernaut; it was flattened by decisions taken a decade ago and hundreds of miles away by men who did not know, mostly, very much about what they were doing, and whose errors and omissions have produced a swath of scar tissue across the land, and across the lives of thousands of people while they, the decision-makers, have gone on to other tasks, writing more memos, readying more juggernauts.

This was to have been the site of Toronto's second international airport – TIA II, in the jargon, for Toronto International Airport II – and it was going to be a dandy. There would be six runways; well, maybe not six, maybe four. Well, if not four, then two. Well, perhaps only one runway, but it would be a nice long one, and there would be a spanking-new terminal building and parking aprons and cargo sheds and all the things that go with an international airport. It would have cost $204 million; well, perhaps $383 million, or it could be $542 million. Well, if you include the rapid transit system and the highways required, more. Let's call it a billion dollars. Okay, if you want to add the user costs, between $2 billion and $3.3 billion. Or perhaps more. Or less. Anyway, this new airport would have solved the problem of the heavy traffic pressures that now come on Malton Airport (TIA I), west of Toronto. Well, not exactly solved them, eased them. It would have taken a lot of the traffic away from Toronto, and everybody knows there is far too much traffic to be handled at the city's present international airport. Well, not too much now, of course, but there soon will be. There will be, by the year 2000, perhaps 198 million people flying through Malton every year. Well, wait, 198 million is too high, more like 96.4 million. Well, maybe not 96.4 million, let's call it either 66.4 million or 61.9 million or 46 million, or, anyway, somewhere between 33.9 million and 60.7 million. Unless, of course, there is something wrong with the figures. A lot of people. It is true, of course, that the traffic realistically expected for the Toronto region could be handled at Malton, but the trouble is that nobody would believe it could be done.

To expand Malton, while perfectly feasible from every physical point of view, would be – we have it on the authority of Transport Canada's most prestigious consultants – "not saleable." Ergo, there was to be another airport, of undetermined size, and God only knows what cost, to handle unspecified numbers of passengers, on this very spot.

In addition, for a mere $408 million more, there was to have been a brand new city southeast of the airport, a city already alive and gleaming on the drawing boards. It was to be called Cedarwood, or perhaps North Pickering. Something, anyway. It was to be put in place by the Ontario government; the airport by the federal government. As with the airport, the reasons for placing the city here were curious, but interesting. The province objected to the expansion of Malton airport – that is why that eminently sensible plan became "not saleable" – because such an expansion would bring the noise of speeding jets over the roofs and into the living rooms of 100,000 people in the Malton area. It would be better, fairer, politically more saleable, to build the airport out in the countryside, out, say, around Pickering. Then the province would plunk 200,000 people down beside that new airport. Perhaps these new people would have no ears, and the noise would not disturb them.

The idea of building a second airport for Toronto became a firm project in September of 1968, although the Pickering site was not settled upon until January 1972, more than three years later. The notion of building a city beside the airport sprang into being in 1971. Both projects were announced on March 2, 1972, and, had all gone according to plan, the airport would be operating today, and the first stage of the city would be occupied. However, all did not go according to plan. The land was seized from local property own-

10

ers, some of whom were delighted, some of whom were not, by means of expropriation. Actually, there were two expropriations. The federal government expropriated the tract of land for the airport – 18,000 acres – in 1972. The province tried to buy out the local landowners for its project, failed, and then applied its own expropriation in January 1974, to a plot that started out as 25,200 acres and then shrank to 17,000 acres. In all, 35,000 acres of land were taken outright. In addition, the province applied zoning controls to another 40,000 acres in such a way that the landowners, who were not compensated in any way, could no longer buy and sell or divide their lands as they wanted to.

The cost to acquire the land and plan the city and airport has never been tabulated. It is well in excess of $500 million, but neither the federal nor provincial government has ever released the full figures.

The airport, however, has not been built and the city has not been started and, God willing, neither project will ever get off the ground. I say "God willing," because there is a powerful push on, still, to go ahead as soon as the money is available and the stench of disaster is gone from the nostrils of the people.

In 1975, after three years of public struggle, the airport was shelved – not killed, but shelved – by the Government of Canada. The proposal for a city, never officially withdrawn, is still glimmering, although tarnished, in the planners' cabinets at Queen's Park in Toronto. Since 1975, Pickering has been in a state of suspended animation. The people who were thrown out of their houses have been allowed back, except where the houses had already been destroyed or moved away. Some of them have taken the opportunity and moved back; they are now renters in homes they used to own, gypsies on the soil that the ancestors of some of them began to till sixty years before Canada became a country. Many more moved away, some to hover on the edges of the wasteland, in new and inferior houses on cramped lots that were all they were able to buy with the money the government gave them for their property. Some of them are still fighting the governments – both governments – trying to get more money or their homes back, or simply asking for a day in court so that they can tell their stories to the world.

A local organization, People or Planes (POP), active in the long struggle to block the airport, still holds meetings every two weeks, waiting for the project to be revived. "You have to watch them every moment," says Pat McClennan, the Secretary of POP, "or the airport will be up and the city will be built, before you know it." POP Chairman Dr. Charles Godfrey says, "We have been fighting this

11

battle longer now than World War II lasted, and we're still throwing shells."

Deliberate deception and pervasive incompetence are evident in the Pickering saga, but, most appallingly, that story also shows that something has gone wrong with the decision-making process in Canada. It has been turned on its head. In theory, governments propose and bureaucrats dispose. In fact, the cabinet ministers involved seldom understood what they were deciding; they simply went along with the civil service. In theory, governments reach out for help in the decision-making process to outside experts who give impartial advice. In fact, the consultants are not neutrals, but allies, sparring partners and, occasionally, the directors of the bureaucrats who sign their requisitions. Public responsibility, the root of democracy, has been elided from the equation by the simple process of concealing any evidence that contradicts the official line. The arguments of confidentiality and cabinet solidarity are then used to block all enquiries and stifle all criticism. Although dozens of civil servants in several departments at both the federal and provincial levels knew that the public was being lied to, manipulated, and conned, none ever took a public stand, and such private demurs as did become public were disavowed. Time after time, civil servants I have interviewed about Pickering have told me that they, personally, knew there was something funny going on, but after all, one doesn't get ahead by rocking the boat. Not even when the boat is the *Titanic*. Canada's Official Secrets Act is so broad, so threatening, that our civil service is reduced, by the fear of going to jail for revealing anything that comes under its all-embracing strictures, to smuggling documents out of cupboards and mailing them in plain brown envelopes. Sir Thomas More believed in forthright courage as the weapon to defend the common weal against tyranny; our lads believe in the postage meter.

The victims of this trickery were the taxpayers in general and, in particular, the people who lost their homes, their families and their health. The phrasing is dramatic, but in the course of the past two years I have talked to dozens of people whose marriages dissolved, whose happiness was torn up, whose health was blighted in the brutal struggle over the airport. Three of the people I interviewed have suffered some form of mental breakdown. Perhaps they were headed for that anyway. I don't know; I only know that the people who cracked under the stress of years of uncertainty and argument and tension did not seem loony to me. In their position, I do not know that I would have fared any better. And the fact that so much of their distress was based on wrong-headedness or plain stupidity seems to me, as to them, unforgivable.

Just as unforgivable was the treatment of those who dared to lash back, who pushed for better deals in the courts. Some of these people were simply greedy; they saw a chance to cash in on the expropriation process and some, alas, were able to do so. Many more, however, were pushed to resist by the simple unfairness of their treatment. They saw that their homes were being taken from them, for no good reason, and they would never be able to buy comparable homes on the money the government was giving them. They saw, too, that officials of both levels of government were using misstatements, threats, and bullying tactics to try to force them to give away their homes at bargain-basement prices. So they resisted. Most of them were simply crushed. The court system, which was supposed to defend them, turned out to be yet another machine for oppression. Some of them could never even get into court. One group of former landowners, dispossessed in 1974, and whose claims of mistreatment were investigated and confirmed by the Ombudsman of Ontario in 1976, are still waiting, not for justice – they have long since given up much hope of justice – but just for a chance to state their case. The Pickering story shows, if we don't already know it, that the courts hold little relief for those who take on the bureaucracy.

Nor did society's other fail-safe mechanism, the public hearing, appear to work. Despite the enormous amounts of money involved, at no time was the Pickering project the subject of debate in either the federal or Ontario parliaments. Federal and provincial law both provide for hearings of necessity in the case of expropriations of this sort. The province met its responsibilities with two measures. In a hasty, late-night session, the Conservative government of Ontario amended its Housing Development Act to give the cabinet what amounts to *carte blanche* to do what it will with seized lands. The law was passed through all three stages in a single night, and opposition MPP's never knew what its real purpose was. They were misled into thinking it was passed to help with federal-provincial housing projects, when in fact it was aimed at Pickering. That action ensured that, in case of difficulties, the province could always win a court battle over expropriation. To make sure it would not have to fight one, the public hearing called for by law was simply eliminated, by fiat of the provincial cabinet.

The federal government met its responsibility to hold public hearings in a slightly different way. First, a hearing officer was appointed to receive evidence on the new airport, but no government witnesses were ever brought before him, so that no planner or expert could ever be subjected to cross-examination on either the

13

need for the airport or the choice of the site. The hearing officer, the late J.W. Swackhamer, was not allowed to make recommendations or draw conclusions, he was only allowed to hear and relay evidence. Nonetheless, he managed to make clear his distaste for the project and for the "ill-considered, incomplete and at times specious" studies on which the decisions were based. His report was filed and forgotten. Then, when public pressure built up for another public hearing, cabinet ministers promised, on ten separate occasions, that this hearing would be open and complete. It was not, and was never intended to be. The day that second hearing was announced, a secret decision had already been taken to ensure that it could come to no other conclusion than that the airport was needed and the site correct. A Royal Commission was established, but its terms of reference set down these two conclusions as the basis of its study. While contrary evidence was brought before the commission in fits and starts, it was never seriously considered. In the commission's terms, the subsequent report was guided by the governing Order-in-Council. In more prosaic terms, the fix was in.

The fix was in, not to smooth the way for a disciplined team of functioning professionals, who could not be turned aside from their necessary tasks to deal with the yammerings of the multitude, but rather to keep anyone from finding out how shoddy the planning process really was. In large part, the technique worked. To this day, the Pickering planning process has, in the main, remained a mystery. Such elements of the work as did come to light revealed glaring errors.

No matter how this project is seen, it is an unmitigated disaster. Suppose, for argument's sake, that the airport was needed, and the city was essential, and that some day they will still have to be built. Then, of course, we have wasted all these years, and much of the money, and everything is still to do. But suppose the opponents of the project were correct, suppose there never was a need for any of this. In that case, we have wasted all that money, and destroyed all those lives, for nothing. In either case, something went fearfully wrong.

This book is an attempt to show what went wrong and why it went wrong. It is a story of incredible bumbling, gross incompetence, and dumb arrogance. If the planners who conceived this project had known what they were about, the airport would now be in place, needed or not. During the course of my research, I have read a great many documents which no reporter was ever intended to see, and which set out the real, as opposed to the revealed, operating techniques of our bureaucrats and planners. The documents show that Pickering Airport was conceived for the wrong reasons, put in the wrong place, and then defended, when the time came for defence, by a long series of misstatements, circumlocutions, and lies. Strong words. The reader may decide for himself or herself if they are too strong.

The secret files make it clear that, had the information available to the government at the time been made available to the public, Pickering Airport could never have been started. Neither, come to that, could Mirabel Airport have been built, for, as we shall see, what happened in Montreal was a dress rehearsal for Pickering. The only difference is that, at Mirabel, the disaster is complete and operating; in Pickering, it is incomplete. Pickering's potential as a money-loser has been temporarily limited, while Mirabel is gobbling up about one million dollars of taxpayers' money with every passing week.

The documents also show that Pickering Airport was not proposed because any expert thought it was the right solution. The overwhelming consensus was that the expansion of Malton would be cheaper and better. It was built because, according to the official version, the experts did not think the public would believe them. The solution was to build the unnecessary airport and then to hide the evidence as to why it was being built. Nor was the site the proper one. Pickering was eliminated as a site for the second Toronto airport as early as the autumn of 1968, because it was not suitable. It was revived only when other sites proved even worse. Even then, it was not the first, not the second, not the third, but the fourth choice of the government planners. The solution, again, was to hide the information about its unsuitability and to construct a fictional scenario in which Pickering appeared to be the end product of a long and painstaking selection process. Nor was Mirabel built because it was needed, nor placed where it should have gone. In this whole damn story nothing was done because everybody in authority truly believed it should be done; it all happened by ghastly accident.

In short, neither Mirabel Airport nor the Pickering wasteland could have emerged from the shadows of a planner's file except for a policy of deliberate concealment, conscious evasion and outright lying that has become as much a part of our political process as ballots, polls, and returning officers. If we do not act to remedy this deficiency and reverse this policy, our history-to-come will be a series of Pickerings, and even more of us will fall victims to the paper juggernaut.

Chapter 2

The Mess at Mirabel,
Part I: The Windup

Margaret Godfrey, activist:
*"There was a man named Luther King, a recluse who lived just down
the road from here. He didn't understand any of this, of course. He
didn't have anything to do with anybody, he just kept to himself. Well,
they expropriated his home and took him to a nursing home in
Stouffville. Within two weeks, he was dead, and his home was
bulldozed."*

Dr. Josef Kates, consultant:
"Most of the people who objected were landed gentry."

Ben Higgins is a cheerful sort, a rotund, shrewd, brisk and charming man, but he is clearly puzzled. He leans back in his lawnchair,
on the sun-dappled grass beside his converted farmhouse just outside Aylmer, Quebec, runs a stubby hand through the remnants of
his grey hair, and smiles a quizzical smile. "What really surprised
me," he says, "was that they accepted my report so readily." He
laughs. "The Transport people were determined to build a second
airport, and once they made up their minds to that, they went
around looking for reasons why they had to have it. The real problem is that in the final analysis, no decision was made. Nobody ever
looks up and says, 'Do we need this thing?' What you argue about
is where to put it. We weren't asked 'Do you need it?,' only 'Where
should it go?' "

Ben Higgins – Professor Benjamin Higgins, Vice Dean for Research of the Department of Social Sciences at the University of Ottawa, author of a number of books on economics, world authority
on regional development – is the man who selected the site of Mirabel Airport. He now admits that "It hasn't worked out as we expected." He now says that "If all the facts had been placed before
us, I suppose I would have recommended the expansion of Dorval." He now notes that "They were in a tearing hurry to get this
done. They kept telling us that every week's delay would cost a mil-

lion dollars, although they never did explain how that came about."
As it turned out, every week's delay saved a million dollars, for that
is the rate at which Mirabel is losing money today.

The puzzlement of Ben Higgins explains a good deal about what
went wrong at Mirabel and what went wrong at Pickering, for the
Montreal and Toronto decisions were intertwined from the very beginning.

It all began, straightforwardly enough, in the boom in air travel
set off by the development of jet passenger planes in the 1950s.
Ocean-hopping became a sport, jet-setters a cliché, and cross-coun-
try travel, even in a country as awkward to cross as our own, became commonplace. Air traffic schedules blossomed, airports bus-
tled, terminals became clogged, and the Department of Transport
(as it used to be called; it became the Ministry of Transport in
1970, and it is now, bilingually, Transport Canada) began to wonder where it was going to put all those travellers. Between 1955 and
1965, the number of revenue passengers served at Canadian airports more than doubled – from 3,249,099 to 7,838,539 – and the
trend seemed likely to continue. (It did, too. The 1968 total was
11,875,000; air traffic more than tripled in thirteen years.)

By the end of the 1950s, the Department of Transport began to
mull over the idea of twinning some of Canada's airports and, in
July 1961, the Civil Aviation Branch brought down a report dis-
cussing such a possibility in concrete terms. The report dealt with
Toronto, where the most spectacular growth was taking place, and
was titled "Study On Need For Second Major Airport To Serve
Greater Toronto." Based on current trends, projected population
growth, and the state of air traffic control procedures – which have
much to do with how many aircraft can be landed on a given configuration of runways in a given period of time – the Civil Aviation
Branch made a series of predictions about air traffic in the Toronto
area through the year 1985.

The predictions were worked out, mainly, on the number of aircraft movements to be expected, and that requires a word of explanation. As aircraft become larger, the same number of passengers can be handled with fewer takeoffs and landings. One 747 jet
equals a dozen Viscounts; with a single take-off, it will remove hundreds of passengers where, a few years ago, its predecessor would
have carried thirty-six. On the ground, however, the larger planes
only make things worse, as they pour a deluge of passengers
through gates and into baggage areas that were designed for the
trickles of a simpler era. Transport experts therefore have two measures of forecasting: aircraft movements and passengers, but there

17

is little consistency in their use. Regrettably, the measure applied in any given case tends to be the one that best suits the argument to be made.

The 1961 estimates of aircraft movement were surprisingly accurate. In 1950, there had been 56,506 movements at Malton, and by 1960, the number had more than doubled, to 132,141. The study suggested that, by 1975, the figure would be 216,800, and by 1985, 294,700 – another doubling. The actual 1975 figure was 238,197; the boys had under-guessed by 9.8 per cent, which isn't bad, over a period of fifteen years. How would Malton cope with this kind of expansion? To find out, the CAB looked at American airports facing the same problem and concluded that, all things considered, they were coping very well, and so could Malton.

The airport had, built and projected, four runways and this is as good a place as any to describe the method of runway designation; it will not only allow the reader to follow what is to come, but lead him to a richer life and popularity at cocktail parties. Runway names are taken from compass headings, with one zero dropped off. The longest runway at Malton runs from, roughly, northwest to southeast, from 140 degrees on the compass to 320 degrees. It is therefore called 14/32. Where two runways are parallel to each other, which is common, they are distinguished by L and R, for left and right. Thus, at Malton, there are two runways in the direction 05/23 (roughly, southeast to northwest). When they are approached from the north, a pilot sees the northern end of one of these runways on his right; it is, therefore, 23R. The southern end of the same runway, approached from the south, is on the left – 05L. The whole runway, then, is 23R/05L, and its parallel is 23L/05R. There is a fourth, short runway at Malton, used for private aviation, in the 10/28 direction. (Note the opposite ends of runways are 180 degrees from each other, so that by adding or subtracting 18 from any runway number, you know its other end; if one end is 15, the other must be 33, and if that isn't cocktail party fodder, I give up.) The map indicates how Malton airport looks in respect to runways.

The capacity of runways depends on a number of factors that determine the speed at which planes can be landed on the same piece of pavement without either bumping into each other or upsetting each other by reason of wake vortex – the whoosh of air behind a fast-moving, large aircraft. A Cessna 240 can land behind another Cessna 240 almost instantly; both are travelling at the same speed, and neither kicks up much fuss; but to land a Cessna behind a jumbo jet is to invite disaster. The small craft may be flipped over by the wake vortex of the larger one. So, one limit on a runway's capacity is the mixture of aircraft to be accommodated, and there are strict rules governing the times and distances (together called "separations") to be maintained between various aircraft under various conditions. Then, too, planes can obviously be landed more easily on a bright, slightly windy day than during a howling blizzard in the middle of the night. The runway capacity is keyed to the inferior flying conditions, when all aircraft are landing by instruments, what the jargon calls IFR, for Instrument Flight Rules.

Away back in 1961, the CAB study found that "Air traffic control systems can at present . . . maintain a flow of 40 IFR arrivals per hour on one runway." There would be times when only one runway could be used, and times when the operation would be shut down entirely by bad weather. Nonetheless, by operating the airport eighteen hours a day (the norm at that time; it is now down to sixteen hours), and assuming a conservative sixty aircraft movements per hour on all runways as a working average, Malton could handle 394,200 aircraft movements per annum (60x18x365; the sixteen-hour figure, in case you were wondering, is 350,400). That capacity could be stretched even further by the simple device of constructing a runway parallel to 14/32. Since the projected traffic for 1985 indicated 284,700 movements per year, there was no need to build a second airport. Or, in the words of the report:

> Having measured the capability of Toronto International Airport by an assessment of the possible aircraft acceptance rates that may be achieved and then, as a separate measure, having compared Toronto International Airport with certain United States airports which are currently experiencing a greater volume of air traffic than is expected to occur at Toronto International Airport in 1985, it is concluded that a second major airport to serve the greater Toronto area will not be required within this period to relieve congestion at the existing airport.

A curious thing happened to this report. It disappeared. Although its conclusions have never been challenged, and its forecasts remain valid, it vanished from the public record. No one of consequence in Transport Canada has ever heard of it. I learned about it by accident. Yet, in this report, the CAB, basing itself on the primitive aircraft handling techniques and instruments of nearly two decades ago, said that Malton was more than capable of handling its predicted load, and if the number went up drastically, the solution was to build a parallel to runway 14/32. The Ministry later declared that Malton's capacity was effectively only 34 movements per hour, not the 60 allowed for in this document, and that 14/32 should not

19

be parallelled. Therefore a second airport became required. There was never any need to answer the contradiction, for the very good reason that the earlier report was buried.

As early as 1961, then, responsible officials faced the problem of whether to recommend the expansion of existing airports or the construction of new ones, and they preferred to build second airports. Why? For one who has watched the work of bureaucrats, my lot for many years, the answer is disarmingly simple. There are jobs and promotions and raises in the process of building things, and none in turning them down. I do not suggest that this reaction is entirely conscious, or that bureaucrats sit down every morning and say to themselves, "Now, what useless thing shall we build today?" I merely suggest that, given two reports, one proposing to build something – an airport, autoroute, or doghouse – and another proposing merely to tinker with the old facilities, the average bureaucrat tends to embrace the former and forget the latter. I put this theory to William Huck, Administrator of Air Transport from 1970-76, and he reeled back, horrified. "You must think there are a bunch of kooks up here who just want to build things," he said. It is an appealing theory, and explains far more than all of the voluminous studies on the record about the building of boondoggles.

So, while the 1961 Toronto study went onto the shelves, departmental experts kept an eye on the growing volume of air traffic, and calculated that existing airports would soon be swamped. Not only was air traffic increasing, however, it was moving inland. The fastest-growing traffic loads were at Malton in Toronto and Dorval in Montreal. Aircraft have not only been getting larger over the years, they can fly further without refuelling. Newfoundland was given a gorgeous new airport at Gander so that it could become the major entry port to North America. The facility was finished just in time to witness jets streaming by on their way to Halifax and New York. Now on most days, you could fire a cannon through the Gander Airport and hit nothing but an unemployed airport worker, sucking on a bottle of Screech. Then a magnificent structure was constructed for Halifax, and it too was completed just about in time to be bypassed.

Paul Davoud, who was the Chairman of the Air Transport Board from 1959-63, contends that he, and others, could see this happening, and tried to prevent it, but in vain. Davoud is a short, stocky, gruff man who now works as Air Adviser to the Ontario government's Ministry of Northern Affairs. Although he is in his late sixties, he still has gravel in his voice and fire in his belly, and he contends that, when he was asked about Gander Airport, he gave his

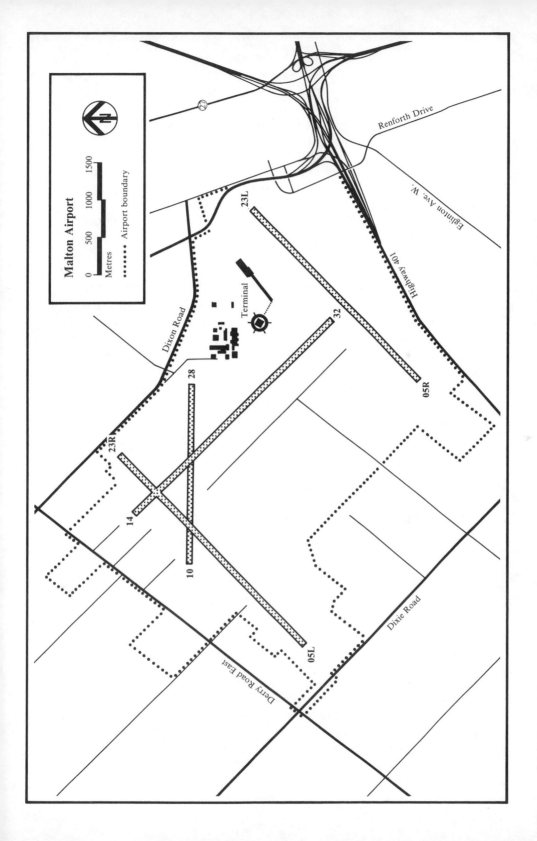

views clearly. "I said, 'By the time you get that built, the planes will be flying right over,' and that's just what they did. I wasn't popular."

It would happen again. In 1966, the federal government commissioned a series of studies on Canada's major airports. Each study was to produce a master plan for dealing with the oncoming crush of customers. In Montreal, the task was assigned to a firm that had no experience in aviation, although it had a good deal of expertise in consulting and planning work. That firm was Kates Peat Marwick, the Canadian branch of the British-based accounting firm, Peat Marwick. The company acquires partners and changes its name accordingly as it travels the world. In the United States, for example, it is known as Peat Marwick Mitchell, among other things. KPM's Canadian president was a slender, wiry, curly-haired, crisp-talking man, Dr. Josef Kates, who was born in Austria in 1921, educated in Toronto, and who was a well-known figure in Ottawa, Toronto, and Montreal as a government consultant. To provide the required airport experience, KPM subcontracted work to an American firm, R. Dixon Speas Associates, of Garden City, New York, and to add a little dash, KPM rang in Van Ginkel Associates, a Montreal firm that had been prominent in planning for EXPO '67.

In the summer of 1967, R. Dixon Speas made a preliminary report. It would be possible to handle the increased traffic projected for Montreal, just as had been proposed in Toronto, by building two sets of parallel runways, instead of the present three-runway arrangement. The problem of additional noise, bound to come with the new traffic load, could be met in part by designing the approaches to stay over the St. Lawrence River to the south and the Laurentians to the north. More land would be required for the expansion, and the bill would not be low – perhaps $300 million. However, there was no need to fall into the trap that had been sprung in other cities – Chicago, Washington, Paris – by building a second airport. Twin airports are expensive to operate, since they require the duplication of facilities for airlines, and the transfer of passengers.

What happened to the Speas study is a matter of some controversy. The company turned itself into a Canadian operation soon after this – it seemed a smart idea, to continue receiving government business – and re-emerged as Aviation Planning Services Limited of Montreal. Marinus Stade, Vice President of Aviation Planning, contends, "Our company said really Dorval can absorb this traffic. There is no requirement for a second airport. So they went to someone else who told them what they wanted to hear."

Eric McConachie, President of the Canadian firm, agrees. "They had pre-determined that they were going to put in a second airport. That was a decision that was made not by the Ministry, but by a consultant. When we took our study to KPM, Joe Kates said 'You've come up with the wrong answer.' We were pretty pissed off; we couldn't see why we had gone to all this work if they already knew what they were going to decide."

William Huck, Air Administrator at the time Mirabel was built, told me that he had never heard of the Speas study and there was, needless to say, no copy on the public record. So I asked Joe Kates about it. Kates left KPM in 1968, although he continued to work for the firm as an associate for the next five years. He became Chairman of Canada's Science Council in 1975, a post he relinquished late in 1978, and he now works, as Josef Kates Associates, out of a suite of offices at 40 University Avenue in Toronto. He was offended by my questions. He said that, while R. Dixon Speas did some minor work on Dorval's Master Plan, "They were only a subcontract to us." It was up to KPM, not Speas, to determine if Dorval could be expanded, and, "You could have expanded Dorval, sure, it would have worked, but it wouldn't solve the problems and it had a limited time span." There would still be noise to deal with, the enlarged facilities could only hold the traffic projected up until 1985, and, in any event, the cost would mount to "billions," not the $300 million cited. I asked Kates if he stopped Speas' report from going to the Ministry, and he replied, "R. Dixon Speas had full access to the department, and there was no reason why they couldn't have told them that." I then asked, four times in all, whether he, Kates, had said to representatives of the American firm, "You've come up with the wrong answer." He replied, on the fourth try, that he could not recall using those words; then he said he couldn't remember saying anything like that. He added, "Most of the meetings with R. Dixon Speas were conducted by Phil Beinhaker."

Philip Beinhaker is the President of IBI Associates, which also operates out of 40 University Avenue in Toronto. Indeed, Kates' telephone is answered in the IBI offices, around the corner on the same floor, with a cheery "Kates Associates" from IBI's receptionist. Beinhaker is a smallish man of medium frame, with thinning brown hair, a scraggly reddish beard and very sharp blue eyes. His father and his late uncle were both developers in Montreal, and he grew up with a natural interest in the process of planning and building. He graduated from McGill University in 1964 with a degree in architecture, worked in France and England for two years – his major effort was on a project at the University of Leicester – and returned to Montreal in 1966. There, he was hired by Van Ginkel Associates, the consulting firm that had a piece of the action, along with KPM, on the Montreal Master Plan. Beinhaker, a quick-witted, smooth-talking man, impressed fellow consultant Kates so favourably, that he was put to work full time on the airport. At first, he was subcontracted from Van Ginkel to KPM, but before long, he became a partner in KPM, and its instant expert on airports.

What Beinhaker says of the Speas controversy is that he doesn't recall "any such meeting" at which Kates told Speas' staff that they had come up with the wrong answer – although he does think it was the wrong answer. His recollection is that Speas did propose the expansion in a letter to Kates, but sent a copy to the then director of air planning in the Department of Transport, who is now dead. That proposal came, Beinhaker says, because "Dixon Speas had a definite bias to think of nothing but expanding the existing airport. They did not want the set of . . . for whatever reasons, they did not want the options expanded."

When I repeated the word "bias" back to him, he wanted to change it. "Well, I don't want to use words like that. I would say that Dixon Speas' professional opinion or opinions, as they expressed it in a number of situations, was just that." If you want to know the difference between a bias and a professional opinion, I would put it at about $50 an hour. However, "It was because we were unable to get the kind of analyses from them that we needed as to capacities and so on that we in the second assignment went ahead and got the Airborne Instrument Laboratories research arm to be our airspace consultants on capacities." Translation: "They went to someone else who told them what they wanted to hear."

The upshot was that, late in 1967, KPM presented the federal government with a report that said that while Dorval could be expanded, the job would be "excessively costly and operationally unsatisfactory." It therefore recommended "establishment of a new airport for the bulk of scheduled passenger and flight operations, using Dorval for general aviation and some short-distance scheduled flights." Dorval would be "de-emphasized" to justify the new airport.

The government then asked KPM to produce another report, this time on sites for a second airport. This is the "second assignment" Beinhaker referred to. The aviation experts, R. Dixon Speas, said expansion was feasible and practical, while KPM, which had never touched an airport in its corporate life, said it was not, and KPM's word was final. Kates explains that his firm's expertise was in "systems planning," that is, problem-solving, and that is why his people

24

were so much smarter than the chaps with experience. Beinhaker agrees.

There were those who did not agree. One of them was Paul Davoud. He maintains, "There is a team at Transport, a team of architects, planners, developers, designers, whose sole survival is based on building bigger and better airports. Mirabel was a classic case. The airlines were going to move to Toronto. Montreal had been the gateway to Canada because you had to land there, the planes wouldn't go any further, but Toronto was the market people were heading for, and when they could overfly Montreal, they would. Now they can. You could see it coming, and the airlines kept on trying to tell the Ministry, but nobody would listen. They had to have an airport, and that was that."

Davoud's bitter analysis is confirmed, in a left-handed way, by William Huck, the former Air Administrator. Huck told me that it would have been better if the government had built the airport at Pickering, but not the one at Montreal. Why? "Because that's where the traffic is, but, what the hell, it takes seven years to build new facilities and you have to do it on the basis of projections and sometimes your projections don't come true."

However, the Ministry wasn't the only outfit with projections. The International Air Transport Association, based in Montreal, also projected more traffic for Montreal, but felt, and still feels, that the solution was to expand Dorval.

For whatever reason, then, KPM was assigned to advise the federal government on the site of a second Montreal airport, which the Air Administrator, the original aviation consultants, and the industry all agree was not needed. In all, twenty locations were looked at, and then narrowed down to five. These were: a site on Ile Perrot, just west of Montreal; one near Vaudreuil, further west; one at St. Jean, on the south shore of the St. Lawrence; one at Drummondville, also on the south shore, but further east; and one thirty-four miles north of the city, just off the Autoroute des Laurentides, near the town of Ste-Scholastique. On April Fool's Day, 1968, under the direction of Philip Beinhaker, the new aviation expert, KPM reported to the Department of Transport, advising in favour of a second airport at Vaudreuil. A facility there would cost less to build and operate than at any other spot, requiring, KPM suggested, an expenditure of $520 million between 1967 and 1985, in construction and user expenses. The location was near the major east-west transportation corridor, and it would work well in tandem with Dorval. The site on Ile Perrot was dismissed as likely to conflict with the air operations of Dorval, and the other sites were shown to be more expensive. Most expensive of all was the Ste-Scholastique site, which would cost $757 million to acquire, build and operate until 1985. It also presented difficulties in the operation of radar and other electronic equipment because of the mountains nearby. These difficulties would vanish. If the Vaudreuil site wouldn't work, KPM's second choice was the southern site, near St. Jean.

The April 1, 1968, report which, like so many, remains sheltered from the rude public gaze, set off a furious behind-the-scenes debate between the Province of Quebec and the federal government. The Department of Transport accepted KPM's advice, and proposed to build its airport west of Montreal. However, the province did not want it on the Ottawa-Montreal corridor. In a series of meetings that began on September 10, 1968, representatives of two governments met to resolve the issue. It is clear that the federal flag was carried by Philip Beinhaker, and that the Quebec people assumed at first that he was with the Department of Transport (he is so listed in the minutes of the early meetings); in fact, he was not, he was still with KPM, and seconded to the Ministry, but the line between an outside consultant and a civil servant seemed to disappear. The minutes of a Quebec government technical meeting, October 1, 1968, show that "*Monsieur Beinhaker a été le principal interlocuteur pour le fédéral.*" The minutes also show that "*le fédéral*" was pushing its western site aggressively, and that if the province wanted a southshore site chosen, and it did, it would have to respond "with strength and precision." That was done, and the result was stalemate. Ottawa felt it could not proceed without at least some support from the province, which would have to supply the roads and services, and Quebec would not accept a site where the development, and jobs, might drift westward into Ontario. On November 29, 1968, Municipal Affairs Minister Robert Lussier wrote Transport Minister Paul Hellyer to say that the federal-provincial committee could not agree on a site. The solution was to bring in a referee.

Besides, there was a new factor. While Paul Hellyer was still Minister of Transport – he would not stalk away from the Trudeau cabinet until 1969 – his was a waning star. The rising star belonged to Jean Marchand, Minister of Regional Economic Expansion, and Marchand said it would be wrong to pick an airport without considering the impact on Quebec's regional base. Who better to do this than Ben Higgins, an acknowledged expert, and an old friend of Prime Minister Trudeau – they had taught together at the University of Montreal, where Higgins was still teaching at this time.

So he was approached and appointed, on December 11, 1968, to determine which of the four sites that remained in the running (St. Jean, Drummondville, Vaudreuil, and Ste-Scholastique – the airspace conflict finished Ile Perrot forever) would best suit the needs of regional economic expansion.

"My terms of reference," Higgins says, "indicated that this airport would be the entry to Canada, perhaps a major entry port for all North America, for overseas flights." There was talk of supersonic jets landing there, and a Montreal paper tried out the name "Concorde" for the new airport. It was not to be. The decision had already been made to add a second airport to the Toronto area, but Higgins was not told that. (The Appendix contains a chronology that makes the dates clear.) He formed his conclusions on the assumption that this facility was to be the major Canadian entry port. He worked, day and night, out of his home on Jeanne Mance Street in downtown Montreal. One of his principal advisers was KPM's whiz-kid, Phil Beinhaker. Higgins says, "He's very bright and apparently made a big impression on the people from DOT. The department would not have gone along with any recommendation to which Beinhaker was opposed."

Higgins began with the assumption that a second airport was necessary. "I always had the impression that the DOT people were set on a second airport and wouldn't listen to anything else." He had never heard of the Speas report. He also assumed that the airport would be served by a rapid transit system; indeed, it made no sense to him if it were not, but again, this was not to be. "I never trusted the DOT people. We were told for example, that there would be rapid transit and a new road system from Dorval and a bridge. That bridge was one of the factors in our choice, because access would be swift and easy." There is no rapid transit, and no complete new road system, and no bridge (this was to cross the Ottawa River near Pointe Fortune, to link Quebec's Highway 29 to the Trans Canada Highway).

The bridge issue was raised privately with Higgins only a week before the professor handed in his report, in an unusual meeting with Joe Kates, on Saturday, January 10. Higgins' notes of the meeting show that the KPM president argued that the new airport "must be a highly integrated part of the Montreal region." However, he wondered, "How can the Province of Quebec build $200 million bridges when it can't meet its debts today?" Despite these reservations, Kates came down for the Ste-Scholastique site, which "contains new concepts to which people must be alerted, makes excellent economic and planning sense." And that's the way it came out in the official report.

In looking at the four sites, Higgins was able quickly to dismiss the provincial favourite, St. Jean, on curious grounds. There were a number of technical objections to the site, Higgins says, but the one given publicly was that it would conflict with American airspace.

"Under an international treaty at the time, airspace over 10,000 feet was in control of the u.s. air force at Plattsburgh, New York." The simple solution would have been to vary the treaty, but the explanation given was that the Americans would not allow it. In fact, the refusal came from Ottawa. "Under some pressure from Ottawa, the u.s. refused to revoke the treaty. We thought there were good reasons for rejecting St. Jean, and that is why we didn't reveal that particular secret."

As a matter of fact, the government of Quebec suspected that there was something fishy with the public explanation, but was never able to prove it. The province had hired Professor Robert Simpson, Director of the Flight Transportation Laboratory at the Massachusetts Institute of Technology, to advise on its site selection, and Simpson said that St. Jean was quite acceptable. "But there was this curious soft spot; the Americans, it was said, wouldn't allow a revision in the airspace treaty. It made no sense, but there it was."

Once the province's pet site was scuttled, Higgins turned to the more serious work of examining the other sites. "Our argument was very sophisticated. We found that the impact of a new airport tends to be concentrated between the airport and the metropolitan centre it serves. [We will meet this argument again, in reverse, when we look at Pickering.] Enterprises move into that area, and people move in around the enterprises. If you put the airport at Drummondville, people would move from areas east of there to the Drummondville-Montreal corridor; you wouldn't help the Eastern Townships, you would hurt them. If you put the airport west of Montreal, it would not help. Growth couldn't come east [i.e., along the corridor between the new airport and Montreal] because that area was already occupied. So it would go west, into Ontario." The province had figured out that much already; it was part of the objection to the western site.

That is how Ste-Scholastique came to be justified. "The idea was that if you put the airport just east of the Autoroute, that would act as a kind of wall, and the growth would go where you wanted it. It was like a balloon effect, one side would get pushed the way you wanted it." East of the Autoroute this far north of the city was barren land and farmland, just the kind of place to put new development. Ste-Scholastique was chosen, then, not because it made a good airport site, but because it made a good balloon. There was, of course, one drawback; if the airport was not really needed, there would be no growth, and no balloon. So it came to pass.

Higgins turned in his report on January 17, 1969, and later complained that he had only seventeen working days to produce it. That brought the tart comment from a fellow professor, Edward McWhinney, "Why on earth, under those circumstances, as a reputable economist, did he accept the federal government's brief? The sensible thing to do, surely, was to point out to the federal government the essential complexity of the problem and to insist on more time."

Higgins' explanation is that he thought he was producing one of a series of preliminary briefs that would be put into the mix. Instead Ottawa was so anxious to be a-building, his hasty document was made the basis for the choice, on March 27, 1969, of Ste-Scholastique as the site of Montreal's second airport.

Quebec wasn't going to like it.

Chapter 3

The Mess at Mirabel,
Part II: The Pitch

Eugene LaBrie, lawyer:
"Mirabel will demonstrate the stupidity of the two-airport system in a way that politicians can understand, namely, the loss of fifty million dollars a year."

Paul Hellyer, former Transport Minister:
"Notwithstanding the inconvenience of the moment, Mirabel will look pretty good in ten or fifteen years."

When the federal government began to blow its trumpets for the choice of Ste-Scholastique as the site of Montreal's second airport, no mention was made of the fact that the technical studies favoured another site, nor of Quebec's vigorous, but so far private, objections to the decision. The price tag put on the facility, $290 million, had little to do with the $757 million that had been used in the Kates Peat Marwick report of April 1, 1968. To get the new figure, all user costs – that is, the cost to airlines of running facilities in two places, and the costs of transferring passengers, were simply ignored, as was the cost of a rapid transit system. (This little trinket was estimated at $250 million for a single line, $438 million for two lines; it had been left out of the KPM report, too.) All that was included were estimates of land acquisition and construction, and these were hopelessly low. The federal government believed its share would come to $175 million, and that the province would pay $75 million for roads and services, and the airlines $40 million. The airport was going to be in operation by the end of 1974, and would serve 3.7 million passengers in its first year, rising to 14 million by 1985, by which time it would be expanded. For this was not to be one of your little airports; the $290 million figure only covered stage one, with one terminal and two runways. Before the government was done there would be three terminals and six runways and lots more money to spend.

When the site was unveiled, the province was furious. *La Presse,*

Montreal's largest newspaper, put its finger on the only point that mattered: "The airport is fifteen miles from Ontario and twenty-five from Montreal." (Actually, it was thirty-four from Montreal, but let it pass.) Premier Jean-Jacques Bertrand telegrammed Prime Minister Trudeau to say the site was "unacceptable," and Trudeau, at a press conference, gave the retort courteous; he said Bertrand was "off his rocker." These preliminaries out of the way, the work began. Because it was clear that Quebec was not likely to prove co-operative in the circumstances, it seemed wise not to trust the province to provide the necessary zoning regulations around the airport. Therefore, a suggestion made earlier by KPM was acted upon, and the federal government expropriated a block of 88,000 acres for the site. Dorval covers 3,500 acres.

Much of the area seized was farmland, some of it scrub, some of it excellent, and one of the farms was called "Mirabel," a happy combination of "Miriam" and "Isobel," two daughters of one of the owners around the turn of the century. That name was adopted for the entire complex.

Many of the locals were pleased to unload their land on the federal government, especially when they could lease it back again, at low rates, to farm on until it was needed. Some were not so happy, and some who started out happy became unhappy later on, when they learned of higher prices paid to farmers around Pickering for the airport there. There were protest marches and demonstrations, but no highly organized resistance. There was no requirement for public hearings under the federal Expropriation Act at the time – Pickering would provide the first trial run for a new law passed in 1970 – and the malcontents were divided, inarticulate and frightened. Even so, the government had to shell out more than it expected. In its 1968 report, KPM had told Ottawa to expect to lay out $20 million for land (an estimate based on 50,000 acres), but the actual bill was $151 million, and there was another $1,280,603 to pay later, for claimants who were able to prove in court that they had been short-changed. This total, $152,280,603, came close to the $175 million given as the entire federal cost; it also made the original land estimate wrong by 760 per cent, which might have caused thoughtful persons to wonder if the planners really knew what they were talking about.

Work at the new airport did not go quickly. The airlines were sore as a boil because they had not been consulted about either the need or location of the facility they were going to have to pay for, through user charges. There was the soundest reason for not consulting them; they would have said things the Ministry did not

31

want to hear. Airlines have discovered in twin-airport systems the world over that it costs a lot of money to run two facilities out of one city, and it causes a lot of inconvenience, and it tends to make the customers – their customers, not the government's – hopping mad. Better to keep the airlines in the dark. The same technique, for the same reasons, and with the same results, was later applied to Ontario.

So the airlines were not really enthusiastic about helping the authorities to lay out their dream airport. It seemed to be out of their hands, anyway. A consortium of planning firms had taken over Mirabel. This consortium did not include KPM, although that firm's Philip Beinhaker was the project's general manager during the initial construction phase. It was not the time for an Ontario-based, English-connected firm to grab off the fattest contract while local boys waited in the ante room. Accordingly, CAIM – Consultants en Aéroports Internationaux de Montréal Ltée. – was formed out of three resolutely Quebec firms: Bland/LeMoyne/Shine and Victor Prus; Surveyer/Nenniger/Chenvert, Inc.; and Beauchemin/Beaton/Lapointe.

CAIM's contract with Her Majesty the Queen, which, like all the other really interesting material, is not for public consumption, is a curious document. It was signed on April 23, 1970, and it called on the new firm to "provide management services for the planning, scheduling, establishment of design packages, supervision of design work, as well as any other services required for planning, design, construction and completion of Phase I of the said airport."

CAIM was responsible for cost controls, and it was to bring in the finished airport in May 1974, at a target cost of $81,113,300, a figure that makes me giggle every time I think of it. It turned out to have what the beauty-lotion ads call "cellular expansion factor." For their work, the consultants were to get a fee of $12,167,000. That, of course, was on top of all expenses, which included the salaries of all employees on the project, plus 65 per cent extra, in most cases, for general overhead.

It didn't work out as planned. Even after a change in provincial governments – Bertrand and his pesky Union Nationale government were replaced by Robert Bourassa and his Liberals in 1970 – federal-provincial co-ordination did not go too well. And then, with the airlines kicking up a stink, and the plans changing all the time, well, nothing seemed to go right.

The airport was planned around a new concept. Instead of the higgledy-piggledy mess at most terminals, with arrivals on one level and departures on another, and restaurants, shops, and booths squeezed in everywhere, all the services would be on the top level and all the passenger movement on the lower level. The airlines didn't like it, and it took time to design, and the terminal cost $80 million instead of the $61 million budgeted. Then there was the question of how to get people on and off airplanes. Permanent gates cost money, about $1 million each, so Mirabel would save some of that. Like Dulles Airport outside Washington, it would be served by Passenger Transfer Vehicles – PTVs – huge mobile lounges that can be shifted around the airport as needed. They cost about $400,000 each, and the government laid on fourteen of them, so that came to $5,600,000. It would have been cheaper to put in gates.

Then there were strikes among construction workers – which you can't expect planners to know about, although they happen on every construction project of this size – and delays in the delivery of materials and foul-ups in co-ordination and changes in design and, pretty soon, it was getting on for May 1974, and no airport in sight.

The CAIM contracts were amended, and then they were amended again, and again, until, on April 20, 1976, the final contract was signed. It contained all the same clauses as before, enjoining the consultant to control costs and bring the airport in on time, but now the target cost was up to $235 million, CAIM's take was up to $25,637,500, and the contract was due to end on June 30, 1976. The bit about the airport being complete by then was very decently left out, because the airport was operating at last. Remember that CAIM wasn't building the airport, it was just supervising the work of others; controlling costs, as it were. And while the costs nearly tripled, CAIM's fee more than doubled. I asked William Huck, the Air Administrator, why consultants are always brought into these things. Why couldn't the government train its own people and do its own supervising? He told me that this way saved money.

When Mirabel's cost overruns began to come to light, the federal government took the usual course – stout denial. Transport Minister Donald Jamieson, speaking in the House of Commons on May 4, 1972, said that the difference between the original estimate – which you will recall was $175 million at the federal end – and the $344,649,000 figure which had then been reached was "quite within the normal difference that one would expect in a project of this size." If doubling the budget within three years is within normal range on any large project, what will the Canadian Arctic pipeline, now estimated at $12 billion, actually cost?

The airport was finally scheduled to open on October 5, 1975, nearly two and a half years late. But it did not – except officially. There was a splendid ceremony, and speeches from the Prime Min-

33

ister and other lofty persons, but no actual movement of aircraft. The Prime Minister added to the dignity of the occasion by saying that Torontonians, whose own airport had been shelved by this time, would soon be down at Mirabel "on their knees," begging for a similar facility. Ottawa laid on $20,000-worth of liquor and $48,000-worth of food and, in all, the federal government spent $81,019 to stage the opening. Quebec, which seemed to get into the swing of things once the ripe contracts began to flow, lashed out $427,865, a sizable chunk of it in hospitality, and $25,000 in advertising.

But there were no airplanes, because the place wasn't ready yet. It wasn't ready on October 26, either, the next official date, due to such minor technicalities as a lack of electricity in some areas, no windows in the cargo section, and an unfinished water system. Airlines were pressured to move out to Mirabel, even in these conditions, because Ottawa was beginning to get embarrassed. When some operators balked, they were told they could remain in business at Dorval for a while longer, as long as nobody ratted to the press.

When Mirabel finally went into operation on November 30, 1975, it turned out that all the people who said it was the wrong facility in the wrong place were quite correct. The Ministry forecast of passengers was wildly wrong; instead of 3.7 million passengers, there were fewer than three million, despite pressure on airlines to use the new toy. The operators noted bitterly that it cost them $32 a head to handle passengers through Mirabel, compared to a North American average of $7. Air Canada alone estimated that it paid out an extra $6 to $7 million annually because of the new airport. Since there was no rapid transit, customers found themselves being nicked up to $35 for a taxi ride out from Montreal, although a metered ride should come between $20 and $25. And there were the confusing, maddening delays, minor outrages, and lost luggage for those who had to transfer from Dorval. (Friends of mine going to the West Indies from Toronto had to leave from Mirabel, which meant flying to Dorval, transferring airports, staying overnight in a hotel and doing it all over again on the way home. Their extra cost: about $250.) The place became a cursing and a byword. Boston's Logan Airport took out newspaper ads to thank Mirabel for being so inconvenient, and inviting customers bound for Europe to fly through Logan instead. Aer Lingus flights from Toronto to Dublin transfer through Mirabel, and the airline reported a drop in business of 50 per cent, as customers found ways around the twenty-nine mile, $30 cab ride from Dorval. Scandinavian Airlines reported a similar drop, of 30 per cent, in its bookings. Corporations, too, were finding costs on the rise. William Turner, President of Consolidated Bathurst, put his company's extra bills down at $50,000 to $100,000 a year, and he told *Maclean's* magazine, "There's nothing wrong with Mirabel that putting it in mothballs wouldn't fix."

A 1976 survey of Ontario travel agents showed that they were avoiding Mirabel "like the plague." The survey was commissioned by Toronto opponents of the Pickering scheme, on the lookout for ammunition. They got it. Of the agents who responded to the survey, 79.4 per cent reported that they avoided booking clients through the new airport, and their comments on experiences with it ranged from "terrible" to "ridiculous." In a typical reply, Dominion Travel Agency of Toronto noted that "Two airport systems are an abomination in air travel that is to be avoided at all costs." The language wasn't elegant but the meaning was plain. The airport wasn't much more popular at home than in Ontario. The de-icing system wouldn't work, and there was a problem with mice in the basement, to say nothing of a series of scandals involving contractors working, or trying to work, at Mirabel. The scandals came out pretty tamely – four men were charged, so far a man and one construction firm have been convicted, and the amounts involved are not large, $1,500 is the highest payoff to come to light to date. Still, it all caused embarrassment.

Meanwhile, the costs kept mounting. Because of the transfer of flights to Mirabel, Dorval began to falter. Its operating profit in 1975-76 was $12.8 million; a year later, it was down to $1.1 million. There were other costs, too. Four thousand acres of land around Mirabel, which was to have been turned into industrial parkland, in line with the Higgins Report, was developed at a cost of $4 million. It stands empty.

As for Mirabel itself, it lost $115 million in its first two years. Otto Lang, the Transport Minister when this figure was given to Parliament on February 28, 1978, said it was unfair to use it, because the amount included interest charges. Apparently, the government had never expected to pay interest charges. Maybe it was going to borrow the money from CAIM. In fact, it is almost impossible to tell what the real cost of Mirabel has been, because the government keeps fooling with the figures. On May 6, 1974, in response to a written question on the Order Paper, the Transport department gave Mirabel's cost as $391,118,000 at the federal level. Two years later, on May 5, 1976, a similar question drew a figure of $322,039,000. The airport had shed nearly $70 million. How? Well, different bookkeeping was used, and different items included. In fact, neither figure appears to take account of the consultants' fees. Besides CAIM's $25,637,500, another $16 million went to other consultants, according to the answer to a question, tabled October 27, 1975 (KPM's share of this was $712,320). The original estimate for consultant fees on the project was $6 million; that cost alone had multiplied nearly seven times.

The generally accepted figure, the one now used by the Toronto *Globe and Mail*, the *Financial Times*, and the *Montreal Gazette*, is that Mirabel's capital cost was $600 million, to which should be added $155 million in operating costs to date. However, that figure is far too low. In June 1978, a draft report was prepared for the government, under the imposing title, "Study of Procedures In Cost Effectiveness, Mirabel Airport." It concluded: "The total cost for Phase I of Mirabel may range between $1,116-$1,426 million."

This tough, forty-four-page document made it clear that "value has not been received for money expended. Economy was disregarded." Not only were the cost overruns staggering, but the traffic forecasts were wrong, and the airport may not have been necessary.

> The revised forecast for the Montreal area predicts 14.6 million passengers by 1990 – the original forecast was for 30 million. Net revenue from Mirabel adjacent land to 1977-78 amounts to a net loss of $7.7 million compared to a forecasted gain of $52.5 million . . . .
>
> In the light of these findings, failure to properly evaluate an expanded Dorval as an alternative was crucial. The prime objective – to make Mirabel self-sustaining – has not and will not likely be achieved for many years.

This report, like so many others, has remained concealed in the desks of all the bureaucrats but one, who sent it to me.

The federal bureaucrats did recognize, in a dim and distant way, that something had gone wrong at Mirabel, and they were anxious to make amends. A white elephant has now been adopted as the official emblem of the airport. However, when the time came to apply the lessons learned at Mirabel to Pickering, the government decided that only an experienced expert could handle the job. That's right; fresh from his triumph in Montreal, Phil Beinhaker was called down to help out the lads in Toronto.

Chapter 4

Looking
for Pickering

Pat McClennan, Secretary, People or Planes
*"First they would send around a man who would say he was offering to
purchase the property, but the paper you signed said you were a willing
seller. If you were smart, you wouldn't sign that. The first batch were
rude, cursing, insulting, they caused several heart attacks. They went to
a man whose family had been here since 1807. He ran a cider mill, but
he sold it and lived in a small, immaculate house. They sent in a guy who
said, 'You may as well sell now, you're going to be expropriated
anyway.' At that time, you couldn't buy anything else here. You couldn't
buy a chicken house. The man said, 'I've never had a mortgage in my
life,' and the government man said, 'You're going to have one now.' The
man was seventy-six. He died a couple of years later.*

*"Then there was Phase Two; they were all sweetness and light, but
still with the threat of expropriation. One day a mother with two kids
came in to the POP office, she told me every day her kids say to her 'Has
Mr.Davis got our house yet?' Another time a woman called and said,
'Well, they've won; my husband had a heart attack today.'*

*"Until the very end, we never had the feeling that anybody would
listen to us. One time a whole bunch of government people came out here
to talk to us, but none of them amounted to much. We asked them if the
protest vote we took at that meeting would be drawn to the attention of
the Minister, and the answer was No. 'Well,' we asked, 'what about the
Deputy Minister?' Still No. Then Monte Dennis got up and said, 'Say, if
you run into one of those guys in the john, tell him, will you?' "*

**Don Stone, former Director, Airside Planning, Toronto Area Airports
Project:**
*"I was excited about it. I was pleased when I got the job. At least the
government was going to sterilize the ground."*

The 1961 study, which concluded that there was no need to build a
second airport in the Toronto area, did not end the matter, by a
long shot. Traffic continued to boom. A spanking new terminal,

completed in 1964, at a cost of $47 million, was designed to process 3.2 million passengers annually, but by 1967, there were already four million people streaming through the facility. A forecast made at that time predicted a traffic load of 6.6 million in 1970, 14.4 million in 1980, and 25 million by the turn of the century. These guesses were pretty shrewd. Toronto did see 6.4 million air travellers in 1970, and probably will handle about 14 million in 1980. (However, some of the guesses made in the cabinet document that contains these figures were not so smart; one notes "Supersonic aircraft may be ready to begin operation from Toronto in 1972 or shortly thereafter.")

The consulting firm called in to help with the Toronto Master Plan to meet the projected growth was John B. Parkin Associates, the company that had designed the new terminal. Parkin, like KPM in Montreal, turned for advice to R. Dixon Speas and R. Dixon Speas felt, as it had in Montreal, that the problem could be solved by expanding the current facilities. This time, the advice was not so snootily received, but then, Parkin had an advantage compared to KPM – it had actually done this work before. In a report on November 9, 1967, Parkin found that "All elements and components of the complex can be developed and increased to a capacity that will satisfy the forecast of air traveller demands to the year 1986, and even to the end of the century."

On July 11, 1968, the federal Cabinet accepted a recommendation from Minister of Transport Paul Hellyer, based on the Parkin Plan. It called for the expansion of Malton airport by building another runway parallel to 14/32 – the same idea that had been raised in 1961 – and new terminal facilities. The government would have to purchase three thousand acres of additional land because, at that time, a separation of at least one mile between parallel runways was considered safe, and that would extend the airport boundaries. Most of the needed land was unoccupied, and Parkin calculated a purchase price ranging "up to $10,000 per acre," or a total maximum of $30 million. Had that advice been taken, it would have been the smartest money a government had spent since the Louisiana Purchase. In all, the expansion would cost $250 million, take twenty years and "extend the life of the airport until the year 2000." The concept depended on some co-operation from the local municipalities and the Province of Ontario to control building in the noise zones around the growing airport.

The Parkin Plan was unveiled by Hellyer on August 2, 1968, along with an announcement of the minister's intention to begin negotiations with the other governments, and a promise to hold public meetings to discuss the project. The open approach in Toronto was in stark contrast to what happened in Montreal, and the government will never make that mistake again. The report had barely landed on the desks of Toronto newspaper editors before their mailboxes began to bulge with the complaints of the locals. Malton ratepayers were outraged. To expand the airport would increase the noise and decrease the value of their neighbourhoods. (The decline in land values seems obvious, but it did not happen. House prices off the noisiest runway in the Malton area have kept pace with those in other sections of Toronto.)

Like people the world over, Canadians are drawn to airport sites because they think the land and housing there will be cheap because of the noise. Once settled in, they begin to call for removal of the noise. In this case, there was more than the usual whining involved. Malton people had known what they were getting into when they moved there, but they had not counted on the noise spreading or the flights becoming more frequent. The argument that if they didn't bear the burden, someone else would have to, did not strike them favourably. It never does. The good burghers of Pickering, when their turn came to face this point, would extend formal sympathy to the Malton victims, but what they wanted, what we all want, is a convenient airport located anywhere but here.

The Malton area had more than a sense of grievance going for it. The province had not discouraged – indeed, had promoted – development around the airport, and one of the local MPPs was a powerful cabinet minister, soon to become premier, William Davis. His home in Brampton lies not far off one of the Malton approaches, and his neighbours and constituents added their roar to the rumble of overflying aircraft. The protestors had a friend in court. They also had loud voices. There were a number of public meetings at which federal and provincial spokesmen were addressed in forceful terms, there were letters to the editor and pamphlets and petitions and when it was all over, the Department of Transport caved in. On December 20, 1968, Hellyer rose in the House of Commons to announce that, because of the obvious opposition to the Parkin Plan, it would be rejected. Instead, the search for a new airport would begin.

The intriguing thing about Hellyer's announcement was that, although the reason given for the decision was the protest, and although all documents from that date forward refer to the December 20 announcement, as if it marked a change of direction, the search for a new airport was already well under way. In a memorandum dated November 26, 1968, C.A. Appleton of the Toronto Project Team of the Department of Transport noted, "A preliminary review has been conducted into the selection of a possible new airport site for Toronto. The various sites have, where possible, been measured against the attached list of criteria based on two alternatives, i.e. with or without the existing airport remaining in operation."

Not only was the Parkin Plan already on the scrap heap, the debate was on whether to close down Malton entirely, something that was never contemplated in the public squabble over expansion of the airport. What is more, the studies had already gone so far as to consider twenty sites in detail, to eliminate fifteen of them and to conclude, "It is recommended therefore that we now embark on a more detailed study of the remaining factors relative to the five potentially acceptable sites."

At this point, the department's minions were supposed to be working on the expansion plan – that, after all, was the political decision handed down on August 2. Here they were, nearly a month before the minister called them off that task, busy on another, and contrary endeavour, and well-advanced in their work. Curious. I do not have to tell you that the November memo was never made public.

There is one other clue. In a position paper, "Re Toronto Airports System," dated June 18, 1971, prepared for the Deputy Minister of Transport and passed by him to the Minister (Donald Jamieson, at that time) it is noted, "During September 1968, the Government decided to develop a multi-airport system to serve the Toronto area rather than proceed with a major expansion of Malton airport." During September? The Parkin Plan had barely hit the fan in September and already "the Government" had canned it. When memo writers refer to government with a capital "G" they are talking about a cabinet decision, and if a cabinet decision was made in September, it must have started in the ranks weeks before. Remember the timing; Parkin turned in his report on November 9, 1967, nothing happened until July 1968, and then the plan was revealed and killed in rapid order. Can it be that the expansion of Malton was dead before it was ever made public, at least in the eyes of the bureaucrats, and that's why they got on with the business of looking for a site while a phoney war raged over Malton?

The official search for new sites began in late 1968, and continued through 1969, and the five earlier selections were simply dumped into the mix. A set of criteria was drawn up by the DOT planners. These were the guidelines against which a new location could be measured, and they changed every time the boys thought up a new place that violated the old guidelines. It was obvious that the terminal-to-be should be within an hour's drive of Toronto – fifty nautical miles was the measure used by the departmental optimists (nautical because airplanes, like ships, use this measure. Cars don't, though; for them it would be 57.5 miles). It was also clear that the area to be purchased should be large enough to hold a full-scale airport, one with at least six runways.

Once the enthusiasm for a new airport got into the air, the earlier forecasts of passenger traffic began to grow like the Blob from Blue Lagoon. Parkin was working from a Toronto passenger load of 14.4 million in 1980, and 25 million in the year 2000. Kid stuff. By simply taking the growth rate of the past period and projecting it forward, the Ministry was able to do much better than that. If the trend at Malton continued at the current rate of 8.8 per cent to 1985, and then jumped to 12 per cent annually – why not? – the department calculated, in a December 1969 report, that there would be 12.4 million passengers in 1980 (lower than Parkin, who thought the rate would go higher, then cut back sharply), 18.9 million in 1985, 32.5 million in 1990, 55.9 million in 1995 and – Wow! – 96.4 million in the year 2000.

Where are we going to put all these people? the planners asked themselves. A better question might have been: Where are you going to get them all? But there it was, on paper. Even if the growth trend was a lousy 8 per cent per annum, there would be 60 million people swarming through the Toronto air by the turn of the century.

This 96.4 million forecast, while impressive, was not the highest that was made. In a flight of zaniness in the spring of 1971, the Bureau of Management Consulting, a government body, handed the Ministry a forecast of 198 million, which it had arrived at by taking "sector projections" and applying them to the earlier figures. Instead of merely measuring the actual growth in air travel and projecting it forward, the expansion of the Toronto area was calculated, wheeled into the equation, and added on. The forecasts had taken on a life of their own; by ignoring all other possibilities – what if Canadians weren't able to produce enough babies to meet the demand? – the planners were able to produce a nice rationale for building a new airport. Even if it wasn't needed now, it would, by God, be needed then. Why not build it now and wait for the country to run out of condoms?

Transport Canada has become sensitive about these forecasts; they are one part of the planning process that has become public. A senior departmental official told me one day that "So far, our pro-

41

jections have been dead on." I replied that the government had made so many projections that one of them was bound to be dead on. The trick was to guess which one. Anyone who cares to go through the material will find that there are sure to be, in the year 2000, either 25 million passengers in the Toronto area, or 198 million, or 46 million, or 66.4 million, or 72 million, or 52 million, or 61.9 million, or 60.7 million or 46 million or 33.9 million or 30 million. The cutback came in forecasts made after 1973, when, what with the oil crisis and running out of bodies to ship and whatnot, it seemed unlikely that the earlier glorious heights would be attained.

The fact to cling to, though, is that when the Department of Transport went hunting for a site in 1968, it thought it was looking for the king-sized model, something that would accommodate between 60 million and 96 million travellers annually. Hence, all those runways.

The planners sat down with a topographical map and a plastic circle representing a five-mile radius, and tried to see how many flattish places of that size could be found within fifty miles of Toronto. It was not written down that simply, of course; there was a whole long memo, "Airport Site Selection Process," divided into sections and written in jargon, to set out how the thing was done. The key part of that memo lies in the "Goal," which was put this way:

1. Minimize the aggregate net costs.
2. Minimize the social and environmental disbenefits.
3. Maximize airport operating safety and efficiency.
4. Maximize the attractiveness and usability of the airport for its users.

In short, find a nice airport.

Memos in hand and circles at the ready, the searchers managed to find 118 patches of land suitable, at first glance, for an airport. At second glance, some of these could be eliminated – they virtually overlapped. That left seventy-nine. Some refinement was now attached to the search – disbenefits came into play. The sites were each given ratings, and measured against a new set of rules. First, there were the built-in constraints. "Existing urban development trends have been projected to their anticipated year 2000 configuration. The areas thus delineated were then to be avoided in the siting of the new major airport." In English: avoid cities and future cities. Then sites that conflicted with currently controlled airspace – around the airports at Camp Borden, Malton, Mount Hope and around the u.s. border – were dropped. Then, "Prohibitive topographic features such as lakes, large rivers, very rough terrain, major swamps, narrow valleys, etc., were also identified in the site selection region and were to be avoided in the siting of the new airport." When you get to be an airport planning expert, you learn things like that. Don't put your runways at the bottom of a lake. Too damp.

Then, it was back to the topographic map and the five mile circles and now, "The number of possible sites falling into unconstrained areas totalled fifty-six." Fifty-six airports is fifty-five too many, so these were tested against each other by means of five weighted criteria, to see which stacked up best. The criteria were: Noise, Airspace, Topography, Consumer Distance, and Ground Transportation. A site whose noise zone would affect more people got lower marks than one with less disturbance, one closer to major existing roads did better than one at the junction of two farm lanes, and so forth. When all that was done, there were nine sites with outstanding marks. One of those considered, and rejected, early in the process, was a site just north of Brougham, in Pickering Township. This is the site that was eventually chosen. One of those that ranked highest was in Beverly Township, west of Hamilton, and we will meet that one again, too.

By the time this process was well-advanced, a federal-provincial committee had been set up. At the technical level, the process was still in federal hands, but the province was able to chip in with bits of advice. For example, provincial representatives knocked out two promising sites "due to their immediate proximity to an important Canadian goose flyway."

The process continued, the sites were sifted again, and came to five, then finally, four. I have put it more neatly than it was done. Some sites were taken out, put back and generally fooled around with until no one knew what was going on. There were twelve sites under serious consideration, then nine, then fourteen. Various departments and various branches of departments chimed in. At one point, it looked as if the job was done: "Site 72 most popular site and therefore recommended for selection." Site 72 was in Nassegaweya Township, Halton County, just northeast of the town of Darbyville, and nine miles southwest of the City of Guelph. However, the planners wanted four sites to look at, one in each of the four sectors around Toronto – north, west, east, and northwest. (To the south sits Lake Ontario.) So four sites were selected for more detailed analysis, although the boys would continue to fool around with a dozen or so.

In 1972, the two governments concocted a thesis that the four sites were merely "representative," and not to be taken seriously. This would help to explain why Pickering was among the missing so early in the process, and then reappeared; but it was applesauce of the runniest variety. All the sites were studied, measured and weighed, and the best in each of the four sectors was taken to the next stage. As you will see, the federal government would have settled for any one of them, so anxious was it to get the airport under way.

The four finalists (see map, opposite) were: a site just south of Lake Simcoe, near the town of Sutton (North), one near Orangeville (Northwest), one near Port Perry on Lake Scugog (East) and one near Guelph (West).

By this time, a Toronto Area Airports Project team had been created in Toronto, under the direction of Gordon McDowell, a longtime Department of Transport employee who has since retired, with a sigh, to his native Edmonton. McDowell signed all his memos "MTAP," and his staff grew, in the way these things will, until it occupied four floors of the Thompson Building on Queen Street in Toronto. There wasn't any airport, but there was lots of hired help. His second-in-command was Larry Potvin, whose title was Manager of Systems Planning on Construction, and who signed himself "TAPS." He is now Director-General, Policy Planning and Programing, Air, for Transport Canada in Ottawa. The government is lavish with titles.

All should have been going merry as a marriage bell, but it was not. For one thing, the province was getting twitchy. Ontario Premier John Robarts had never been wild about the second airport, which he thought might involve "heavy financial outlay for new highways and transit systems." He had to be soothed, and he finally decided that the feds probably knew what they were doing, and withdrew his complaints. Then some of his underlings began to kick up. They wondered if Ottawa was thinking of shutting down Malton altogether (they were, too) otherwise, why were they searching for such a bloody big airport? They were set straight in a letter dated October 28, 1969, from G.A. Scott, Assistant Deputy Minister, Air, in the federal Department of Transport, to W.Q. Macnee, Deputy Minister of the Ontario Department of Transport. Macnee was promised that Malton would continue to exist, and that the second airport would be built, and that "There is no intention on the part of the Federal Government to reconsider the full development of Malton as a viable alternative." "Viable" was the big word in 1969. That letter, written a decade ago, is still government policy.

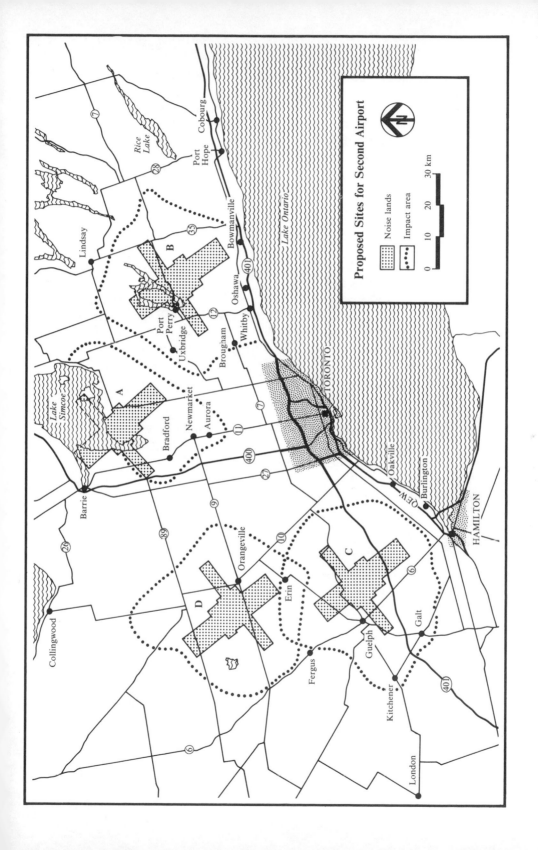

Proposed Sites for Second Airport

Noise lands
Impact area

0 10 20 30 km

Then the province began to unlimber its plan to develop the Toronto area, which was called the Toronto-Centred Region concept, or TCR. It was first mooted in 1969, and ripened through the next two years. One thing the TCR plan was likely to do was to emphasize growth to the east of the city, rather than to the west, which was already becoming crowded. That, at least, was the general feeling of those in the know. One of those was Dalton Bales, then Attorney General of the province. He, with two partners, bought a ninety-nine-acre parcel of land in Pickering Township, east of Toronto, on September 13, 1969. The land was subsequently expropriated for the province's North Pickering development, at a handsome profit. The transaction came to light, Bales resigned, and turned his profits over to charity. His sympathizers said there was no need for him to quit, because he did not act on insider information. This did not wear well; a common assumption was that the Attorney General must have been in on something, but the planning process was so screwed up that, if Bales knew where the airport was going in 1969, he was the only man in Canada who did. Just the same, it is hard to feel sorry for the man. It is possible to be a land speculator, or the Attorney General of a province. Not both. If the province wanted to shift growth eastward, that might not work so well for the federal government's highest-rated site – Guelph.

Uneasy lies the head that dictates the memo. This new worry had barely landed on the table when the whole selection process began to go sour. The four sites so proudly siphoned out of all that verbiage and all those reports, with all that computer time, turned out, each and every one of them, to be so many crocks.

The phrasing is mine, of course. That is not the way bureaucrats write. What they said was that each site presented difficulties, although all could be worked around. They became, however – crushing word – "problematic."

The Guelph site (West) was the cheapest to develop, at a mere $890 million, and the best from the point of view of weather, but "In terms of air operations and control this site is ranked last because its airspace requirements overlap with those of Malton, a factor which will eventually impose limitations on their combined capacity." If you have an airport whose operation may lead to airplanes knocking into each other, you have a problem.

The Orangeville site (Northwest) was fine from the airspace angle, but it was ten miles further from Malton than the West site, and it would cost more to develop, "Due mainly to larger expenditures on Access." The price tag for this one was $920 million. What is more, the weather was poor. If you have an airport likely to be socked in by blizzards, you have a problem.

The Sutton site (North) was a washout. "On the basis of an initial evaluation, the Federal/Provincial Committee decided that the North site was unsuitable for the following reasons:

- a very large number of people would be disturbed.
- the airport would disrupt a prime recreational area.
- there would be severe conflicts with regional recreational traffic."

Forget the North site. It wasn't even given a price tag.

The Port Perry site (East) was fine for airspace, but that was because it was so damn far from Malton – sixty miles. It would cost the most to develop, $960 million, it would displace "numerous summer cottages and about 5,500 people," and, "its weather is in fact only slightly better than that in the Northwest."

I am not making any of this up. It really did take the federal/provincial planners months and months and months to find out that Guelph is close to Malton and that Orangeville is snowy and that there are a lot of tourists around Lake Simcoe.

Well, never mind, nothing is perfect in this life, and so the planners decided to keep going with their four crummy sites. They were turned over, for provincial analysis, to Dr. Gerald Hodge, of the University of Toronto, who would consider them from the standpoint that concerned the province most – regional impact. Hodge was Ontario's Ben Higgins, but he was harder to rush. He turned in an Interim Report on January 27, 1970, and his final version early in March. The report was fine as far as it went, but from the federal point of view, it went too far. Hodge analyzed the four sites and listed them in order of preference: Orangeville was best, Port Perry next, Guelph third, and Sutton fourth. That is, remember, from the point of view of regional impact. Hodge knew nothing about airspace conflicts and other wonders. So far, so good. But then, being a conscientious man, he went on to wonder, in an appendix, just what the feds were up to, anyway. He had read the forecasts of air traffic as part of his work and, in a thoughtful little piece called "Perspectives on the DOT Forecast of Air Passenger Movements for the Toronto Region," he tore them to shreds.

"Air passenger forecasting," he began, "is one of the lesser sophisticated varieties of forecasting today." What the feds had done was to take the growth trends of the past years and project them forward "with no indication of a levelling off in the next thirty years." This made no sense. When automobiles had been the big, new thing, consumption growth rates were phenomenal, but the market reached a saturation point and growth slowed. Wouldn't the same thing happen to air travel? Like anyone reading the forecasts, Hodge was rivetted by the way the bureaucrats had traded common sense for thinking big, to come up with 96.4 million passengers in 2000.

"In terms of totals, this 96 million would represent the present combined activity of all three New York airports, Chicago's O'Hare, Los Angeles, Atlanta, San Francisco, Washington (National), Miami, Boston, Dallas-Fort Worth, Detroit, Kansas City, and Seattle-Tacoma."

In his polite, academic way, Hodge was asking, "Are these guys nuts?," but he put it differently: "Air Traffic of 96 million passengers in an area with a maximum year 2000 population of approximately seven million persons seems unrealistic."

All of this radical stuff was deleted when the feds summarized Hodge's report for internal consumption and for such higher-ups as cabinet ministers, although it did come out later.

So here we were, in the spring of 1970. The search for a second airport had been now under way officially since December of 1968, and unofficially since September of that year. Eighteen months, and nothing to show for it but a pile of reports, memos, and bills, four mediocre sites, and a kick in the butt from some academic smartass who hadn't even been asked for his advice on the forecasts. It was time to do two things: first, to look again (sigh) at the possibility of expanding Malton, and secondly, to call in Phil Beinhaker.

Chapter 5

The Plan is Saved

Helen Auld, retired:
"When we first heard about the airport, we laughed. How absurd. It's a long time ago, now, and we are not young. Six years. Six of the years we had expected to pass in peace and quiet; instead, we've had incredible trauma."

Gordon Auld, retired:
"Helen's great-grandfather built this place to retire in in 1840. He had three sons who were involved in the 1837 Rebellion, and he had to borrow six hundred pounds to get them out of hock."

Helen:
"We tried to fight against it, we tried our best, but it was too much. My health was affected. I was in a state of nervous exhaustion, so we gave in. It is a dreadful feeling that you have lived in a place all of your life, and someone can just come along and take it away. You have done nothing wrong, but one day there will be a knock on the door, it is the sheriff and he has come to evict you. That is a dreadful thing for an old couple to face."

Larry Potvin, Director-General, Policy Planning and Programing, Transport Canada:
"It would be nice if people didn't have to be disturbed, but the fact is that to do these things people do have to be disturbed. I, personally, would not want to be expropriated."

When we last saw Philip Beinhaker, he was packing his bags after his triumph at Mirabel Airport, and preparing to move to Toronto, as a partner in Peat, Marwick and Partners, which is what KPM became after Josef Kates left.

An advisory committee was established to help plan the Toronto project, under the chairmanship of D.R. Hemming, Director of Corporate Planning for the Department of Transport. Kates was on that committee, keeping his hand in, and so was Beinhaker. The other members were: Professor Hans Blumenfeld, a Toronto urbanologist who had done some work on the Montreal project, E.R. Wilby, a partner in Parkin Associates, and Clayton Glenn, Vice President, Operations, of Air Canada. Of these, the most important was Beinhaker. One of those closely involved at this time described him as the "swashbuckling leader," and he began to buckle his swash even before he left Montreal. On April 22, 1970, he was handed the reports on the second Toronto airport to that date, and asked to evaluate them. It was going to be a snap because, as Beinhaker noted in a letter, "The contribution of KPM will also ensure that full advantage is made of the experience gained on the New Montreal Airport Development during the similar stage of that project."

On May 11, a mere nineteen days after he received all the documents, Beinhaker was ready to pronounce, in a series of letters to Hemming. There were nine letters in all. Beinhaker studied the forecasts and found some problems with the methodology, but the work "appears to be adequate." That must have been nice to hear. Unlike that rude Dr. Hodge, who actually looked at the numbers, Beinhaker confined himself to what he called "the forecasting methodoloby [sic], rather than the actual forecasts." Thus, he didn't have to worry about where the people were going to come from. He suggested more studies. Then he looked at the land cost estimates for the airport-to-be, and he thought they might be too low. He suggested more studies. He looked at the development costs of the four favoured sites, and thought the work done there was pretty good. "On the other hand, changes in the airport plan runway/taxiway layout should be anticipated." Guess what the government would need more of for that? He thought the Toronto team was overlooking the money to be made out of land-banking a huge parcel of countryside, as was done at Mirabel, and he dealt with the delicate issue of the airspace problem at the highest-ranked site, Guelph. Perhaps the problem wasn't that bad, he suggested; all four sites "could be made to operate." But if there was a real difficulty, he had one bit of advice: the boys should get their story straight before anybody went public. "The only suggestion is of a strategic nature; to ensure that all groups within Transport at least agree on the significance of the difference in sites from the aviation point of view, as identified by the different approaches. The significance of the difference can then be viewed within the overall perspective of all the other issues. This is apparently appreciated and this suggestion is only made by way of confirmation."

Beinhaker was getting $45 an hour to write this way, but never mind, it would soon go to $50. He was saying what Ben Franklin once said, that the boys should all hang together, or they would all hang separately.

In the covering letter to Hemming, summing up all his work, Beinhaker put his foot in it.

> The costs to develop a new Toronto International Airport are indeed very great. The aggregate capital costs will be at least twice those for Montreal . . . . The present weakness of the economy and the aviation industry, coupled with these high costs, certainly raises the question as to the timing of the new airport.
>
> It perhaps also raises the more basic question as to the alternative solutions for the aviation system in the Toronto-Centred Region. The work has focussed on where to locate a new airport and Ontario in the Goals plan, recently made public, alludes to a new international airport. The issue I am raising is, what to do, rather than where to do it.

Oh, dear. Actually, it was not so strange that work had focussed on where to locate a new airport, since the decision to build one was now ancient history, but Beinhaker plunged on to suggest more study – naturally. He lined up six possibilities:

1. Expand Malton, and compensate nearby residents for the noise annoyance. (The whole board should have lit up and registered Bingo at this point; it was, and remains, the answer, but Beinhaker hurried on past.)
2. Build a series of airports, to work with Malton.
3. Integrate "aviation and surface transport systems" with a series of airports joined by "surface linkages" – trains, I guess.
4. Develop the Toronto area with multiple airports for domestic travel, while siphoning off all the international travel to Mirabel.
5. Build a new airport for international travel, and use Malton for domestic.
6. Build a "new Toronto International Airport integrated with an urban and transportation development."

Beinhaker did drag out once more the old question of expanding Malton, and that was really bad news, because a separate report had been done by the Toronto Planning Team (before it became the Toronto Area Airports Project) on this very subject, and it came crashing down the same day Beinhaker reported. It said, in brief, what the 1961 study had said, and what the Parkin Plan had

51

said – the expansion of Malton was not only feasible, it was the cheapest and smartest way to go. The study looked at the four sites under consideration, and calculated the cost of opening and running them, including user costs, to the year 2000. It found that the cheapest, at Guelph, would cost $2,812,000,000. The capital cost, which had earlier been reckoned at $890 million, was only the beginning; there were airline costs and transfer costs and infrastructure costs and carrying costs and, in short, all the costs governments don't tell us about when they announce mammoth projects. The total was close, therefore, to $3 billion. Malton, using the same methodology, could be expanded and run to the same date for $1,990,000,000.

"On the basis of costs, a Malton expansion to 2000, representing a total saving to the economy of approximately $820 million, must be preferred to a second airport. Analysis of another somewhat costable criterion, air operations and control, indicates that Malton as the single major airport in the region could be cheaper than a two-airport system by something in the order of hundreds of millions of dollars."

This was dreary reading indeed. Not only were these people saying that the forecast traffic loads could be met by that old standby, building a runway parallel to 14/32, they were saying the operation would save something over a billion bucks.

Well, hell. The boys, as Josef Kates either had or had not said in another context, had come up with the wrong answer. They were told to go back and try again. This they did, in a sixty-two-page report dated August 1970, which unabashedly came to the same conclusion: "The most desirable alternative from a cost standpoint would be to expand Malton."

Since the last time anyone had looked at the Toronto airport seriously, in 1968, there had been a number of technical advances in aviation. It was no longer necessary to keep parallel runways a mile apart, and it was therefore unnecessary to buy the three thousand acres of extra land mentioned in the Parkin Plan. In stating this, the August 1970 report was not breaking new ground. Close-in runways, with separations of from 720 to 1500 feet, are called "duals." One runway is used, at any one time, exclusively for landings, and its parallel for take-offs. This is done, and has been done for years, at O'Hare airport in Chicago, at Los Angeles, in Newark, in New York City, and elsewhere, from San Francisco to Athens, Greece. However, Transport Canada maintains to this day that it either can't be done or isn't worth doing. It isn't safe and it isn't efficient, and the fact that O'Hare and Los Angeles and San Francisco and

La Guardia do it doesn't count. The Airport Inquiry Commission would report, in 1974, that "The dual lane runway concept offers little or no increase in runway capacity in cases where an instrument landing is required," and "The Commission has a real concern for the risk to safety due to wake turbulence where parallel runways are separate at a distance of 2,500 feet or less." That is the current gospel.

I stood, not long ago, between the dual runways 28L/10R and 28R/10L, at San Francisco airport. These runways are 750 feet apart. I stood there for about an hour, while my wife took photographs of large and small and intermediate jets landing on one runway and taking off on the other, and even, just for the hell of it, landing at one end of one runway while another jet took off from the other end. I told Frank O'Malley of the airport staff, "They can't do that, you know." He replied, "Been doing it ever since I can remember."

Three days later, we did it all over again, on the two sets of duals at Los Angeles International Airport, where I told Ethel Pattison of that airport's staff that I had it on the best authority that we were watching an illusion. She said, "Oh, yeah?"

But wait, perhaps San Francisco and Los Angeles are not efficient. Oh, yeah? In 1977, San Francisco handled 338,675 aircraft movements and 19,334,730 passengers in an area of 5,207 acres. Los Angeles handled 491,346 movements and 26,858,857 passengers on 3,500 acres. Malton's total that year was 244,800 movements and 11,322,200 passengers on 4,200 acres. The table on page 55, which compares a number of world airports, shows just how under-used Malton is.

As to safety, San Francisco and Chicago both have had exemplary records. Before the tragic crash at O'Hare on May 25, 1979, in which 275 persons died – a crash that had nothing to do with runway alignment or airport safety factors – the last mishap reported there was in 1972, and produced no fatalities. Not bad for the world's busiest airport. Pilots are not fond of the Los Angeles facility, but not because of the dual runways – because of smog. At all of these airports, aircraft are required to meet the same standards of separation as anywhere else – including Canada.

To continue to assert that duals don't work, in the face of common sense and lengthy experience, requires a steadfastness, not to say a boneheadedness, that is awesome. That steadfastness would be used to smash down the August 1970 report, which stubbornly went on to insist, "Runway capacity analysis indicated that additional taxiways, specialized Air Traffic Control equipment and a new close-in parallel 14R/32L direction runway can acceptably accommodate all area carrier movements to beyond the year 2000."

What is more, there would be nothing for the excitable burghers of Malton to get up in arms about, because, "By positioning the new runway between its acceptable spacing of 700 feet to 3,500 feet from the existing 14/32 runway, it was found that the currently utilized noise contours would not be appreciably expanded (and not at all at the lower end of the range) during the planning period to the year 2000 . . . . In a more general sense, newer generation aircraft will definitely be less offensive with regard to noise and air pollution and this trend will be accelerated as government certification requirements regarding noise and air pollution become more strict."

Equipment was getting better, planes quieter and governments tougher; put them all together and they spell: expand Malton. "In light of these developments a fully expanded Malton to the year 2000 has emerged as a viable airport system alternative to a Toronto II-Malton system." This option would also save money. Boy, would it save money.

"On the basis of costs, a Malton expansion to 2000 represents a total saving to the economy of over $2 billion and must be preferred to a second major airport. Analysis of another criterion, Air Operations and Control, indicates that Malton as a single major airport in the region would be substantially better than a two airport system by at least $217 million."

So that even the meanest intelligence could grasp what was intended, the planners concluded their report. "Accordingly, it is recommended that: Malton should be expanded to meet the major air carrier transportation needs of the Toronto-Centred Region over the time from 1970 to 2000."

Later, the Transport folks would pretend that the plan to expand Malton was born and died in 1968, and that all other studies showed the expansion to be impractical. When the 1970 report then leaked out, they said, oh, well, yes, one lousy little report, but it was all wrong. There were dozens of other studies that contradicted this one memo. Like so much of what was said, this was bear-oil. At this point, the expansion of Malton had been recommended by the 1961 report, the Parkin Plan, two 1970 reports and even by good old Phil Beinhaker. It had been negated, not by any technical study, but by the political decision announced on December 20, 1968 – at a time when the bureaucrats were already working on a second airport.

This was getting embarrassing. You send these guys out to do a study and they bring in the wrong answer; you send them back

SOME AIRPORT CAPACITIES

Airport	Size (acres)	Annual Passengers	Air Transport Movements	All Air Movements
Chicago O'Hare	7000	41,376,100	611,900	718,100
Atlanta	3800	27,299,200	440,900	490,000
Los Angeles	3500	25,983,100	356,500	482,600
London Heathrow	2715	23,241,500	256,300	278,100
New York Kennedy	4900	21,033,000	287,100	305,100
San Francisco	5207	17,564,000	293,500	342,500
Denver	4600	13,698,700	264,600	418,400
Frankfurt	2520	13,170,100	196,700	212,200
Toronto Malton	4200	11,322,200	176,700	244,800
Paris Orly	2666	10,670,800	144,500	152,000

Sources: Report on Airport Capacity, May 1977, U.S. Department of Transportation. British Airports Authority Annual Report 1976/77.

again and they bring it right back, wronger than ever. There was only one thing to do, take it away from them.

The Toronto team reports were given to Hans Blumenfeld, the urbanologist on the advisory committee. I asked William Huck, the Air Administrator at the time, why the work of his own experts, confirmed by a second study, had been set aside, and Blumenfeld brought in. I was expecting him to say that the department wanted a fresh look at the subject, from someone who had not taken a position. I was then going to lay on him a study that Blumenfeld did in 1968 in Montreal, in which he made his views clear on the subject of airports. He thought the existing ones should be closed down, and new facilities built, further out. However, Huck fooled me. He couldn't remember who Blumenfeld was, and then he couldn't remember that the studies had been turned over to him, and when we got that straight, he couldn't remember why. He suggested that I ask somebody else, and when I reminded him that he was the man in charge at the time, he looked grieved.

Blumenfeld stomped all over the Malton expansion in an eleven-page letter dated August 17, 1970, to D.R. Hemming. The whole point of the exercise was to get away from noise at Malton, he said, and expanding the airport would not work. The thing to do was to close down the Toronto airport, sell off the land, and build a whole new shooting match. "I strongly agree with the paper's emphasis on the disadvantages of split operations. But I believe that the only satisfactory answer is not 'Malton alone' but – after an inevitable transition period – a new airport alone."

For the site of this new marvel, he favoured Guelph. Close down Malton, build a rapid transit link, and open a new airport at Guelph. The province's apparent preference for putting growth in the east could be ignored: "I personally consider their reasons for preferring development to the north and east very weak – and intend to say so publicly. In any case, the province appears to be reconciled with accepting site C." (C was Guelph; it was also called West.)

Land sakes, now Blumenfeld had come in with the wrong answer. Malton could not be closed. The province had already expressed itself on this subject, and had been assured that it wouldn't happen.

Yet another study came in about this time, also favouring Guelph. It was called "Second Toronto Airport Site Selection," it was signed by the Toronto Airport Planning Team, and dated September 1970, but that is only the filing date. It was clearly done earlier – Blumenfeld's letter indicates that he had access to it. This report was mainly a roundup of some of the earlier studies. It described the site search so far, mentioned that fifty-nine sites became semi-demi-finalists (the number was fifty-six in an earlier report) and indicated why Pickering had been knocked on the head so early. In this study, four criteria were used: distance, forecast urban growth, airspace, and topography – Pickering flunked every standard but the first one. This report concluded that of the four finalists, Guelph had the edge, and it mentioned, in passing, that the total cost of a second airport would be in the area of $5 billion, when user costs were added to capital and operating expenses. This report was not too significant at the time, since it was a summary of earlier information; it only became important because it was later leaked to the press.

For the moment, then, the government had two reports strongly favouring the expansion of Malton and two pushing Guelph, a site that wasn't much good. It was time to bring Beinhaker back up to bat.

All the earlier studies and Blumenfeld's letter were turned over to Beinhaker and, on September 8, 1970, he came through with his masterpiece, "Strategy Paper Relating Aviation Systems to Broad Policies and Programs of Public and Private Sectors." This was the foundation on which future policy would be erected, and if the structure was a little shaky, you couldn't blame Beinhaker. You couldn't blame him, in part, because it was hard to work out exactly what he said, although it all sounded good.

He admitted, on page three, that "Unlike Montreal, a new International Airport to accommodate most, or all, of the traffic is not the least cost solution." So, you could expand Malton, and the complaining neighbours could be paid compensation. But there was a catch. Always is.

"The problem is that noise from aircraft flight operations is felt to be objectionable in the adjacent communities. It is also questionable if Malton is equipped or can be made to accommodate the unforeseen possible developments in aviation technology to the year 2000."

This last sentence, which sounds so rotund and wise, is Bunker C. Somebody might think of something between now and the year 2000, and for some unaccountable reason that bright idea might be applicable to a new airport, but not to Malton. Why? Who knows.

The real rub, however, is that while Malton could be expanded, such a course might be "politically unacceptable." Besides, it provides no "fall-back position." By "politically unacceptable" Beinhaker presumably meant that the locals would raise hell – a fair

57

guess. The "no fall-back" crack is another of the buzz sounds that permeate our language. It seems smart, but means nothing. Beinhaker tacked to and fro with this logic for some pages. "Not only is a new airport not an obvious answer at this time, but technological developments of the next decade may bring the real answer to the airport system plan for the Toronto-Centred Region . . . . Significant reductions are promised in the noise generated by aircraft engines . . . . Then Malton may be able to continue to accommodate the majority of traffic beyond the next decade."

This sounded as if our lad was siding with those rotters who wrote the August report, but no fear. "However" – there is always however – "the public will likely question now if improvements will occur and may not believe it."

The issue was not airports, but credibility.

"The fundamental problem is as follows: the reconfiguration of Malton to accommodate all traffic is quite likely not to be accepted as a long range answer and, indeed, may not prove as good as present promises of engine noise reduction would indicate."

What to do? If they don't believe Malton, and if two airports are too expensive, why not a whole covey of airports? The idea was called "Design for Aviation," and it flew.

"The concept is to acquire land for a major airport facility, to develop an intercontinental airport for charter and some scheduled activity now and to preserve flexibility of expanding the role of the new airport if necessary in the future."

The government should lay its hands on the land for one new airport now, while planning a series of "Metro-ports," as Beinhaker called them – expansions of regional airports, and new airports. Perhaps some more land should be protected for one of these. STOL – short take-off and landing – aircraft were coming into vogue; perhaps a STOL-port should be built. What was required, in any event, was to "preserve flexibility" and provide a "fall-back position."

When all was said and done, Beinhaker had dismissed the expansion of Malton, not because it couldn't be done, but because people might not believe it could be done. This wasn't planning, it was faith-healing. However, Beinhaker had presented the lads with an excuse to build a whole damn brood of airports. That was nice.

The Toronto Planning Team reports were brushed aside and never mentioned in polite society again, except with a sneer. Blumenfeld was brushed aside. Beinhaker was accepted. He produced an expansion of his concept which didn't make much more sense, but hung in there with flexibility and fall-backs, and then he accepted an assignment "To develop strategies to be employed by the

Minister to secure approval in principle from the Government of Canada to the overall approach developed in the first and second strategy assignments."

I used to think that when a cabinet minister came up with an idea, he took it to his colleagues and said, "Guess what?" No such thing. He hires a consultant, at $50 an hour, to mount a PR campaign to put the thing across. This campaign began with a meeting between Beinhaker and Transport Minister Donald Jamieson on September 18, at which the Minister swallowed Design for Aviation in a single gulp. Beinhaker later wrote of this meeting, for the record, that "It was generally agreed, and decided by the Minister, that Malton alone is not saleable and that the plan must include provision of a new airport to maintain flexibility." That was just Beinhaker, laying on the old oil; in a private description of this same meeting, in a letter to Hemming dated January 13, 1971, the consultant makes it clear that Jamieson didn't decide anything, he just accepted: "The Minister concurred with this approach, as presented in the paper."

It is important to get straight what the federal government was being told about these events, because it, after all, was supposed to be making the decisions. On October 5, 1970, Cabinet Document 656-20 was circulated to members of the Trudeau cabinet. It was signed by Donald Jamieson, as Minister of Transport, and it constituted a review of what the ministers needed to know to make an intelligent decision. It was called "Re Toronto Area Aviation System."

This paper stated that the proposal to expand Malton had been made on August 2, 1968, and rejected on December 20, because such an expansion could not meet the test of "land use compatibility around the airport." There was a brief description of the site-search, and acknowledgement that "Four sites were selected for detailed study and agreed upon by the joint committee." Nothing was said about the fact that all four sites had now become problematical, nor was there anything to support the later contention that they were merely "representative." Instead, it was made to look as if the department was just being thorough, in examining all possibilities. "In parallel with the examination of alternative sites, the overall aviation system requirements for the Southern Ontario/Toronto region were studied. The aviation system includes all the components of airports, airspace, and airlines, as well as the effects of new technology and the effects of regional development. The study was to determine the optimal utilization of a possible new airport, the existing Malton airport and other airports located in urbanized centres of the region."

So, the ministers were not told that Malton expansion had been looked at again, or that two studies concluded that it was a marvellous solution, or that a third, Beinhaker's, had concluded that it was the right idea, but "politically unacceptable." Instead:

Malton will not likely be capable of handling satisfactorily the projected growth from 5 million passengers in 1970 to 40-60 million passengers in the year 2000 because of
(a) the noise problem
(b) limitations of the airport land
(c) curfew restrictions.

It appeared, then, there was really no choice except to build another airport; even if it did not have to be built at once, "A new airport will ultimately be required."

The four sites were described, briefly, and it was clear that the two favourites were Guelph and Orangeville. The Lake Scugog site was described as "Unfavourable, as the majority of users, as well as Malton airport itself, are separated from the site by Metropolitan Toronto."

This argument applied just as well to an airport at Pickering as to one at Port Perry, but it simply disappeared when the Pickering site was up for approval. Nobody outside the Cabinet heard it.

The document went on to lay down the outline of Design for Aviation and to recommend its adoption. No intelligent minister, reading that material, could come to any other conclusion than that the expansion of Malton was impossible, and that the only real choice still to be made was among the promising sites that had already undergone examination.

On October 15, Beinhaker made a presentation, on flash cards, to members of the Cabinet Committee on Government Operations, summarizing Design for Aviation. It went down well. On October 21, the Cabinet Committee recommended the new policy to the full Cabinet and, on October 27, that august, but ignorant body authorized four steps:

(a) Land for a new major airport should be protected. If full acquisition proves necessary, cost would be $80-150 million, depending on the site.
(b) The development of a program at Malton airport which is common to any possible role of the new airport, at a cost of $105 million, of which a little more than half is already committed.
(c) Consideration of the development of the initial phase of the new airport at a cost of about $50 million-$100 million. This initial phase could be in operation by 1975-76. [Ho, ho.]

(d) Consideration in the future of the development of Metroports, including the Toronto waterfront, Hamilton, and Oshawa and including the use of STOL vehicles if operational.

Design for Aviation had gone from a somewhat garbled letter to government policy in forty-nine days. Not only were we saved, flexibility-wise and fall-back-wise, but instead of all those billions of dollars hurled around in the planning documents, the government thought it was committed to $200 million or so. The rest of the bill would come later.

Speaking of bills, the ones submitted by Peat, Marwick and Partners were interesting. I have no record of what Beinhaker was paid for the May 11 letters. He refers to the charge in the letter to Hemming on January 13, 1971, but all he says is that the fee was "$5000 below the amount authorized by you." That one must have been charged on an hourly basis. Then there was the Design for Aviation paper – that cost $25,000. Then there were the papers expanding on that, "Strategy Assignments," they were called, and they came in at $18,500 and $21,000. (Part of the job on this $21,000 contract was to help prepare a survey of local public opinion on the airport and, if possible, to float the four sites out for reaction. This was Jamieson's idea, part of the heady stuff of participatory democracy, then in vogue, and neither the bureaucracy nor Beinhaker thought much of it. It was dropped, which saved a lot of embarrassment, since the site that would eventually be unwrapped had nothing to do with the four then lined up.) Then, there was another $21,600, because, as Beinhaker wrote to Hemming, "You indicated the need for experienced professional staff to be available to contribute to the overall on-going effort, as well as to possibly undertake special studies." Standby money, with a split infinitive thrown in for free; cheap at twice the price. So that's $86,000 that we know about, plus an undisclosed figure, for advice. Small change.

In all, KPM received $2,147,077.92 for consulting services at Mirabel, and firms that Beinhaker was connected with – Peat, Marwick and Partners, KPM, and his own company, IBI, drew $1,494,113 (up until March 31, 1977) out of the Toronto project. The fees for Design for Aviation were the merest trickle in this golden stream.

Beinhaker's high profile was, by this time, beginning to irritate some bureaucrats. Larry Potvin, second in command in the Toronto office, wrote to his boss, Gordon McDowell. "In reading the description of the ongoing work as contained in Mr. Beinhaker's letter, one can easily get the impression that the work is in fact being done by PM&P . . . . Besides the important aspect of professional recognition, there is maybe a more substantial point with respect to

61

any audit of the consultant involved. Frankly I feel that Mr. Bein-haker should contain himself [presumably Potvin means confine] to describing the work that PM&P will do for us."

A few months later, Potvin complained that "Mr. Beinhaker continues to report progress," and noted, "I am rather surprised at the number of partners we now have employed on the team." This last was recognition of the fact that the consultants were bringing in lower-paid employees, training them on the government stipend, then promoting them as partners. Once they got to be partners, their rates went up $10 an hour.

None of these quibbles had the slightest effect on Beinhaker. From the Ministry's point of view, every dollar spent was well worth it. By late October of 1970, the frights of spring had been banished. The prospect of an expansion of Malton was writhing on the ground with a stake through its heart, and the planners were back where they had started, with a second airport back on the books.

Now, if they could only find some place to put the damn thing.

Chapter 6

Who Picked
Pickering?

Anne Wanstall, journalist:
*"I was with the delegation that went to Ottawa to interview Donald
Jamieson, when he was Minister of Transport. He was like a great big
St. Bernard puppy, all very friendly, and he just rolled over you. We
came out of the meeting, and the* Toronto Star *already had the story of
what he had said to us, which was that he wasn't going to listen to us. At
one point I asked him if we would get our property back if the airport
was cancelled, and he said the government would hold onto it. 'We might
need it in case of war.' I wondered if I'd forgotten English. Were we
speaking the same language?"*

Donald Jamieson, June 14, 1972:
*"It troubles me to think that there are those who have not known what
questions to ask or whom to address. Likewise, I am troubled to think
that there are those who have received answers, but no satisfaction."*

While all the argybargy over whether to expand Malton or build
one more airport or move to a multi-airport system was going on,
federal and provincial representatives were meeting to talk about
zoning controls on the noise lands around any new facilities, and to
begin the haggling over cost-sharing that makes confederation such
a treat. Premier Robarts indicated, on December 11, 1970, that
while he was prepared to buy the Design for Aviation concept, he
might not want to announce it, or to make a final decision on site,
for as much as a year.

This was bad news; the feds might not have a site yet, but they
were certainly anxious to announce one. They went back to mulling
at the four choices they still had and, with time, came to like them.
So a firm cabinet decision was made early in February 1971, that
no sites would be announced. Yet. Instead, they would keep pick-
ing away at the candidates until they got one that worked, and announce that. Transport Minister Jamieson, the cabinet memo covering this decision shows, was inclined to announce all four, to test

public reaction. He had more or less promised to do that in the House of Commons on May 19, 1970, when he said, "I am prepared to release the full details of our findings and to withhold the final decision regarding the site until there has been adequate opportunity for all appropriate submissions to be received and considered thoroughly."

The difficulty was that only one site could be protected, legally, under the Expropriation Act; to announce four would be to invite land speculation on a massive scale. So the earlier commitment was wiped out. Why not? It was only the word of a cabinet minister given to the House of Commons.

Then Premier Robarts resigned and, on February 12, 1971, William Davis became Ontario's new premier. He had to be educated into the new concept, and he had already let it be known that he favoured an airport east of Toronto.

Accordingly, on March 16, 1971, Deputy Minister of Transport O.G. Stoner sent Jamieson a briefing book for a meeting to be held between the minister and Davis on March 18, in Ottawa. The brief was a dilly and, had it been made public, would have destroyed much of the federal government's later argument for putting the airport at Pickering. It is worth a look. The brief begins with a note from Air Administrator Huck to Stoner, explaining what the documents are for. Then there is Stoner's memo to Jamieson, telling him how Davis can be manoeuvred into accepting a site – almost any site – and how that site can be announced on April 12, 1972.

Re: Toronto Airports Project
I attach an aide memoire for your forthcoming meeting with the Premier of Ontario.

As Mr. Davis was not directly involved in your previous meetings, it is possible that the discussions will have to commence with your basic strategy for the airport system – new airport, major ongoing role for Malton, and Metro-ports – to bring Mr. Davis along to the point of understanding which you reached with Mr. Robarts in December, and to then proceed from that point. The issues involved may be summarized below:

1. The Airports System: Does Mr. Davis agree with the decision as did Mr. Robarts? The system is to consist of the new airport, Malton in a major ongoing role, and Metro-ports. Points likely to be of special interest to Mr. Davis are the interim expansion program at Malton, and also, in view of recent announcements by (Ontario Treasurer Charles) MacNaughton, the role of Short Take-Off and Landing aircraft in the Metro-port concept.

2. The approach to a decision: Does Mr. Davis agree the approach of choosing a site, protecting it under the Federal Expropriation Act, and conducting public hearings under that act with additional dialogue if necessary? Will Mr. Davis provide protections for the adjacent lands at the chosen site, and the broad regions at the other sites by administrative holdback?

3. Timing: Does Mr. Davis agree to move immediately, or does he wish to delay a decision? If he wishes to delay, is he prepared to make a written request to that effect?

4. Site Decision: Does Mr. Davis agree to the West or Northwest site as a tentative decision on site? The West is the least cost, most convenient site. The northwest is equivalent in airport cost, greater in transportation capital costs and convenience, the degree of this being directly related to how soon and how much traffic is assigned to the new airport. The East is equivalent in airport cost, and like the Northwest, greater in transportation capital costs. However, it is very poor in terms of user convenience. This major problem of the East can be solved only with major expenditure in high quality sophisticated access transportation.

Never mind the bad grammar and jargon, and note what this memo is up to. Jamieson is being both stroked and guided. He is told the strategy is his, but he is twice reminded of his strategy, in case he has forgotten. He is prodded, gently, to ask Davis about protecting the noise lands; money could be saved if the province would simply freeze a chunk of land by regulation, and to hell with the people who owned it. This, in the end, is what happened. Then he is told to pressure the premier on timing. Robarts had been too smart to put his stall in writing, so that if delay added to the costs of the project, the feds would not be able to pin it on him. If Davis was a rube, Jamieson might be able to mouse-trap him. Fat chance. Finally, the minister is reminded to make sure he gets Davis to agree to a site, any site. Note that the Ministry favoured the West site – Guelph. However, a fall-back position, always a favourite, is provided. If Davis won't take Guelph, offer him Orangeville. It isn't as good, but it's better than nothing. The East site, at Port Perry, is bad and expensive, but Davis has already indicated, curse him, that he wants the airport east of Toronto, so Jamieson needs a strategy to deal with that. Stoner gives him one, culled from the memos of Transport underlings:

"If Mr. Davis is adamant about the East, you might: i) Suggest assisting Provincial regional objectives by acquiring land for a

Metro-port site in the East in combination with either the West
or Northwest site."

This is the carrot; the province could have its airport in the east if
it would agree to another where it was actually needed, west or
northwest.

"ii) Ask him to satisfy you that the additional investment in
ground access to alleviate the East's problem of user convenience
would be forthcoming."

This is the stick; if the province wanted the airport where it had
no right to be, let the province pick up the tab.

"iii) Move to acquire either the West or the Northwest site unilat-
erally."

This was another stick; if the bastards won't play ball, we can always do what we did in Quebec, and go it alone.

With specific reference to the timing of any announcement, you
may wish to note that documentation for Notice of Intention is
complete for the East, West and Northwest sites. Assuming you
reach agreement with Mr. Davis prior to your leaving Ottawa on
March 26, a Cabinet submission relating to the tentative decision
on site could be prepared for April 12, to be ready when you return. The Province will require approximately one month from
the date of agreement to initiate the administrative holdback procedures but this need not delay an announcement.

This aide memoire is supported by attached reference documents which deal more fully with important issues which may
arise.

Both governments would later contend that the sites mentioned
here were only trial runs. Bazphaz. On April 12, if Davis could be
pushed into agreement, the federal government was going to announce the airport, and the Ministry didn't really give a damn if it
was West, Northwest or East. Indeed, only the North site had been
definitely ruled out. The feds had gone so far as to prepare documents to seize the land in all three places. This was despite the fact
that the supporting documentation that Stoner sent Jamieson
showed that the problems facing all three locations were still un-
solved.

There was this little nugget in one of the supporting papers:

None of the sites proposed for the new airport are [sic] perfect.
Concern has been expressed by the officials of the Air Administration regarding the air traffic control at the West site, when operated jointly with Malton. At both East and Northwest sites the
weather is less favourable than the West.

And this:

> The Eastern Site is poor from the users [sic] point of view as the majority of airport users would have to cross the Metro area and would at some time experience conflict with recreational traffic.

This crippling liability which, I remind you, applies to Pickering, was spelled out further in Attachment C to this same document:

> The Eastern site, would suffer from three major disadvantages related to the time spent by users in travelling, and is hence unattractive. This [sic] disadvantages are:
> 1. Conflict with peak recreation traffic in the Eastern transportation corridor.
> 2. Wide separation from Malton with resultant loss of flexibility.
> 3. The fact that most of the users are separated from the site by Metro Toronto.

The only way to get around the problem was to build a rapid transit system, estimated to cost a minimum $119 million. It was this $119-million bill that Jamieson was to hand to Davis:

> If Ontario wishes to make this additional investment in ground access in the interests of regional development to make the East site more accessible to users located in Western and Central Toronto, the East site may be regarded as acceptable.

Jamieson was even told how to whipsaw the premier:

> Should Mr. Davis continue to press for the East the Minister might wish to adopt the tactic of turning the tables, i.e. by requesting Mr. Davis to show how he would solve the ground access cost and user convenience problems associated with the East.

So Guelph was a bad site and Port Perry was a monster. Orangeville, too, had major drawbacks. It was fifty-three miles from downtown Toronto and forty-three from Malton. It would therefore be expensive, not only in access roads, but in extra costs to airlines and the public. It would not meet the province's wish for growth in the east, it would drop noise and pollution problems on the Niagara Escarpment, it was no hell for air traffic control, and worse for weather, although it was not, the memo notes, as snowy as Dorval.

A special fourteen-page memorandum was included to point out the faults and failings of Orangeville, because Jamieson had already decided that he liked it. A group of local politicians had come calling on him in Ottawa, to press the case for an Orangeville airport, and he was impressed. The Ministry, however, preferred Guelph, and so the long memo. While a cabinet minister is usually easily handled by his staff – they, after all, know what is going on, and he only knows what they choose to tell him – he is, in the end, the boss. He is approached as if he were a rhinoceros, dumb but dangerous, and likely to take offence if not properly stroked. The memo concludes:

> This memorandum summarizes what currently appear to be the most likely objections to be raised to the Northwest site. It is understood that should the Minister choose to protect the Northwest it is his policy not to be wedded to his initial choice, and that should the objections listed above, or other which might emerge subsequently, attract sufficient support, the Minister would give consideration to changing his tentative decision.

This unctuous oil was wasted. On March 18, 1971, Jamieson marched into a meeting with Premier Davis, determined to sell him the Orangeville site. He almost did. Davis was too smart to put anything on paper, too wary to commit himself, and determined to have something built east of Toronto, but he indicated that, if the feds wanted to pick Orangeville, he would make no public objection.

So that was it; Toronto would have a second airport, and it would be at Orangeville. What would it cost? Something over $1.5 billion. The background documents give the capital, operating and maintenance costs as $836 million, and user costs as $697 million, for a total of $1,533 million. It would not be announced that way, of course; all the user costs would be dumped and the other costs fiddled. Governments like to work these little fibs on their parishioners. The October 27, 1970 cabinet decision contemplated a bill of around $200 million. We were in for eight times that, at least.

Orangeville lasted as the selected site for less than a month. While one group of locals was for the airport, another was against it, and the opponents included an Air Canada pilot, Charles Burbank. He began writing letters to the papers to point out that in driving from his Orangeville home to Malton, he had noted that "The weather is many times poorer in this location than below the Niagara Escarpment." In addition to snow, there was "dense radiation fog."

Joseph Ernst, who taught history at the University of Toronto, and was one of the key figures in the anti-airport lobby in Orangeville, phoned a man he knew to be working on weather studies for the feds, and this expert confirmed that an airport at Orangeville would be shut down, by weather, fifty per cent more often than

Malton. The study was confidential, but Ernst spread the word, and pretty soon the newspapers were full of warnings. (Ernst later wrote a book, with Sandra Budden, about their experiences, called, *The Movable Airport*. Toronto: Hakkert, 1973.)

If you are going to have a bunch of busybodies poking into every little thing, you can't build airports. On April 1, Administrator Huck wrote to Deputy Minister Stoner to assure him that the Air Administration was now in agreement "Supporting the Northwest site as the best long-term decision from the total point of view." All the negative thinking in the fourteen-page memo to Jamieson was not withdrawn. "You will appreciate that the paper 'Northwest Site: Possible Objections,' which you felt was defensive, was not intended to state the Air Administration's view as such, but to appraise [sic] the Minister of some negative reactions that we anticipate may emerge."

The belly-crawling was complete: "The Air Administration concurs with the minister's view that the Northwest site is the best long-term decision from the total point of view."

What total point of view? There were no explanations, no new studies, nothing had changed except that Jamieson had been able to slide the site past Davis. Civil servants are supposed to give their political masters their best judgment, and if they are overruled, so be it. But that's not the way it works. As we see here, the second airport had been so oversold, and the problems with the sites so tempered, that Jamieson got the bit in his teeth, and plumped for Orangeville. Why not? He had the boys' word for it that all the sites could be made to work. So, they curved back on their own tracks and even denied having a view.

However, all this sycophancy went for naught. On April 21, Russell Gwilliam, one of Beinhaker's colleagues at PM&P, wrote to Gordon McDowell, chief of the Toronto Area Airport Project, enclosing the fourth and final draft of a document for the cabinet on the site selection. This was the paper that would lead to the formal declaration of a second airport, at Orangeville. Gwilliam noted that "Ontario agrees aviation system in principle" and that "The Minister has discussed possible sites with Ontario and has reached a tentative decision to which the Province will not object. This is the Northwest site . . . Hence objective is to acquire the Northwest site."

Attached to this memo is a copy of an earlier Huck memo on the Orangeville location, which says, "The weather at this site is less favourable than the West, but acceptable." That was the new doctrine. Beside this is a handwritten note, "May not be in light of new

69

data." The study on which Joe Ernst's pal was working was now finished, the Ministry could no longer ignore the fact that the weather in winter in Amaranth Township features blizzards, and Orangeville was finished before it ever got officially to cabinet. The fact that Ontario had accepted the site would be covered in the usual way – no one would ever know.

Within days, there was another rocket. On April 27, a task force assigned to look at STOL came back with a report suggesting that the system was so useful that it might take the pressure off Malton. Why not hold off any decision, it suggested, until this was settled?

Then came another blow. On May 5, the province announced official confirmation of its Toronto-Centred Region plan, with fanfare about the need to move new growth east of Metro. Now that Orangeville was buried in snow, Ontario was pushing east again. Things looked dark indeed for our side, until the feds dug back down into their bag of tricks and came up with a reworking of Phil Beinhaker's multi-airports system. It was called "Airport Strategy: A Revised Approach." It was really "Son of Design for Aviation." It is undated.

Just about the time the TCR plan was confirmed – the date is uncertain – a senior official in the Ontario government got word from one of his colleagues at the federal level. "He said none of the four sites works, but not to worry. They had two new sites for us to look at. It came out of the blue."

The new sites were, in fact, a couple of the oldies. One was Peter's Corners, in Beverly Township, southwest of Toronto – No. 79 in the earlier run-through. The other was at Brougham, in Pickering Township, the site that had been scratched years earlier. In that first look, however, the feds were looking for a great big airport; now they would settle for two smaller ones. Or, in the words of "A Revised Approach," "This paper examines the advisability of acquiring two 5-10,000 acre tracts of land for possible future airport developments located at the western and eastern airport sites, rather than a single 15-20,000 acre site at one location."

If the province wanted an airport in the east, they could have it, as long as they accepted one in the west first. "The intention would be to develop facilities at the western site first, and subsequently at the eastern site as demand develops."

So, scrub all the work on North, West, Northwest, and East. They were all dead. The new stars were Southwest and Northeast, and they would be run up the flagpole together. The Beverly Township site had ranked second in the original weighted study, but the difficulty with it was that it intruded on Beverly Swamp, and that was likely to outrage environmentalists. Besides, there was that nice Guelph site near by. When Guelph was scrubbed, Swamps Preferred took a sharp nosedive. Anyway, a smaller airport would do less intruding. The Pickering location had been scrapped for the simple reason that you couldn't put a major airport there; the land was marked by rolling hills and two large streams. But a little, tiny, 5,000-10,000-acre airport – that is, one larger in area than either Dorval or Malton – that was no problem.

Ontario could be made to swallow the concept: "The Provincial Government could accept this proposal without embarrassment as they would not have to go back against their public commitments with respect to announced regional development concepts."

The two smallish airports would handle short-haul passengers only, that is, those going on trips of up to 500 miles. Malton would handle the rest. Then, there would be a STOL-port in downtown Toronto, which would also handle short-haul traffic. The Southwest airport would attract between two and four million passengers annually, making it, the strategy paper claimed, "larger than Malton today." Well, no. Malton at that time was handling over seven million passengers, but never mind, in planning reports it isn't accuracy that counts, it's the swing of the thing. The Northeast airport "might attract one to three million" passengers by the year 2000, and "a downtown STOL-port would attract two to three million passengers in 1985." (Why 1985? Because the STOL study was done separately, and only looked ahead that far.)

The biggie was yet to come: "If regional airports and a STOL-port handled only short-haul traffic, then the remaining traffic in the year 2000 would be 48-55 million. Therefore land is required for new airport facilities to provide flexibility to offload more traffic from Malton."

Zowie. This paper was assuming up to 65 million passengers in Toronto, and it proposed to handle them with five – count 'em – airports: Southwest, Northeast, STOL-port, Malton, and a really big new airport we'll call X, because no one knew where to spot it.

The Southwest airport was going to cost $921 million to build and operate and the Northeast one, $895 million. No figure is given for either the STOL-port or X, but obviously the total bill would be in the billions. This was not to accommodate passengers now, or even ten years from now, this was to anticipate a crush of folks three decades hence. With five airports operating at that time, even if the planes didn't keep banging into each other, passengers would need airline schedules, a road map, and a bird dog just to find the appropriate terminal. Well, never mind, it made perfect sense to the planners, and they set out to put the new strategy in motion.

71

On June 21, George Sladek, another Beinhaker sidekick at PM&P, went out to have a quick dekko around the two new sites, and he reported on June 30 that both appeared to "have potential." He thought the Beverly Township location would work better, though. An airport at Pickering would interfere with community development plans, lead to the loss of "high quality farmland," and had no potential for expansion. "Beverly could accommodate four runways and possibly a six-runway airport . . . . In the case of Pickering, a two-runway airport appears to pose little difficulty. A four-runway airport also appears possible, but with considerably greater difficulty."

This didn't sound too good. On July 8, Sladek went back to Pickering, with three civil servants in tow – we couldn't leave everything to the consultants – but couldn't come up with anything more cheerful. "Pickering is probably too restricted for a four-runway airport," this report noted, unless a lot of money was spent flattening the place. The deed would also require the "phasing out" of the town of Claremont. The report commented again on the "high quality" of farms in the area. This quality would drop later on, as the need to justify Pickering emerged, until, by the time of expropriation, it became nothing more than "a typical part of the Toronto urban fringe." The difficulty about putting in more than two runways would simply disappear from the memory of man. So would most of the projected costs. If you can't kid the voters, what's the point in politics?

It was a good thing the department had come up with this bundle of new airports because, in May 1971, all of the earlier planning memos had been turned over to the department of Urban Affairs (since gone to rest). Urban Affairs called in a consultant, naturally, to look at them. The consultant's report came bouncing in on July 20, and it was a shocker. It said flatly that the work done so far was so poor that the only thing to do was to start all over again. The forecasts were dumb, the methodology suspect, and the logic a mess; "We have come to the conclusion that a rational and defensible decision on the future development of airport facilities cannot be made at present time."

Transport's planning techniques were so sloppy that they "will be difficult to defend in any public scrutiny." The boys had them there; there would be no public scrutiny. "Several important social and economic implications relating to future development of airport facilities have not been considered." And, the crusher, "A detailed investigation of . . . the expansion of Malton would appear to be necessary." The whole exercise had been based on "a six-runway airport by the year 2000. It is not clear that such an airport would ever be needed."

So it went, for seventy-nine devastating pages. There was only one thing to do – again, send for Phil. Our consultant can lick their consultant. Accordingly, the Urban Affairs study was turned over to Beinhaker and, in one of his bravura performances, he buried it in marmalade. Beinhaker prepared a paper for the department in draft form; minor changes were made and then it was sent on, by Air Administrator Huck, to Deputy Minister Stoner on September 8, 1971. It was presented as the work of "The Toronto Airports Project Team," but it wasn't, it was just Beinhaker, defending his baby. Huck told his boss in his covering letter that the damaging crack about a rational decision not being possible was "based on an examination of the studies made up to early 1970," and so should be dismissed. Poppycock. A simple glance down the footnotes would have shown Huck, or whoever drafted this misleading sentence for him, references throughout 1970 and early 1971. Beinhaker took much the same position, though.

He began no less than nine paragraphs acknowledging some body-blow to the planning work with the phrase, "The project team agrees with this comment." The team agreed that "The existing studies are questionable," that it was "not clear that such an airport would ever be needed," that "It is misleading to calculate cost of noise by calculating financial loss of a land-bank account" (a little fancy counting in one of the studies), and even that "Costs have not been discounted and should be."

However, he had the ultimate riposte: "Similar points were raised internally in the Air Administration as early as summer 1970 and the work of this project team during the past year had been directed to respond to most of these issues."

There wasn't going to be any six-runway airport, by cracky. There were going to be four or five airports. And if the Ministry had screwed up earlier, well, just watch its smoke from now on. Beinhaker wanted to say that all the earlier studies were "no longer particularly relevant," but that seemed too brazen – after all, there were still all those bills to account for – so the phrase was softened to "useful only as background material." Guy Lafleur has never gone around a gaping defenceman more easily than Beinhaker stickhandled past the Urban Affairs report, although his performance rather begged the question: if the planners had done such a lousy job to date, what guarantee was there that they would do any better in the future? History finally answered that question. They didn't.

Before this hassle was cleared away, the pressure was being applied once more to Ontario. On July 23, 1971, Transport Minister Jamieson met with Ontario Treasurer Charles MacNaughton, and the senior staffs of both men, in Ottawa. Jamieson laid the two new sites on the province, and tried to wring a hasty approval of the Southwest site out of MacNaughton. It didn't work. The minutes of that meeting note that Jamieson began by saying he would like to "make an announcement to the effect that the West site is considered to be a good solution for Toronto, and, while not wedded to it, the MOT wants to obtain the public reaction before proceeding further."

Actually, it wasn't the West site Jamieson wanted. That was last week. What he wanted was the Southwest site, and what he wanted most of all was for the province to swallow it without belching: "He stated he hoped the Province would not immediately oppose this selection after he made it."

MacNaughton refused. "The province's whole TCR plan would 'fall apart' if the only airport built were to the west of Metro Toronto, and as they were committed to this plan, they cannot agree to a single airport in the west, alone."

With this hint, the feds knew it was time to sweeten the pot. "Mr. Jamieson then added that he would develop an airport facility east of Metro Toronto when circumstances warranted it. The minister stated he would be prepared to get a parcel of land now if the Province could agree to our overall proposal. He wanted to make a public announcement that the Ministry is ready to move on the choice of airport sites without further delay."

This wasn't really offering much, so MacNaughton stalled. There would have to be agreement on cost-sharing before anything could be done, he said, and besides, "He wished to consult his Ontario cabinet colleagues before giving his reaction to the modified airport development program."

The vulgar subject of costs was not brought up at that meeting, but Jamieson went to it with a report in his briefcase called "Airport Strategy," dated June 24, 1971, which gave the cost of the Beverly airport at $895 million. No cost estimate was done for the Pickering site, so confident were the feds that they could sell Beverly, but a figure of $16 million was included to buy the parcel of land in the Pickering region referred to by Jamieson. "Ground Access costs" – mostly a provincial responsibility – for Beverly were listed at $314 million, a sum that would have scared the pants off MacNaughton, and a sum $14 million lower than Jamieson would subsequently claim for the entire development of an airport.

MacNaughton went back to Toronto to brood and, the more he brooded, the sorer he got. On August 9, he sent what can only be called a shirty note to Jamieson, complaining about the way the feds kept chopping and changing.

"Members of your staff have related the major elements of your new proposal to the Provincial study team.

"I have discussed this proposal for a new site location with the Honourable W.G. Davis and certain of my Cabinet colleagues. It is of concern to us that your study team have indicated that the evaluation of this new site in the Southwest part of the Toronto region be completed by August 26, 1971. It is our opinion that a satisfactory evaluation of a completely new site cannot be completed within a four week period, and in light of the fact that some 18-20 months were required to evaluate the four earlier sites, I am concerned that the possible expenditure of millions of this government's tax dollars will be conditioned on such a brief and obviously cursory analysis."

That was telling them. MacNaughton wanted another four months to decide, and what's more, he wanted the feds to look harder at the Pickering site. "I understand that after some reluctance, your staff has agreed to evaluate an eastern airport site . . . . I think you should be aware of the Ontario government's concern over the extremely brief investigation being carried out in the evaluation of this new site."

Thank heavens that letter never came to light; it would have wrecked all the later claims about the care with which Pickering was selected, and the agreement on its merits. MacNaughton's letter was written in part because the province was beginning to get uneasy about what the feds were up to. One of the Ontario planners told me, "What really threw us was the suspicion that they didn't know what the hell they were doing. Where were all these sites coming from? First it was Guelph, and then Orangeville, and then, whammo, Peter's Corners. It was spooky."

On August 21, Ontario, which was beginning to be a bit of a nag, released a status report on the TCR plan which said that any airport in the region should be built "in accord with the plan" – that is, east of Toronto. That same day, provincial planners laid the federal site scheme for Pickering on their own TCR map. It was in direct conflict. The province planned to put a string of communities along Highway 7 east of Toronto, and to reserve the land north of them for agriculture and recreation, but the airport would wipe out two of the towns-to-be, Brock and Audley, and wreck the agriculture and recreation reserve.

There was worse to come. Two days later, the Toronto team reported to Ottawa on a preliminary airspace check. The Beverly location would work, but not Pickering. "The sw site will present little or no airspace interference with the existing Toronto International Airport . . . On the other hand, an airport at the proposed Northeast site is expected to have a major influence on the operation of Toronto International."

The federal strategy, if that is the term for lurching around, was unravelling day by day. On September 17, Jamieson, after numerous drafts prepared by his underlings (the first was written on September 1; it took sixteen days to get it right), replied to MacNaughton's angry note of August 9, agreeing to postpone a site decision, and to have another look at Pickering. On October 21, Ontario voters went to the polls, and Davis was returned to office with a large majority. His bargaining position was now unassailable. That same day, the federal Cabinet Committee on Government Operations caught up with, and accepted, the new three-airport approach. It was really a four-airport approach, with one in reserve; in fact, it was really the old multi-airport approach of Design for Aviation, re-treaded. The full Cabinet accepted it six days later and it became, for a brief and secret time, Canada's official policy.

About the same time, urbanologist Peter Oehm did a quick, eight-page study for the province to compare the Beverly and Pickering sites from the point of view of regional development. He found, to no one's astonishment, that Pickering suited the TCR concept better. Ken Foley, Director of the Economics Branch of Ontario Transport, wrote the feds to say, "Our early evaluation of these new sites indicates both have major problems" and "neither site appears to be totally acceptable" – but the Pickering location was less awful than Beverly, even though it wiped out Brock and Audley. Perhaps, the letter hinted, a little deal could be worked.

The feds were bloody, but unbowed. In early December, they gave their last gasp. This was a weighted study of five airport sites: the three old crocks from 1970 that had not been completely massacred – Guelph, Orangeville, and Port Perry – and the two new boys, Beverly and Pickering. The study was, not to put too fine a point on it, stupid. The sites were judged on the basis of seven criteria, and certain criteria immediately knocked an airport out as "Unacceptable." Lack of "Airspace compatibility" was fatal in this study, as was "Urban Sprawl." Guelph was knocked off on both these points. The airport the Ministry wanted to announce in April was doubly disqualified now. Likewise Orangeville, because of "Severe Winter Storms" and Port Perry because of "Poor Passenger Convenience." Cost was not a criterion in this measure, which seems odd, and no weight was given to the fact that of all the sites, Pickering presented the greatest "Social Disruption." You had to get a black box on your criterion to be ruled out, and Social Disruption didn't rate a black box. And guess what? When all was said and done, only two of the five sites were acceptable, and those two were Beverly and Pickering. The choice between them, however, was no contest. Beverly rated higher than Pickering on six of the seven criteria, and equal on the seventh. The planners were so excited they set down their findings all in capitals:

"TWO NEW AIRPORTS REQUIRED AS A MINIMUM – ONE TO OPEN IN 1978 (PREFERABLY THE SOUTHWEST). BOTH TO BE OPERATIONAL IN THE EARLY 1980S. IF DECISION MADE TO ACQUIRE ONLY ONE SITE NOW, *SOUTHWEST RECOMMENDED* [This was underlined]."

Last year's new, improved site was now a washout, but this year's ultra-new, super-improved location contained the secret ingredient, capital letters. The province still wouldn't buy. At a federal-provincial meeting on December 16, Ken Foley told the feds that Ontario had already committed substantial funds to sewer and water facilities east of Toronto, and could not afford to duplicate them in the west. Ottawa could either put its airport at Pickering or go it alone.

Ottawa caved. On December 22, Jamieson and MacNaughton met once more, and Jamieson agreed, tentatively and reluctantly, to Pickering. That was the end of the three-airport concept. It was never mentioned again. Indeed, the third airport may have been stuck in there simply for bargaining purposes. That was also the end of the small, 5,000-10,000-acre concept. Pickering, despite all the warnings that it wouldn't work, was going to be a full-blown monster.

There were still some rough edges to smooth out, such as the airspace interference. That was fixed in a report dated December 29, in which Walter McLeish, Director General, Civil Aeronautics (he is now Air Administrator) ruled that "The capacity effects on the airspace system that could result from the development of this site are not considered to be of a magnitude which would preclude development of a major airport at this location."

Exactly one week after the minister accepted the Pickering location, the airspace problem disappeared.

The TCR plan problem was solved, too. During February 1972, at a series of meetings between federal and provincial planners, the TCR map outlines were shifted around until, by golly, the site was no longer stamping all over them. The lines had been confirmed only in August; now they were unconfirmed, but nobody was told about the change. Later, when opponents of the airport did their own map overlays, they thought they had caught the planners in a blunder, and made much of the fact that there was a conflict between the TCR and the airport site. The boys replied stonily that no conflict existed (it did, on the land reserve, but not the towns) and let it go at that. There was even a bonus in this; the province decided to push ahead a plan already on the books, and to develop a major urban centre just outside the airport. It would be called Cedarwood, and it would house, eventually, 200,000 people.

Then there was the matter of an environmental study. Pickering had been thrown in so quickly that nobody had looked after this, so, in January 1972, an environmentalist was sent out for three days to see how the place looked in the middle of winter. He said it looked okay to him.

On January 28, 1972, the Toronto team's top dogs, and Beinhaker, went to Ottawa to present their new notion to the higher-ups. They liked it. The scheme was put to the Committee on Government Operations on February 1, and to the full Cabinet on February 7. They liked it too. This was not the multi-airports scheme they had approved before, nor was it the Son of Design for Aviation they had also approved. It was brand new. The Cabinet was shown a four-runway airport laid out at Pickering, and told that it was necessary in order to accommodate 62 million passengers in the year 2000. It was not told that the planners had preferred the Beverly site and had been whipsawed into Pickering; it was not told that Ontario had major reservations about the site, nor that the province had accepted Orangeville, and then had to be diverted. Instead, the ministers were led to believe that, because of the drawbacks attached to the four earlier sites, "It was decided to re-examine the sites which had been identified in the preliminary analysis." They were given the weighted study of the five sites that showed Beverly and Pickering to be acceptable. Then they were told, "The relative merits of these five sites were analyzed and it was concluded that the Northeast site represented the best location" – which was simply not true.

The Cabinet said, yes, yes, fine, fine, and approved. Who could blame it? Who could follow all this? Who even knew half of it?

On March 2, 1972, Darcy McKeough, who had replaced Charles MacNaughton as Provincial Treasurer, and Donald Jamieson got up in their respective parliaments and read a joint statement announcing the selection of Pickering as a site for Toronto's second airport, and the creation, on paper, of a magnificent new city called Cedarwood.

"The scenario they gave," as one provincial planner put it, "had very little to do with what actually happened." Both ministers managed to present an entirely misleading history of the airport choice. It was like saying that Mickey Rooney married seven times because he liked girls; there was some truth in the facts, but all the juicy bits were left out.

Both announcements said that "The choice of a site northeast of Toronto has come after an exhaustive federal-provincial evaluation since 1968 of fifty-nine potential airport sites within a fifty-mile radius of Metropolitan Toronto." This left the impression, and must have been intended to leave the impression, that Pickering was one of the fifty-nine. It was not.

The statement went on, "It has now been decided that for a number of compelling reasons, the Pickering Township site is more suitable than any of the other sites studied." That wasn't a lie, it was just tricky; it depended on what was meant by "suitable."

When he finished the joint statement, McKeough went on to refer to the "important environmental study," which he said had "encompassed such considerations as air quality, vegetation, wildlife, soil, water, minerals, and open space." That was true. The environmentalist had found that Pickering contained air, vegetation, wildlife, soil, water, minerals and open space. What they were like, he hadn't had time to discover.

McKeough also said that Pickering would add "Major stimulus to the Toronto-Centred Region Concept." This was confusing. When Mirabel was chosen, the justification was the Higgins Report argument that buildup tends to come between an airport and the metropolis it serves, but if that was correct, growth would go between Pickering and Toronto, not eastward from Pickering. It would add to urban sprawl, and urban sprawl was why Guelph had been knocked off the list in the December 1971 report.

Jamieson gave the cost of the airport as $300 million. That was totally misleading. It was apparently based on an internal document prepared by Larry Potvin, who, on March 1, fired off a note to his colleagues to use the cost of $288 million "in any discussions." The sum was made up of $63 million for land, $55 million for runways, $85 million for terminals, $15 million for ancillary buildings and $26 million for "miscellaneous," including navigation aids, project management and design. Gone were all the user costs, the cost of a rapid transit link, the cost-sharing deal to be made with the province, and much else. The figures were absurd. To date, the federal government has spent more than $200 million, with no runways, no terminals, and no ancillary buildings, just a heap of miscellaneous.

79

The compulsion to justify a second airport was so strong that every objection was quashed, and the need to conform was so strong that even the men who knew what was happening got along by going along. Gone were the fundamental objections to an eastern site, gone was the logic of all the earlier studies, gone was Design for Aviation, gone was everything except the forecast of 60 million passengers and the Holy Grail of a second airport. Perhaps the men responsible now felt it was too late to turn back – more than three years and millions of dollars had been invested in a bum decision, and it would certainly have been embarrassing to admit failure now. But the fact is that they didn't have to admit failure because, with luck, no one would ever know what happened.

Who picked Pickering? No one did. Nobody wanted it. Until it was launched on March 2, nobody would vouch for it. When, on January 30, 1973, Transport Minister Jean Marchand, who succeeded Jamieson on November 27, 1972, asserted in the House of Commons that "The Ontario government also reached the conclusion that the airport at Pickering best suited their planning," Premier Davis promptly wrote to set the record straight. "The words 'best suited' do not accurately describe the circumstances," he wrote. Once the federal government pressed its case for one of the final two sites, the province preferred the eastern one, even though it required "some adaptation" of the TCR plan. It did not follow, however, that Ontario agreed with the site.

When it was all over, and federal-provincial teams were working on the new airport, an embarrassing question came up. D.W. Stevenson, Director of Policy Planning in the Ontario Department of Treasury and Economics, asked the feds, "Why can't we expand Malton?" He got no answer, because answer there was none.

However, the subject would not die. The March 2 announcement, with its attendant expropriations, made Pickering a public issue, and the Transport chaps were about to find out that the toughest shots of the provincial planners were nothing compared to what would be laid on them by the band of loonies who lived on the land that had been so abruptly whisked away. They were about to kick up a terrible stink in its defence.

Chapter 7

The Bitchers
and How They Grew

Brenda Davies, nurse:
"We quickly divided into two groups, those who were angry because they didn't think they were getting enough money for their homes, and those who didn't care about money, who said, 'You've got to show me a better reason than anything I've seen yet to make me give up my home.' When the government people came around they told us firmly not to dicker over price and not to try to fight expropriation. You won't get more and you'll likely get less. I had read the [Expropriation] Act and there were certain rights, certain things you would get. I asked the government man if these would be refused if you fought expropriation, and he said 'It stands to reason.' Of course, that was false; the people who fought got much more. I have tremendous respect for the idea of government, and I tried to instil this in my children, but in the circumstances it didn't take. A whole generation of youngsters grew up with this example before their eyes. They hate government. That is a terrible thing."

Jim Allward, airport planner, Transport Canada:
"The public are not aware of the interlinkages, don't understand how fragile the fabric of society is. They showed us a film with rats in enclosures and at first they were living quiet and peaceful and then it got more crowded and more crowded and they began to eat each other, and they got apathetic. Because it was too crowded you had a total breakdown. You can see something like that at times at Malton."

When the decision to plunk a new airport and a new city down in the heart of Pickering was announced on March 2, 1972, many of the local residents simply refused to believe it. Peter McCowan, who owns his own cement company in the area, recalls, "It just seemed nuts to me at first. I paid no attention whatever." Housewife Pat McClennan couldn't believe it, either. "We could make nothing of it; anyone could see you couldn't put an airport here."

The members of the Pickering Township council were stunned. They had recently worked out a long-term planning proposal with the province; now it was gone, in a puff of smoke. There must be some mistake. Others accepted the plan, stoically. Governments move in mysterious ways, and this was just another mysterious move. They began to calculate the value of their properties. Still others, most of them local farmers, were delighted. Carson Armstrong was one of these. "The ones that complained, they were city folk, mostly," he says. "Some farmers I know were millionaires out of the deal. You don't hear them complaining." Armstrong had already sold his land to a developer; all the takeover meant to him was that he could rent it back, cheaply, while continuing to enjoy the money he had made on the sale.

In all these mixed reactions, however, there were a handful of people who were certain, at once, that the projects were real and serious, and equally certain that they should be stopped. Among these was Hugh Miller, a farmer whose family has been raising crops on the same property since 1839 and who, at sixty-one, intends to keep on with the tradition. There was no way he would stand still for expropriation. "I am just bright enough to know that anyone who has worked hard all his life and suddenly stops won't enjoy himself and won't last long. Those that sold out, they look twenty years older. Alfred Baggy, he was seventy-two when they expropriated him for the marshalling yards. He got $400,000 and he went to Florida for six weeks. He came back in a coffin. He never had learned to loaf."

Then there were Anne Wanstall and Aileen Adams. Wanstall is a British-born journalist, who was working at that time as a food expert for the *Toronto Star*. Adams works in public relations. They had bought a ten-acre lot on the Brock Road in 1964. It was an historic house, and the bell on its rooftop rang during the Rebellion of 1837. It would ring again when the airport was shelved in 1975, and then it would disappear, after Wanstall and Adams were forced off their land. The bell is now buried; it belongs to the federal government, but it was stolen before it could be claimed, and put away against the day when, and if, the airport is officially abandoned. The two women had picked this property in part because of its historical associations, and they spent thousands of dollars and eight years of their lives refinishing and refurbishing it, and when the airport announcement dropped on them like a bomb, they were determined to fight back. They got on the telephone and began to call neighbours, friends, anyone who might be interested, to a meeting at Melody Farm the very next day.

As it happened, there was already the nucleus of a protest organization in the neighbourhood. When a development called Century

City was slated for Pickering in the late 1960s, a local group sprang up to fight it, headed by Clark Muirhead, an Uxbridge councillor who owns his own engineering firm. Muirhead dug into the Century City planning documents, and found glaring deficiencies. When he began to hammer at these in public, he was joined in battle by farmer Hugh Miller and Dr. Charles Godfrey. Godfrey, the director of rehabilitation medicine at Wellesley Hospital in Toronto, had been farming in the area on a part-time basis since 1952. He is slender, balding, quick-witted and energetic, a man of great charm and natural leadership abilities, who managed to earn the grudging respect of the civil servants. "At first I thought he was a son-of-a-bitch," one Transport official told me. "Then I thought, 'Boy, would I like to have this son-of-a-bitch on my side.' " Godfrey saw the Century City project as a disaster. "It was a land assembly by Revenue Properties; it would be an instant community. But there was no industry here to support Century City and we didn't want it."

Lorne Almack, who combines farming with a career as a planning consultant and partner in the firm Price Waterhouse Associates, and Terry Moore, a family court judge in Newmarket, helped in the Century City battle. The climax came at a meeting to approve the plan. The developers' spokesmen laid on an impressive display of charts and drawings to show that the city would be good for the area. They were not expecting any substantial rebuttal. Then, one after another, the five local men stood up, each to deal with and demolish one aspect of the plan. When they were done, one of the Century City lawyers commented, "You're obviously a forecaster, Dr. Godfrey; can you tell me how long I'm going to live?" "A long time," Godfrey replied. "The good die young."

Century City died on the drawing boards. Although no one knew it, that battle was a warmup for the longer, larger conflict over Pickering and Cedarwood, and it had left the victors with two important lessons. One was that if they organized, they could meet and beat hired experts at their own work; the other was that a joke is worth a dozen charts. Both lessons would be put to work again.

When protestors began to gather at Melody Farm on March 3, the Godfreys – Margaret Godfrey was, and remains, just as active as her husband – and Hugh Miller were among the early arrivals. The house was soon jammed to overflowing but, since no one knew much about what was actually proposed, not much planning could be done. However, a decision was taken to form a protest group, and it was given a name, People Or Planes. No one is sure exactly who first suggested the title. There are half a dozen claimants, and it was first given as People Over Planes, but it soon became People Or Planes, and, more usually, just POP. The meeting also named Hugh Miller as chairman, pro tem, until an election could be held.

A second meeting took place at Brougham Community Hall on Saturday, March 7. POP's minutes show that, at that gathering, $748.04 was collected in donations in buckets, including $200 from "an overflow crowd gathered in a nearby church, receiving the broadcast from the main hall." Passing the bucket for funds remains a feature of the POP assemblies, which remind me of gatherings I have attended of the Social Credit League in Alberta, and the Co-operative Commonwealth Federation, before it went high-hat and became the NDP, in Saskatchewan. Righteousness abounds, funds are short, and coffee is free. Stirring speeches were made by Miller, Godfrey, Frank McGee, who wanted to be the federal MP for the Ontario riding on behalf of the Conservative Party, Norman Cafik, who was the Liberal incumbent, and William Newman, the area MPP, now Minister of Agriculture. Cafik said, among other things, that he was "unalterably opposed to the airport" and that he had first heard about it "only one hour before the announcement." That was funny; on March 1, Charles Godfrey, a Liberal at the time, attended a party fund-raising dinner at the Royal York Hotel in Toronto, and he says Cafik told him about the airport which he, Cafik, thought was a splendid thing indeed. Anyway, on Saturday night, he was unalterably opposed. Later, he became less unalterable, and before long, he was alterably in favour.

At this second meeting, Godfrey became chairman pro tem – Miller didn't really want the job, and Godfrey did – and, on March 24, 1972, he was formally elected to the post he holds to this day. POP was off and screaming.

It was, and is, a bizarre organization. On the left is Bill Lishman, who is described in the history of the town of Brougham as "a sculptor of repute, a skilled wood carver, blacksmith and welder." He also rides motorcycles, flies hang-gliders, and ran for the NDP, in vain. On the right is Clark Muirhead, a square-jawed free enterpriser who regrets almost everything that has happened in politics since they repealed the Corn Laws. In POP, they get along just fine.

The organization joins feminine activists like Anne Howes, who complains with some justification that POP is a male-dominated lobby, and others who, like Hugh Miller's wife, Elsie, could step into the pages of a Victorian novel as the busy homemaker, with no questions asked.

There are slickers like Brian Buckles, who combines farming with an executive job as Vice President of Corporate Operations for

Manufacturers Life, and who did many of the analytical studies for the group. There are down-home folks like Gordon and Helen Auld, whose farm families go back more than a century. There are artists and sculptors, nurses, doctors, lawyers, salesmen, actors, designers, writers, stockbrokers, labourers, housewives, retirees and ne'er-do-wells. There is a strong admixture of part-time farmers, city folk who moved out here in the 1950s and '60s, and who still combine agriculture with a salaried job. All in all, a mixed bag.

Transport Canada, which never understood POP, and probably never will, dismissed them as greed-driven speculators, on the one hand, or hobby-farmers who were upset because their idyll was being interfered with, on the other. "They're just fat-cats," one Ministry official told me. But they are not; at least not most of them. They are resolutely middle class, generally conservative, and genuinely enraged by what they consider to be the shoddy planning and bullying tactics of two governments.

Brenda Davies, a registered nurse who became one of the zaniest of the POP activists (she has a sign on her front door demanding a fifty-cent entrance fee from all government men; she wears a hat that features a plastic model of a jet airplane) is, in private, a serious and concerned woman, and she contends that "If the governments were so dumb about the things you knew about, how could you trust them to decide whether they needed an airport, and where to put it?"

It wasn't greed that held POP together, and it wasn't looniness, although the organization has streaks of both; it was a collective feeling that impersonal forces, misdirected forces, callous forces, had been set loose by the two governments, and that they had to be opposed.

Pat McClennan remembers the beginning of her involvement this way: "We were driving along and heard this announcement about the airport; we were absolutely stunned. The announcement said there would be a plan in the provincial government's Brock Road office, so we went there. On the wall there were two army survey maps from about 1914 Scotch-taped up there with blue marking pen around the airport site. It was as if they had said, 'Well, let's have one more gin and tonic and draw up an airport.' I got mad that day and I've stayed mad ever since."

Peter McCowan had a similar experience. Although he dismissed the first announcement, he soon received an expropriation notice, with an accompanying map. "The map was all off; the roads were going the wrong way and the railway was running through the wrong concession. I went to the federal government's trailer on the

Ninth Line and Highway 7, and they said, 'You've got to go to Brock Road, the provincial office.' So I go there and I walk in and on the wall are pinned a series of topographical maps put together with Scotch tape. It was obviously done at the last minute. There is a woman at the counter and I explain to her about the map they sent to me being all wrong. She says, 'It doesn't matter, we're going to expropriate it all anyway.' I'm completely stunned."

McCowan is a handsome man in his middle forties, a self-made businessman, competent athlete, world traveller; one of the beautiful people. Pat McClennan is somewhat older, a good deal less confident, much less experienced. One brief encounter with bureaucracy made them comrades in arms, and they joined the swelling ranks of POP. A group so diverse was bound to have internal squabbles, and it did. One member got up at a meeting to argue that POP should stop fighting the idea of the airport, and concentrate instead on getting it shifted to some other locale. The minutes of that meeting note grimly, "It was lucky he left early or he'd have been lynched."

POP's bible became a booklet that Anne Wanstall brought to an early meeting: *The Householder's Guide to Community Defence Against Bureaucratic Aggression*, by Antony Jay. Jay had been a cabinet minister in the Wilson governme..t in the U.K. He had advice to offer from both inside and outside government, but his most telling comment was this: "When the enemy is the referee as well, when a government official will be adjudicating between you and an arm of the government, then you have to fight ten times as hard for the same chance of success." POP took that to heart.

Fear, anger, humour, and hard work were the prods that kept the protestors going. As word of the airport and city spread, and as more and more people began to receive expropriation notices, they flocked to meetings. Some appeared at a few gatherings, sat, listened, then drifted off. They thought the battle was hopeless, or that the protestors were too radical or – far more often – the newcomers were simply unable to spare the time, energy, and emotional involvement the project demanded. In a number of cases, one partner in a marriage became involved with POP while the other did not, and the result was domestic strife. There were a number of divorces on this account. One man, who lost his wife this way, now bitterly resents the organization. "I wish to God I'd taken the first money they offered us and run," he says. "At least I'd still have a family."

The active members were divided into cells – this was one of Antony Jay's suggestions – and a cell captain was made responsible for each of the twenty-one communities involved in the airport and

Cedarwood schemes. Whenever volunteers were required, to gather petitions, distribute leaflets, or just turn up at a meeting to heckle a government spokesman, they were turned out by the cell captains. Late one afternoon, Sinclair Stevens, the Progressive Conservative MP for York-Simcoe, the neighbouring riding, telephoned the POP office to say that a display of strength in Ottawa would be a good idea. Within two hours, three busloads of volunteers had been rounded up; the next morning, they were marching around Parliament Hill with placards.

At first, most members of POP believed the group should concentrate on stopping the airport, and let the city be built. At a Steering Committee meeting at Hugh Miller's house on March 11, 1972, Isobel Thompson's argument, that "The purpose of this Committee should be to stop the airport and Cedarwood," was dropped in favour of Charles Godfrey's motion: "The object of this committee is to stop the airport." However, the resolution was reversed on April 9, less than a month later, and POP carried on a two-front war, against both the federal and provincial government schemes. (The province kept saying that, even if the airport died, their new city was such a grand idea that it would go ahead anyway; they still say that.)

The war was carried on, in large part, through subcommittees. There are always subcommittees, and for POP the crucial ones were the Executive Committee (as the Steering Committee became), the Legal Committee, Fund-Raising, Technical, Diplomatic (the lobbying committee), and Publicity. The most active, and effective of all these was the Publicity Committee, thanks, among other things, to the combined talents of Anne Wanstall, Isobel Thompson, and Libby McCowan, Peter's wife. Wanstall knew whom to contact in the media, and how to get out press releases; McCowan was a tireless worker, a fearsome heckler, and a terror on the telephone. Thompson added flair. A Whitevale housewife when the battle began, she now works for the provincial government, a fact that never fails to tickle her husband, Tommy. Like Wanstall, she was born and brought up in England. In civil rights matters, the British are trouble-makers, no doubt about it. She is a comely woman who had some training as an actress, and used it to good effect; POP didn't put on demonstrations, it staged dramas. Libby McCowan is a slender, pretty, troubled woman. The battle took too much out of her, and she came perilously close to complete mental collapse. That is why, in the end, she and her husband gave up, and sold out. Peter still comes back to see the lovely property they used to own, now rented, and which is being demolished by stages. Libby doesn't; she can't bear to. For months, this trio worked full time – Wanstall took a leave of absence from the *Star* – churning out publicity, and stirring up trouble.

POP staged a lot of dirty tricks, some of which were authorized by the various committees, many of which were carried out on a free-lance basis.

The Ontario government brought out a tabloid newspaper: *Airport Information, A Special Supplement*, whose front page featured a two-column picture of Darcy McKeough and a lot of misleading jargon about the chunky goodness of the airport, and city-to-be. It also carried, inside, an eight-column reproduction of the famous wrong-way map. Within two days, POP had produced its own version, *Airport Information, A Special Supplement, Part Two*, which used the same typography and make-up. It even had the picture of McKeough in the same place, except that it had been doctored slightly; he was wearing a People Or Planes button. The material in this edition was a frontal attack on both the airport and Cedarwood. POP members drove around to the federal and provincial sites, picked up all the official publications, handed out their version, and told the government workers, "This is an updated version." One bureaucrat grumbled, "My God, they never tell us anything," but accepted the switch and, for a few days, people calling for information got the POP paper.

The Publicity Committee also produced a document that looked exactly like an expropriation notice, but instead contained information on how to fight expropriation, and how to get in touch with POP.

There were other gimmicks, some not so cute. One of the Ministry of Transport's public relations men, Nigel Dunn, lived in the area, so POP members made a practice of ordering food from take-out restaurants, and having it sent to his place in the middle of the night. They also worked the old wheeze of calling him up several times during an evening, to say they wanted to leave a message for Sam. After Dunn had indignantly denied several times harbouring anyone named Sam on the premises, someone would phone and say, "This is Sam. Any messages?" Dunn eventually moved away, and later switched jobs. He is now a PR man for the post office, which makes POP members think there is a God, after all.

Then there was the old frozen fish trick. Several trailers were set up for government officials to work out of, and the children of some POP members slipped frozen fish under the trailers, to melt and rot.

There were other dumb stunts. The Department of the Environment had put up a meteorological tower, and two youngsters went out one night to loosen all the bolts on the tower supports, hoping that, with the first strong wind, the tower would come crashing down. However, they loosened too many bolts, and the structure came down, almost on top of them. They lost their tools, buried in the debris.

In the main, however, POP used a more sophisticated brand of humour. At one meeting, when a government spokesman had finished singing the praises of Cedarwood, Godfrey replied shortly, "Don't tell us it's a unique opportunity to plan a community. Eve said that to Adam."

POP was good at nagging. Jay's booklet had admonished the reader to go to the top of the official tree and to persist; so, every morning, someone was detailed to telephone Premier Davis and Prime Minister Trudeau. One day, Libby McCowan got through to Trudeau, but he had nothing much to say.

Far more effective were the group's combined drama and fund-raising efforts. There were expropriation kits and training sessions; there were letter-writing contests in the schools, with a prize for the best essay on the airport; there were bumper stickers, buttons, lawn signs, and helium balloons with messages – all of them sold for a profit. POP produced its own movie on the issue, which it rents for $6 a showing to interested groups. An automatic typewriter was put to work churning out letters of protest; there were parades, picnics, motorcades, walkathons, art sales, newspapers, a lovely book of drawings of historic houses, by Jane Buckles, and even a time capsule. There was an Earth Day, a Media Day, and a Bavarian Night. The Bavarian Night alone cleared $1,000. To dramatize the plight of the local farming community, POP trucked milk, fruit, and vegetables down to Toronto's City Hall, and gave it away, with a pep talk. Protestors flooded onto T.V. and radio, wrote letters to the newspapers, and turned up at public meetings all over the province to heckle cabinet ministers. POP even put a float in Toronto's Santa Claus parade.

They were always putting on a show for the benefit of the media. They learned that the press didn't really care about the rights or wrongs of their case, and couldn't be bothered to read the long documents on either side of the argument. That was too much work. What the journalists wanted was something to see and photograph. So POP gave it to them. Isobel Thompson says, "It took us a long time to realize they weren't interested in words, they were interested in action. Once we had a few things with real razzamataz, they were willing to listen." To get a donkey's attention, you are supposed to hit him on the nose with an axe handle; to get a journalist's attention, stage a parade the television cameras can photograph.

At the annual Sportsman's Show in the Canadian National Exhibition grounds, signatures and letters of protest were collected by the thousands. Since federal government spokesmen had promised to respond to each and every protest individually, POP gathered the letters into batches, and then sent them to Ottawa in odd lots. One day, two letters would be sent, the next 1,100, the next forty-seven, and so on. The idea was that the Ministry of Transport would bring in extra help to answer the letters, and staggering them would make it impossible to know when to lay on extra staff.

Another committee was set up to broaden POP's appeal, and to canvass the neighbouring communities for support. It was called the Metropolitan Toronto Airport Review Committee – MTARC – and, under the chairmanship of Toronto lawyer Douglas Turner, who has a farm near Uxbridge, MTARC set out to fan the flames of regional discontent. Ratepayer groups from Stouffville, Claremont, and other communities – including Toronto – joined MTARC. The Ontario Federation of Naturalists, of which Lorne Almack was a member, joined up, as did a number of environmental groups, including Pollution Probe. MTARC gained the support of Toronto Mayor (now MP) David Crombie, and of Alderman William Kilbourn, both of whom added prestige, savvy, and clout to the anti-airport lobby. MTARC is really POP under another name (something the federal government never did figure out), although it confined itself to dealing with technical issues, and left the rough stuff to POP.

When the Department of Public Works began to put down survey stakes, one ingenious POP member suggested imitating Ali Baba, and driving in hundreds of phoney stakes, to foul up the surveyors. That was turned down, and stayed down. So were suggestions to pave the lawn in front of Queen's Park, to release chickens in downtown Toronto, to float paper airplanes across the Ontario legislature, and to petition the Queen.

Many of POP's best ideas came out of bull sessions. In the early days, the group worked out of members' homes; later it graduated to an abandoned schoolhouse, and today is ensconced in the Cedarwood Community Hall. (There is a town formerly named Cedarwood in the area; this name was to be used for the new project. However, that was later dropped, and the city-to-be – if there ever is one – will be called North Pickering.) Wherever the office was, the ladies of the Publicity Committee would gather to answer the telephone, or use it, and they would kick around ideas. Some were simple, such as a contest with a prize of $25 for answering the telephone with "I support POP." Some were a little more complicated. One day, during one of these sessions, someone suggested that the only way to keep airplanes away might be to put up a dirigible, the way the British did in the Second World War. That turned into a scheme for gathering publicity by hiring a balloon and sending it up with a message, and that turned into a Balloon Ascent Day at Lorne Almack's farm, which featured side shows and games of chance, and brought in loads of money and publicity. There was a Trillium Tour, for the more genteel, a card draw for the more conventional, and the flying of a hang-glider over the House of Commons for the more daring. All came off.

So did a couple of freelance projects by Aileen Adams. When Public Works Minister Jean-Eudes Dubé came to a local country club to explain his department's work on the airport, Adams crashed through his aides and handed the startled minister a bag of horse manure. "This is some of our lovely soil," she told him, smiling sweetly. She may have felt that she was simply returning a favour. She looked frail, but she had the guts of a burglar. POP staged a roadside demonstration on Highway 7 one day, but it was being ignored by passing traffic, so Adams stepped out into the busy road and created a one-woman roadblock.

POP was not the only lobby in the airport business. In the area around Malton, a group called New Airport Now – NAN – grew up out of a ratepayer's association opposed to the expansion of Malton. NAN was run, in large part, by Miriam Mittermaier, a Rexdale housewife whose husband, Arthur, had once worked for KPM. Although he left the consulting firm before his wife became involved with NAN, POP used the coincidence to make it look as if Mrs. Mittermaier was simply trying to get work for her husband. Mrs. Mittermaier appeared on open-line shows to state her group's case – that the noise level around Malton was so bad that anything, including the opening of another airport at Pickering, was worth doing; whenever she did so, POP members would get on the line with tough, and usually well-informed comments. They gave her a very rough time.

Mrs. Mittermaier says of POP that "They had incredible expertise at their beck and call," a reasonable comment. Jean Bickley, a neighbour and friend who did publicity for NAN, says, "POP had a terrific sense of PR," and that is certainly true. However, both say that POP was "quite ruthless," and there is something in that, too.

Closer to home, an outfit sprang up in Pickering called POW – for Progress Over Welfare. Its argument was that an airport would create jobs, and its chairman was David Binger, who ran a small store in Brougham. Binger and his wife contacted the Ministry of Transport for help and got it, but discreetly. Larry Potvin, second in

91

command of the Toronto Area Airports Project, went out to Brougham on the night of April 10, 1972, with Jack Shelton, then, as now, a Transport PR man. They came away with the feeling that POW, however splendid its aims, was no match for POP. It needed help. POW was holding a public meeting on April 14, and Potvin noted in a memo to his boss, Gordon McDowell, that "We should . . . lay out a well-organized program, so that we do not lose control of the meeting." He proposed sending a strong MOT delegation, headed by McDowell. He also suggested that the department should provide a public address system, since POW couldn't put up the necessary $300. McDowell agreed to provide the PA system, and to send a four-man team, but he wouldn't go himself, Potvin filled in. The meeting was not a success. POP translated POW into "Pave Our World," and the group faded and died.

POP, on the other hand, continued to grow. At its height, it claimed a membership of 2,200, but not all of these were active members. That number is roughly the number of objections the group was able to gather for a public hearing under the Expropriation Act. However, only 815 properties were expropriated in the federal development, and only 130 of these filed formal protests. Most of the other properties were in the hands of people who were content to let events take their course, or in the hands of developers and speculators, who kept their mouths shut and their heads down until it was all over. The federal government made much of the fact that, as one cabinet memo puts it, "Of the 2,163 intervenors, only eight per cent were land owners being expropriated." What right had these other needle-nosing busybodies to kick up a stink when they weren't even being turfed out of house and home? Rapists, I understand, feel much the same way about street-corner loungers who call the cops on them.

It didn't matter if POP could properly claim 2,200 supporters, in any event. The work turned, in the end, on the efforts of a few dozen activists; they were the ones who attended the meetings, turned out reports, knocked on doors, made telephone calls and engaged the interest of their colleagues, neighbours, and the community at large. Some of them did well out of the battle – Hugh Miller and Lorne Almack both got to keep their farms – some, like the McCowans, did not do so well.

However, POP, with all its kinks, was a splendid and successful organization, and compared to its competition – NAN and POW and the MOT – it was a Supergroup. In its first three years of operation, it raised $130,000, which went on legal fees, publicity, and research. In the end, it stymied two governments that spent millions. The

MOT spent $39,000 on a single display at the CNE to promote the airport, while POP made money out of its CNE excursions, and drew more attention to boot. When the protestors claimed that the government had overlooked a gull flyway, the feds set out to investigate. The study cost $253,035, and included charges for three ornithologists, at $2,500 a month each, one field supervisor, at $3,500 a month, one biologist, five assistants and two consultants. The notebooks, paper, and copying budget for this little caper came to $400. The study concluded that gulls would not present a serious hazard to aviation in the area, and it had spent about twice as much as POP laid out in its entire campaign.

The government was handicapped in its dealings with the protestors because it never could fathom what made that little group of zanies tick. Why were they so excited all the time? For the MOT folks, the whole exercise was a matter of shoving memos around; they never did grasp that people resent being displaced for something as dumbly planned as the airport. The departmental files are full of memos, many written by MOT's public relations people, predicting the imminent collapse of POP. Some of these are worth examining, not for what they show about POP, but for what they reveal about the bureaucrats. It is like having a peek into the files of Nixon's aides.

For example, Nigel Dunn, whom we have already met, wrote weekly reports to his bosses on the activities of the protestors, and in one of these he says that he has found out what really frightens POP. It's him – Nigel Dunn. No kidding. "POP considers that the main threat today to its entire case is MOT Public Affairs generally and Nigel Dunn specifically." He doesn't say what he has done to make him such an object of fear – maybe he finally got the message for Sam – but he does go on to protest that POP plans to "tape record information personnel in the process of giving out information to the public." Dunn says this would constitute an attempt to "gag" Public Affairs. What it constituted was an attempt to stop the PR men telling different tales in different places.

In another memo, Dunn describes how he managed to sway *Toronto Star* reporter Gary Oakes into turning out a story that took no pokes at MOT. "That MOT came out quite free of criticism is due largely, I am satisfied, to the fact that I spent several hours with Oakes – a good friend and former colleague – carefully explaining the Ministry's position."

In yet another report, Dunn noted, "POP is still alive, but it's not nearly as healthy as a year ago. There is no doubt they are strapped for funds. POP has been weakened by its lack of restraint . . . I understand that the creator of the hanging episode [a mock hanging of Trudeau and Davis], Bill Lishman, has been expelled from POP because of his lack of judgment." Actually, the creator of the hanging scheme was not Lishman but Clark Muirhead, who was nearly expelled from his home by his wife, who thought the stunt was dumb. Lishman was not expelled. He was, however, criticized within POP because he went ahead with a rock concert after the Executive Committee had – it thought – vetoed the idea. The executives were sure a rock concert would bring out people smoking strange substances, which it did, and that it would result in terrible publicity, which it did not. Dunn may have terrified POP, but he did not know much about its workings.

Another MOT PR man, Paul Roach, reported to McDowell on the POP demonstration at Toronto City Hall. Before the event, Roach wrote to say that it was coming up and that "A discreet representative will be in attendance to take a sounding."

Roach, as it happened, was the representative, although he was not all that discreet. He found the whole show pretty much a waste of time, which was funny, since it generated considerable newspaper, radio and television coverage, most of it favourable. In his report, Roach says that he walked around engaging in verbal duels with POP members, all of which ended in the same way: "visible embarrassment" on the part of the POP people. He did not ever identify himself as an MOT official, but, for the rest, he was happy to set the protestors straight. "I located a number of active discussions, listened for a moment and then, when asked to sign a petition, stated, 'Well, I'm not exactly pro-Pickering.' The millde-aged [sic] POP participant answered, 'Well, you have your views. What we're trying to do is present our views.' "

I like this exchange. I don't understand it, but I like it. I think a "millde-aged" man must be a chap in his sixties; we all get milder then. And I think Roach meant to write that he had said "I'm not exactly anti-Pickering." Otherwise, the exchange, which he reports produced "visible embarrassment" on the face of the foe, makes no sense whatever. Roach's general impression of the City Hall affair was "that of a teen-age demonstration." This was the reassuring guff to feed the troops.

In the publicity contest the bureaucrats, with all their resources, were never able to compete effectively with POP. On another level, concerning the technical arguments that revolved around the airport, they did not fare much better, as we shall see in the next chapter.

Chapter 8

Unravelling
the Threads

Bobby Baun, former hockey star:
*"When the airport announcement came, I couldn't give a shit whether
they built it or not. I was a fence-sitter. We had bought out here to farm
and raise cattle, and that's all I cared about. Our first assumption was
that we were going to make a fortune, but they didn't expropriate, the
province just froze this land for the noise zones. The expropriation
stopped west of us. That was that. We were living on loans, and the loans
were supported by the equity in the farm. When the freeze went on, who
the hell was going to buy the farm? So the equity disappeared and the
bank pulled out. I figured my place was worth about a million dollars,
with that big house, but the bank couldn't see it that way.*

*"I went into voluntary bankruptcy. We lost everything. I'm not
complaining, because I can still work and we'll come out okay, but it
sure doesn't seem right, especially when the goddam result is that they
haven't built anything anyway."*

Bruce Small, consultant, Transport Canada:
*"The decision went flip, build it, flip, call it off, flip, build it. It's on
another flip now. Such decisions are made for personal reasons, then
we're called in to provide the logical rationale. Sometimes you say,
'There just isn't the logic there, it can't be done.' Sometimes you find the
logic."*

When POP began in 1972, its aims were limited, its resources minimal and its motives mixed. Most of the local objectors were not opposed to a second airport – what did they know of airports? They
were opposed to a new airport and a new city in Pickering. When
the provincial government confirmed its Toronto-Centred Region
plan in August 1971, the locals assumed that they were safe from
the ravages of development; most of their area had been designated
Zone 2, "Agriculture and recreational development." When the
March 2 announcement came, they felt betrayed, and it took the
Pickering Council only four days to say so, in a resolution passed
March 6: "That this Council is opposed to the construction of a
second Toronto airport in the location suggested." They didn't

want an airport – in their backyard; they didn't want urban sprawl – beyond their fences; but the argument went no further than that. As Mrs. Frances Moore, one of POP's key members, put it, "My original reaction was 'Oh, God, not here.' It was a selfish reaction. But then you began to delve into it and found out how stupid it all was."

As snippets of background material began to come out, it dawned on POP members that the airport proposal was based on appallingly weak logic, and, since Cedarwood leaned on the airport, if POP could demolish the first, the second would come crashing down. So POP's Technical Committee concentrated on the airport argument. The Technical Committee consisted, in fact, of four men: Al Graham, Clark Muirhead, Lorne Almack, and Brian Buckles, but the bulk of the work was done by Almack, part-time farmer and Price Waterhouse consultant, and Brian Buckles, part-time farmer and insurance executive.

Almack came to the area in 1957. He had lived in Scarborough, but had always wanted to indulge his passions for farming and ornithology. He and his wife Rhoda, an enthusiastic gardener, bought 107 acres on Brock Road, just north of Brougham. Almack looks and sounds like a middle-aged farmer. His boots are muddy, his voice raucous, his manner direct, and his fuse short. He commutes to Toronto on a Go train, and it is my theory that as soon as he arrives in the railway station, he ducks into a telephone booth, chucks his jeans and galluses, and emerges, attaché case in hand, as a suit-clad, computer-punching consultant. He is familiar with all the analytical games of the consulting business, and it was his job to take apart the government's case. Considering that he only had the material the governments chose to release, he performed remarkably well.

Brian Buckles is quite different. He looks like the vice-president of an insurance company. He is nondescript, quiet, precise, and bespectacled. He has a B.A. in philosophy, an M.A. in history, and a background in engineering. He and his wife Jane, an artist, moved to the area in 1968, when Buckles was twenty-eight, and bought twenty acres with an 1840 farmhouse on it. Buckles' job was to take apart the government's noise studies and forecasts, based on his own intimate knowledge of computers. He did so well at it that he was held in considerable awe by the MOT folks. One memo indicates that at least seven people were involved in planning how to fend him off in a single interview.

Almack says, "This was bullshit"; Buckles says, "We had difficulty following the government's logic." Almack says, "I was going to fight those bastards"; Buckles says, "I like the space and silence out here." Part of Almack's farm was expropriated, but later released; his theory is that "They said, 'Oh, God, let's not tangle with that bastard.'" Buckles was expropriated, and he moved ten miles further north into a newer house that he doesn't like nearly as well. "I don't feel hard done by," he says. He got $160,000 for his old place and paid $144,500 for the new one, which is larger, although further out, and devoid of historic value. Hard done by or not, he remains convinced, from the work he did with Almack, that the government case for the airport is unsupportable.

The first break came on April 10, 1972, less than six weeks after the airport announcement. That day, Clark Muirhead, the Uxbridge councillor and POP stalwart, released a document that had been passed to him by someone in the provincial government. This was the September 1970 report we have already met in Chapter Five, the one that showed that Pickering was not even among the fifty-nine sites on the government list. You will recall that this report plumped for an airport at Guelph. POP called a press conference and released the study which, if it did nothing else, showed that both governments had been misleading the public. The MOT public relations office swung into action with a press release saying that the 1970 document was only "preliminary" – always a nourishing favourite – and that "later studies showed quite clearly that the proposed Pickering site is the most ideally suited location" – which was peach fuzz.

The embarrassing fact that Pickering was not even among the semi-demi-finalists, although two cabinet ministers had said it was, was ignored. When Andrew Szende of the *Toronto Star* asked Ontario Treasurer Darcy McKeough about the Pickering choice, McKeough replied that it was "just one of those that rolled in at the last." Szende didn't ask him how that squared with the March 2 statement about the careful selection from a list of fifty-nine. Nor did any newspaper dig into the minor discrepancy between the $300 million price tag that the government was giving for the airport and the nearly $5 billion cost cited in this paper (and that was for the cheapest airport site, at Guelph; the paper gave a $6.17 billion cost for an airport at Orangeville, and $6.4 billion for one at Port Perry). You can't expect us reporters to notice every little thing.

The April 10 leak should have tipped off the media that there was something seriously wrong with the story they were being told, but it did not. However, four days later, on April 14, POP released its first technical paper, attacking the federal position with the best in-

97

formation the protestors had available, which was the fact that the Pickering site finally chosen violated three of the four criteria the government was using when the September 1970 report was written. The guidelines in that document measured an airport by its distance from the "demographic centre," the forecast urban growth in the area, airspace interference and physiography. Pickering was close to Toronto, so it passed that test, but it was bound to produce urban sprawl, interfere with Malton airspace, and was on rolling lands.

The next day, April 15, there was another leak, this time of an ecological study which had been done for Pickering Township Council, and which showed that the airport was a potential disaster area. The study concluded, "It would be wishful thinking to hope for any kind of ecological balance for Pickering Township if an airport is built on this site, for it is impossible."

In the Ontario legislature, Environment Minister James Auld was asked whether the airport didn't violate the province's environmental guidelines and answered: "I won't say yes or no," which was forthright, but not helpful. Premier Davis and Darcy McKeough also came under tough questioning about the province's role in selecting the airport, and attempted to lay the whole thing in the lap of the feds. Not surprisingly, this led to demands for release of the background planning papers. Up to this point, nothing had been let loose, officially, but PR releases from Transport, which Jamieson said were "distilled" from the earlier studies. Distilled was a very good word for these documents, for they were so much moonshine. It was obvious that the feds were going to have to open up, or face a veritable flood of leaks as provincial officials began the time-honoured political pastime of covering their own asses. On April 22, in response to a question from John Diefenbaker, Jamieson told the House of Commons that he would release background documents when he met, on April 26, with a delegation from POP.

The meeting took place in the Transport headquarters in downtown Ottawa. The government's PR people thoughtfully provided the press with a briefing on what had happened at the meeting before it even broke up. This is known as anticipatory journalism. Both sides kept written minutes – POP's are virtually verbatim – and they are in general agreement as to what happened. The POP spokesmen – Godfrey, Almack, Muirhead, Buckles, and Wanstall were the most vocal – followed a list of written questions, which provided a framework against which Jamieson set down his philosophy of airports. He held, roughly, that a country can't have too many of the things, and that Canada was in need of many more.

Jamieson was surrounded by ten departmental officials, one observer from the provincial government and, of course, Philip Beinhaker.

Beinhaker's task was to correct the minister without ever seeming to do so, and to answer the technical questions. For example, Jamieson said that traffic at Malton would be doubled from between six and seven million passengers in 1972 to 12 million – it could not hold any more. "The peak will be 12 million. Put in 12 million passengers, you double the same noise problem."

Oh, dear. Malton could handle more than 12 million passengers – it does so today. What's more, noise doesn't double when passengers double. It could be much less, if larger or quieter planes are used; it could be more, if there are more flights. There is no direct correlation between the number of passengers and the degree of noise annoyance. It is not considered good form, after a cabinet minister lays down a clunker, to say "Pay no attention to the foregoing. Chap doesn't know his elbow from Mount Royal," so Beinhaker didn't do that; instead, he switched off the discussion into a treatise on the difference between the problems of airports in Montreal and those in Toronto, and the gaffe was covered.

The POP people did not make much impact on Jamieson. They didn't know enough, yet, to interrupt his ramblings about the need to build a whole flotilla of airports. They did, however, wring from him an undertaking to release the background documents on which the decisions were based. "Our information is freely available," Jamieson said. It was one of the richer japes of the season. The documents released over the next three months were the ones that conformed to the government scenario on the planning process. There was nothing to indicate that Orangeville had been chosen, and rejected; that any airport east of Toronto was regarded as unworkable; that the feds had been backed into Pickering by Ontario; that an attempt to blackmail the province into putting up the money for a rapid transit to their lousy site had failed, or that a "major conflict" with Malton airspace had been discovered, only to disappear, magically.

Chances are that Jamieson didn't have more than a vague grasp of what was going on, anyway. During the meeting with POP, he was asked why Malton couldn't be expanded, to handle 30 million passengers, as Chicago's O'Hare Airport was then doing. He said it could, but such an expansion would be "very expensive." His own department's papers indicated the opposite; expansion was cheaper than a new airport, but the problem was that it couldn't be done. Jamieson must have forgotten that.

The cabinet minister is the captive of his staff. During a later visit to Ottawa, POP members cornered Finance Minister Donald Macdonald to outline their case against the airport. He listened in silence, and then said, "If what you're telling me is true, then everything we have been told by our own experts must be wrong. I can't accept that."

On another occasion Isobel Thompson's daughter, Gillian, went down to see Jean Marchand, after he became Transport Minister. The meeting came about because Marchand's executive assistant, John Fairchild, had been rude and overbearing to the seventeen-year-old girl in a telephone conversation (he was calling Mrs. Thompson, got her daughter, and got into an argument). Gillian's mother raised seventeen kinds of hell, and induced author Pierre Berton to write a blistering note to Marchand. The upshot was an invitation for Gillian to come and see Marchand personally, which she did, in the company of a friend, Mrs. Fran Wiser. Marchand was feeling both defensive and expansive; he told his visitors what he had already told the public, that his department was in "a mess." He also told them that he didn't want to be the "French Canadian who could be accused of not giving an airport to Ontario after having given one to Quebec." He said there were great pressures on him to build Pickering, that if it was his decision, he might not do it, but "he had to be guided by experts and their recommendations, which were to proceed with Pickering."

That is the crux: bureaucrats decide; ministers accept and defend. It's not what we read in our political science texts, but it is how the system works.

The protestors went back to report to their Steering Committee that "The Minister did not give us very much information to work on" – and to hector the provincial government.

On June 6, Darcy McKeough released the province's background papers, which showed, among other things, that, contrary to his public statements, Ontario had really done very little work on Pickering. It had taken the word of the feds on the need for an airport, and concentrated on trying to shove the thing east of Toronto. Two days later, McKeough met a POP delegation that included the Legal Committee, which put a number of written questions to him, including this one: "In acquiring land in the Cedarwood area, is the Government proceeding under the authority of a specific statute, and if it is, what is the statute under which the Government is proceeding?"

The point was that the government was not itself going to build Cedarwood; it was going to assemble the land and turn it over to the mercies of private developers. POP's legal experts didn't think the government could do that; the assumption in expropriation law, the doctrine of "eminent domain," is that the seizure is for a public purpose, not for private profit. McKeough's answer was typically vague. Ontario was hoping to acquire the necessary land by negotiation, he said, and would resort to expropriation only if necessary. When the time comes, "the Government does not know which statute it will be proceeding under."

POP had raised a valid point, and a check with the province's own legal adviser suggested that there was indeed a problem.

On the evening of June 29, 1972, Attorney General Dalton Bales moved an amendment to the Housing Development Act of Ontario that would authorize the government "to acquire land for purposes of building a development as defined in the Act and to dispose of any such land on such terms and conditions as he [the minister] may determine."

The amendment was rammed through three readings and passed at 11:57 that very night. The opposition parties were asleep at the switch. Liberal MPP Vernon Singer did think there was something funny going on: "I would just appreciate it if the minister could tell us what the real objective of this act is, because it certainly doesn't appear on the surface of it." Michael Cassidy, the NDP housing spokesman, and now that party's provincial leader, was all for the amendment because he thought it meant the province was going into the land-banking business. But Bales straight-armed them both: "The present act . . . requires an agreement if there is a joint project with the federal government. We anticipate that there will be developments in the future where the provincial government alone will be involved. For that reason, we need the additional clause to be added to this section."

That quieted everyone down, and the amendment zipped through. Bales was only funning. The development the amendment would aid was Cedarwood, and the province now had the power it needed. It could expropriate for any housing development and, once it had the land, do with it what it chose – give it to a developer, put up a bowling alley – it didn't matter. This dreadful power is still in the hands of the province, and it was the power used to expropriate in Pickering, when the time came.

The POP members didn't know that they had tipped off the government until much later. By the time the Housing Development Act amendment was slipping through Queen's Park, they were hard at work planning for the public hearing, before J.W. Swackhamer, Q.C. This would be the only round they clearly won.

101

Chapter 9

Hear Today,
Gone Tomorrow

Sandra Salverson, housewife:
*"Serenity is a lovely word, and I have almost forgotten what it means.
We were finding it gradually, and my daughter got her horse, my son got
a goat and some ducks, pet ducks and geese, we already had a Collie
dog and cat, both of whom loved it all as much as we did, all this on less
than one acre of land. But we looked out on the fields and a mill-race, a
beautiful, tranquil view. Then, suddenly, in March 1972, a man on the
radio announced the plan of the federal and provincial governments to
expropriate land in Pickering Township, in order to build a new airport
and a supercity to be called, at the time, Cedarwood. My first feeling
was complete shock. Then came the anger, and it has never left me. No
warning, no discussion with the people, just an arbitrary government
decision, made by the federal Liberal government and the provincial
Conservative government . . . . We have felt this horror hanging over our
heads. Unlike the people of Malton, we moved here in good faith, never
dreaming that anyone would consider building an airport in this area, let
alone a city. I know of at least one heart attack as a result of these
events. Tension has grown to such an extent that if the divorce rate has
not increased already I am sure it probably will. I know my intake of
tranquillizers has at least doubled. My son is becoming almost a rebel
with no respect for politicians or government, and who can blame him?
What kind of future citizens are we creating?"*
> *– from the Transcript of the Airport Inquiry Commission,
> April 10, 1974.*

Cabinet Memorandum, January 16, 1973:
*"The objectors contend that the real social costs implicit in the
Pickering decision have been neglected.
Two of the fundamental objectives of the Toronto-Centred Region plan,
as recorded in Design for Development, are:*
- *the improvement of the quality of life.*
- *the better use of the natural environment.*

*By working closely with Ontario to integrate the new Toronto airport
into regional development plans based on these objectives, the Federal*

Government has contributed in a very positive way to the achievement of Provincial Goals based on these objectives."

The 1970 federal Expropriation Act set down quite clearly how the 815 properties to be seized for the airport site should be dealt with. First, the owners would have to be told about the coming cataclysm – they were told, in a general way, on March 2, 1972 – and then notices of intention to expropriate were to be delivered to those affected. Then, the government would have to affirm that the intention was real, and would be acted on. This was done on June 29, when the federal Cabinet agreed "that the Government should reaffirm the need for the second major international airport, and proceed with the expropriation of the site." Then, there would be a hearing into the expropriation, and Toronto lawyer J.W. Swackhamer was appointed to that task. Then, the government would decide to confirm, or not, the expropriations on the basis of the hearings and then, by jingo, there could even be a public inquiry under the Inquiries Act to look at the whole thing again.

It looked pretty fair, but it would have been more honest, if less politic, for the Minister of Transport to announce that "We're taking this land because we want to, and anybody who doesn't like it can kiss my tush."

The cabinet decision taken June 29, 1972, committed the government "to interpret generously the provisions of the Expropriation Act which relate to Public Hearings." And that was announced out loud. What wasn't announced was that there was a catch; the agreement was "to hold a further examination after the confirmation of expropriation, not to question the need for the airport, but to discuss matters such as airport roles, timing and integration of the airport into urban development plans."

So, there would be a hearing, and there would be an inquiry, but both were scheduled to come to a pre-determined conclusion. The expropriation would be confirmed, and the inquiry would not be allowed to investigate whether there was any need for the airport. In the end, the inquiry would not report until December 1974. Its major conclusion was written on June 29, 1972. Saves wear and tear on the bureaucrats' nerves.

Still, the formalities had to be observed, and POP, which still thought the debate was a real one, girded its loins for what was to become the Swackhamer Hearing. John J. Robinette was hired to represent the protestors at this hearing. Nobody knows how many bumper-stickers, loaves of bread, works of art, raffle tickets, and la-

103

pel buttons were sold to raise Robinette's $7,500 fee, and nobody doubts that the money was well spent. He was not only a prestigious, thoroughly Establishment lawyer, which would upgrade POP's image, he was a damn smart fellow. It was Robinette who acted for objectors to Toronto's Spadina Expressway, and the expressway was stopped, at least temporarily. Not only that, he scared the bejabbers out of the feds. A federal cabinet memo dated August 2, 1972, notes that "It is expected that POP counsel J.J. Robinette, Q.C., will receive good press coverage during the hearing."

This would be so even though, the memo claimed, the press was fed up with POP: "The People or Planes Committee is still the principal opposition group in the area of North Pickering. POP morale is somewhat lower at the present time because the Toronto press is getting bored with its public statements and, to some extent, feels that it is being used by the Committee. POP can only gain more public attention by resuming demonstrations of various kinds, as most of the potentially embarrassing documents to the Ministry case have now been utilized by POP."

I like that last touch; the feds were safe because the rest of the embarrassing material was beyond the reach of the prying outsiders. The main thing to worry about, then, was Robinette, and the Transport officials who prepared this memo wondered whether it mightn't be best just to postpone the whole hearing business for a while. In the end, though, that wouldn't do much good, because if there was no hearing, the pressure would double for an inquiry:

"The Metropolitan Airport Review Committee . . . was quiet until it was announced that Mr. Robinette would receive government documentation. This group then immediately made a request for the material, and it can be anticipated that after studying it will have some comments to make to support its case for a Public Inquiry. It appears that the most effective way to counter this suggestion would be for the hearings under the Expropriation Act to be under way."

This passage suggests two things about Transport thinking. In the first place, the lads never tumbled to the fact that MTARC was simply POP in another dress, although a hint might have been gleaned from the fact that MTARC's studies were signed by Lorne Almack and Brian Buckles. In the second place, the department, a cabinet decision notwithstanding, was still hoping to duck an inquiry. Better to keep the thing confined to a hearing before Swackhamer, because the feds didn't have to show up at it.

The Swackhamer exercise was for the purpose of registering objections to the expropriation; it was not an examination of the merits of the land seizures, just a bitch-in. What's more, the hearing officer was not empowered to pass any judgments or make any findings; his job was merely to summarize what he heard and go home, and if the government chose to ignore his report, so be it. Neither the federal nor the provincial governments submitted a scrap of evidence to Swackhamer, so there was no opportunity to cross-examine any of the people who made the decisions as to whether there was a proven need for the airport, or whether Pickering was the proper site. There has never been such a cross-examination, and I doubt if there will ever be one.

Within his limitations, however, the late J.W. Swackhamer produced a devastating summary of what he heard. That evidence consisted of technical evaluations from POP, complaints about the loss of farmland, complaints about secrecy, and direct and powerful attacks on both the need for and placement of the airport.

POP received from the government and its own sources the documents showing that a major expansion of Malton had been proposed and rejected, not because it wouldn't work, but because it was held to be "not saleable." They were able to show that Pickering had been rejected in the preliminary screening, and that Guelph had been preferred. They showed, too, that Pickering was resurrected in 1971 only because of the failure of the other sites, and, even then, it was ranked behind Beverly. There were a good many gaps in POP's knowledge, but they were able to show, as Swackhamer put it in his report, that:

1. By far, the weight of the background material contradicts the government's position as to need and site.
2. Material in support of the governments' decision is manifestly ill-considered, incomplete, and at times specious, if not spurious, in its analysis. This latter material cannot bear even the most perfunctory of examinations.

This was precisely what the Urban Affairs department had said, although nobody knew that.

Although the province kept away from the hearings, three men who had done work for Ontario did turn up, and they had some disturbing things to say.

Kenneth Fallis, an agrologist with the Department of Agriculture, who lives in Pickering, said that his department "had not once been consulted with respect to the siting of the proposed airport." Although the province had produced a study purporting to show that Pickering's farmlands were in poor condition, "This study must have been studiously misinformed or deliberately misleading." Most of Pickering's farmland was Class I, and "It is important to note that only eleven per cent of all agricultural soils in Ontario are Class I."

This testimony would encourage POP to argue that the federal and provincial governments were threatening to take 43,000 acres of farmland out of production (the 43,000 figure came from the original provincial site of 25,000 plus the 18,000-acre airport site). In fact, however, crops are raised around airports all over the world; I have seen cows grazing at Schipohl Airport near Amsterdam, and watched sheep browsing within a hundred yards of the runways at Prestwick in Scotland. POP weakened its case by exaggerating. When the federal Department of Agriculture was finally consulted, the department said that the airport would, in fact, destroy good farmland, but refused to say how much – certainly not 43,000 acres. The loss on the site wasn't what counted so much as the loss of lands for access and services.

The nub of what Fallis had to say was that, given a choice between Pickering and Beverly, the governments, if they wanted to preserve good farmland, should have gone to Beverly with their airport. And, far more important, the studies used to support the choice of Pickering were not merely suspect, they stunk out the joint.

Dr. Gerald Hodge, Professor of Urban and Regional Planning at the University of Toronto, and the man who produced the provincial report, "Regional Impact of a New Toronto International Airport for Toronto," also appeared before Swackhamer. His was the document that dealt with the four sites under discussion in March 1970 – Sutton, Orangeville, Port Perry, and Guelph – and which suggested that those at Orangeville and Port Perry would work best for Ontario's regional planning. Pickering, now that he had had a chance to look at it, would not work at all. It would have a negligible effect on growth east of the Pickering site, because "Pickering is too close to the magnetic effect of the Metropolitan Toronto area."

Hodge also expanded on his earlier attack on the federal forecasts, and expressed annoyance that his work was being misused to support the government case. Darcy McKeough had written an article in the *Ontario Economic Review* (Volume 10, No. 3), in which he said that "Hodge forecast the annual flow of air passengers through Toronto would reach 54 million by the year 2000 . . . roughly in line with the federal estimate." Hodge had said no such thing. He had objected to the government's zany 96.4 million figure, and had used 54 million as a figure between the high and low forecasts then being used, all of them suspect. His own judgment,

Hodge told Swackhamer, was that the air traffic in the year 2000 would be around 31 million. Like Fallis, what he was really saying was that the governments' abuse of facts was evident.

Peter Oehm, the urban planner whose hasty study showed that Pickering was more suitable as a site to move growth east of Toronto than Beverly, also gave evidence. He said that of course a site east of the city would work better to this purpose than one west, any nit could see that, but he had spent exactly a day and a half preparing his report, which he called "an eight-page wonder." The main point, Oehm said, now that he had had more time to look at the concept, was that "The proposed airport and Cedarwood Townsite are in direct conflict with the Toronto-Centred Region concept."

Swackhamer never did find out why Ontario was going along with an airport which the experts it had hired itself were saying was bonkers, because the necessary documents were still in cold storage. As we have seen, the crucial point for the province was its commitment to water and sewer services in the Pickering area. To preserve that investment, a minor massacre of the TCR plan was permissible, as long as it was not admitted. So Darcy McKeough was trotted out on several occasions to announce that the TCR was still *virgo intacta*, and the baby was buried behind the house.

The Swackhamer hearing also delved into another and contentious subject, which keeps cropping up whenever airports are mentioned, and I therefore propose a small discursive expedition to study it now. I am referring to noise.

Noise has always been a problem in urban environments. Fifty years before the birth of Christ, Julius Caesar banned chariot traffic in Rome at night to reduce noise levels, and we have been trying similar stunts ever since. Airports, in particular, represent huge sources of noise pollution, and science, ever alert to opportunities to measure things, has come up with dozens of ways to classify and forecast the amount of noise likely to be produced, and the level of racket likely to be accepted around an airport. The measures include the Composite Noise Rating (CNR), the Noise Exposure Forecast (NEF), Community Noise Equivalent Level (CNEL), the Aircraft Sound Description System (ASDS), the Noise Number Index (NNI), the Isosophic Index, the Total Noise Load Index and, my favourite, the Mean Annoyance Level.

Only two of these played much part in the Canadian government's plans, the Composite Noise Rating and the Noise Exposure Forecast. The CNR was a logarithmic formula based on a bundle of components – the noise characteristics of various aircraft, the frequency of aircraft movements, and whether they occurred during the daytime, or at night. A set of three contours was developed, based on the CNR, which could be laid on the map of a community around any airport to predict response. People in Zone 1, exposed to less than 100 CNR, were not expected to complain much, although at times they would find noise interfering with outside activities – a jet overflying conversations around a barbecue, for example. People in Zone 2, exposed to 100 to 115 CNR, would be subject to loud noise, frequently. They would complain, and complain vigorously; they might even take community action to protect themselves. People in Zone 3, with a rating higher than 115 CNR, were bound to complain, early and often, and almost certain to take concerted action. With the CNR, the government knew what to expect, at least.

However, this system, which was in use in Canada until 1972 – that is, until just before Pickering was announced – did not include any factors to account for noise in airport ground operations (running up jets, for example, in overhauls), nor did it measure the background noise in a community (if you live beside a bowling alley, a passing jet is less offensive than if you live beside a babbling brook), nor did it measure the tone and duration of sound. High noises are more irritating than low ones, and ten minutes of jet roar are more irritating than one, but you wouldn't know that from the CNR.

In 1969, the U.S. Federal Aviation Administration came up with a slightly more sophisticated measure, the NEF, which we adopted in 1972. This measures the total noise forecast to be received at any given point from all the aircraft operating within hearing range of that point. It takes into account the kind of aircraft engines used, the glide-path followed, the frequency of flights, and the maximum tone and duration of sound. All of this knowledge produces a forecast of community response, not unlike the CNR. A measure of 25-30 NEF is roughly equivalent to 90-100 CNR; thus, at 25-30 NEF, there will be interference in the community because of noise, but few complaints; 30-40 NEF will produce vigorous complaints, and, at any figure higher than 40, all hell will break loose.

However, NEF did not measure background noise any more than did the CNR, nor could it predict community response in an area not previously exposed to aircraft. As with the CNR, it could produce contour lines of predictable response on a map overlay, but it was a crude tool, for all its computer read-outs.

Noise, whether measured in CNR, NEF, or Mean Annoyance Levels, does more than irritate; it can produce deafness, strain, psychosis, heart attacks, and alcoholism. No fooling. A University of California study released in the autumn of 1978, showed that "The tension, anxiety and the fear associated with the tremendous noise" of overflying jets could actually reduce the lifespan of people living near airports.

The people in the Malton area have known about the damaging effects of sound for years. In 1967, Miriam Mittermaier moved with her family onto Kendleton Drive, off the east end of the northernmost of the two parallel runways 05/23. This runway was later lengthened, so that it became noisier after the Mittermaiers moved in. "We bought in reasonable good faith and with reasonable prudence," Mrs. Mittermaier says, but noise, a minor irritation when she arrived, became a brutal problem later on. She joined a local community group, which became involved in the battle to block Malton expansion, and is now Secretary of New Airport Now.

"Noise is cumulative," says Mittermaier. "Most of the winter, except at the Christmas rush, there is no problem. Windows are closed. The problem is in the summer when you're outside a lot, and it comes on gradually. After it has been quiet for a while, and when the planes start up again, I say to myself, 'This isn't as bad as I remember it.' That's the first day. The second day, you tend to become more irritable. By the end of the third day, you're a wreck, screaming at the children for no reason."

Constant complaints from people like the Mittermaiers have led to the shortening of flight hours at Malton, and the parallel runways are no longer used as parallels, but one at a time.

The Mittermaiers, like the Pickering residents, thought they had a deal with government. When the decision was announced in 1968 not to expand Malton, they thought that at least there would be no expansion of the noise lands. Local municipalities, on the basis of that decision, permitted building in areas where it would otherwise not have gone, and the result was to create an enclave crowded with people who were bound to oppose any change at Malton.

Local councils like larger tax bases, so they approve development where common sense should tell them that development ought not to go. In the fall of 1978, after ten years of battles and warnings, the Etobicoke Council approved a 450-unit housing development in an area just south of the airport. The local community association requested that there should at least be a study of noise, and pointed out that a rough reading gave an NEF of between 35 and 40. But the Ontario Municipal Board said that was not necessary, and the Ontario cabinet upheld the OMB, and the development is under way. In a couple of years, that will produce another 2,000 or so residents screaming about airport noise and wondering how they got into this mess.

Noise produces political problems around airports, and governments tend to argue the case whichever way suits their thinking whenever the subject comes up. All of this was clear back in November 1972, when J.W. Swackhamer was considering the subject of noise. He only heard one side of the argument – from POP – and POP maintained that technological improvements would see noise zones reduced around airports until, eventually, the real noise would be confined to the airport lands themselves.

Different landing techniques could be employed; if aircraft approaching a landing stay quite high until they are close, and then make a sharper approach than normal – e.g. a six-degree glide slope instead of three – the noise on the ground will be more confined. Jet engines are being modified to reduce noise, and the cost of retrofitting – modifying engines already in operation – is much cheaper than building a new airport. Changes in air traffic control equipment and techniques have made it possible to place runways closer together, helping to shrink the noise zones. And most important of all, in the United States jets are forced to meet strict noise standards.

In 1969, the U.S. Federal Aviation Administration promulgated Part 6 of the Federal Aviation Regulations, which set strict rules for the amount of noise any transport aircraft may produce. This regulation, FAR 36, is equivalent to a standard adopted by the International Civil Aviation Organization, to which Canada belongs. Any new jets flying into Canadian airports will perforce be quieter.

Later, FAR 36 was strengthened to apply the same noise standards not merely to new aircraft, but to those already in service, and these standards, too, apply in Canada. By 1985, all transport aircraft will be required to meet the new noise levels. Common sense suggests that, by 1985, the governments will have a handle on noise around airports, and since Transport's own forecasts show that the need for a second airport doesn't emerge until after 1985, the POP witnesses argued that noise was not going to be the problem the feds said it was.

John M. Duggan, an American airport consultant and noise expert, was brought up to appear before Swackhamer, and Duggan concluded, "For the post-1985 period, therefore, aircraft noise should not be a factor of significance at any but the oldest and smallest of our busy airline airports. The combination of quieter vehicles, divided between long and shorter runways, and noise-optimised flight procedures shall, hopefully, have won aviation's share of the battle for a quiet environment. The noisiest aircraft around should be the unmodified wide-bodied jets being hailed today for their quietness."

So, POP argued, as the new aircraft and new techniques replace the old, noise should go down at Malton; even adding more traffic would not increase the racket. And, even if that turned out not to be the case, there was no reason for dumping noise into a new community to avoid its increase around an old one.

The Swackhamer Report was given to Public Works Minister Jean-Eudes Dubé, the minister responsible for physical development of the airport site, on January 4, 1973, along with the "Response" prepared by the Ministry of Transport. The response was a beaut. In dealing, for example, with the now-familiar argument that there was no need for a second airport, except to justify a political judgment, the response says, "Technical experts were indeed challenged by their colleagues over the five years of work, but in no instance were technical experts overruled in technical matters by decision makers either elected or appointed."

This is the stuff that grows roses. It was the decision that Malton was "not saleable" that led to the rejection of reconfiguration; the subsequent reports started from the base of that conclusion. They didn't deal with expansion except to dismiss it; instead, they provided arguments, most of them ridiculous, for selecting other sites, none of which was Pickering. To test this assumption, in late 1978 I asked Philip Beinhaker, the man whose work, more than that of any single individual guided the government, about it. It is worth noting exactly what I put to Beinhaker, and his response. This is from the tape recording of our interview:

STEWART: Well, when the decision was finally made, it was made on the basis of your argument that the expansion of Malton was perfectly feasible but not saleable politically at this time. It was a political issue, not a technical issue.
BEINHAKER: Well, if you could solve . . . if you could solve certain political problems, then you had the basis of a technical solution. The political problems you had to solve were the value you placed on the impact on the communities around it and the noise, which is not unlike the Dorval situation, and that political problem still exists. It's a problem, not politics in the sense of party politics, but in terms of policy. Are you going to recognize the complaints of those people as to the impact on their environment, or are you going to put a lesser value on that? It's a matter of politics, a sense of policy. The next political issue was one of the planning issues related to the municipalities. Are you going to

get agreement from Etobicoke and Mississauga and the others to protect the necessary lands so that you don't get further encroachment to further residential development, which causes further aggravation and further problems in the future, and further curfews and further limitations on airport operations? And thirdly, are you going to get the other level of government principally involved, i.e., the province, to provide the necessary infrastructure for a further expansion? Now all these things can be, once all these things are agreed to, there is nothing technically that can't be solved. And the amount of money you have to spend in order to expand Malton in a massive way is not substantially different than the amount of money you would have to spend to provide major expansion at Metro-ports or through a series of Metro-ports, I should say, or at another major airport. Those are, therefore, it is a political issue. Since those other parties, people around Malton, the municipalities and the province, have indicated that they are not necessarily prepared by any means to accede to all those things, you have fundamentally a political problem in that it is not saleable.

A simple "Yes" would have done, but I am content with Beinhaker's statement, seven times, that the problem was political, not technical, and willing to lay it beside the "Response" contention that it was technical, not political. (Incidentally, Beinhaker used the occasion to promote the latest gospel, which is that the real reason for building a second airport is that it's just as cheap as expanding Malton. Later in the interview he admitted there were other costs attached to a second airport not attached to expansion – user costs, duplication of equipment, and so forth.)

It was baloney, and baloney cut in the very thickest slices, to say that the technical documents supported Pickering. But how did Dubé, to whom the response was directed, know that? God knows, he wasn't going to read all the background bumph. If he wanted to read more than the response, which dismissed each and every POP argument with replies as daffy as the one on Malton expansion, he was given a covering cabinet document on January 15, 1973, to explain things for him. This document invited every minister to grab at Pickering. Not only was it the best thing since sliced bread, it wouldn't cost a dime. The memorandum holds that the arguments against the airport are "largely based on a single report produced in the summer of 1970 and subsequently rejected by government experts as being technically and socially unfeasible. This report was released prior to the hearings in the interest of full objectivity along with the 167 other documents contained in some 35 volumes."

Almost none of this was true. POP did latch onto the August 1970 report, but that was not an isolated document, it was the second review of all the Airport Planning Team's work to date. Its conclusions had not been rejected, simply ploughed under. Finally, it was not released "in the interests of full objectivity," it was let go to stop POP making hay out of leaked papers.

The Cabinet was told that opposition to the airport was fading and support was growing. What's more, there was no need to worry about where the money was going to come from. "It has been established that the expansion of airport facilities in the Toronto region will be financially self-sustaining." The cash would come from the Airports Revolving Fund, which had been established to loan money out, at normal market rates, to build air facilities all across Canada. This money would be paid back by user charges on the airports. To make this argument work, the new airport would have to be both busy and efficient – unlike Mirabel – the cost of duplicating facilities would have to be ignored, all the costs to airlines would have to be ignored, and a new airport tax to be levied on every airline ticket would have to be treated as revenue, instead of as a cost to the customer. But who knew that? From the papers they had in front of them, the cabinet members could only conclude that the knocks against the new airport came from a shrinking band of local loonies who based their whines on a single, out-dated, wrong-headed report, that most people were for the project – a political plus – and that, as the document trumpeted, "The new Toronto Airport, as with other major air transportation facilities, will not compete for government funds in the traditional sense."

Who could turn down such a deal?

You may think I exaggerate the ignorance of cabinet ministers faced with these complex issues. I don't. Consider a note prepared for the MOT confidential file on a meeting with Transport Minister Marchand on January 15, 1973, nearly two weeks after the Swackhamer Report and the MOT response were circulated. In this meeting, Marchand asked: "What is meant by Malton reconfiguration?" – a subject that had been under discussion for six years – and "Was there any other site involving fewer people?" – the answer, evident in the background material, was that every other site involved fewer people – and "How committed is the Province to the Airport?" – the subject of dozens of letters, reports, and memos in his own files.

Clearly, he didn't know what was going on. However, that did not prevent him, along with the rest of the Cabinet, from deciding on January 30, 1973, that the expropriation of the Pickering site should be confirmed. At the same time, perhaps because some of

113

the Swackhamer comments hit home (the cabinet document says, with a note of grievance, that the report was "eloquent"), the MOT's hopes of doing without an inquiry were dashed. There would be such an inquiry, and it would be, the announcement of the Cabinet decision said, "full and open."

That was hogwash, and every member of the Cabinet who could read and understand either of Canada's official languages knew it to be hogwash. We shall see why.

Chapter 10

The Commission Sits

Libby McCowan, activist:
"The place across the way from our place was boarded up but I asked them to save the milkhouse, out by the road. The kids used to go there to wait for the school bus. It was shelter. They said they would save it. Then one day I saw them over there with their big, fat machines. I went over and spoke to the guy in charge. I said, 'You know they promised not to tear down the milkhouse, don't you?' He said, 'Lady, it's all coming down and there ain't nothing you can do about it.' I went completely berserk. I started to scream and shout; I said I'd go and get a gun and hold it to his head. He said he was going to call the police. They did call the police, and I went and called Peter, my husband, and I told him 'If you don't want me going off in a little yellow car, you'd better do something.' "

Peter McCowan, businessman:
"They had no business doing what they did with so little purpose. They don't have the right to put their subjects through what they put us through because of their stupidity. I'll never forgive them."

Mr. Justice Hugh F. Gibson, Royal Commissioner:
"People who declare war on airports often do not really have all the facts, nor weigh all the issues . . . . They overlook the enrichment of life which air transportation has brought. All the facets offered by the air transportation system add up to a way of life which the travelling public has not shown the slightest interest nor the slightest sign of giving up, and why should it?"
— from the Gibson Report, p. 230.

Mrs. Isobel Thompson slugged Nigel Dunn on the evening of April 10, 1974, at Pickering High School. Both were attending a hearing of the Airport Inquiry Commission, chaired by Mr. Justice Hugh F. Gibson of the Federal Court of Canada. Thompson was an active member of POP, Dunn was a MOT PR man, at the time of the assault.

115

Regrettably, it is an assault which Mrs. Thompson acknowledges freely, and without remorse, although she deposes that her husband, Tommy, did not approve. The way of it, she says, was this: "An old man got up to ask a question about his property and Gibson was really rude to him. I jumped up and said something, sprang to his defence and Gibson told me to sit down. Dunn came up to me afterwards and put his arm around me and said, 'Nice try, sweetheart,' and I just took my hand and slugged him. He was shocked. I was astonished. So was Tommy, he saw it. I went up to a policeman and said, 'Did you see that?' He said, 'It certainly is hot in here, Ma'am.' "

Why would a petite, genteel, and generally non-violent lady like Isobel Thompson smack an inoffensive man like Nigel Dunn? Because he was handy. She was giving vent to the rage and frustration that hundreds of residents of Pickering felt because of the way in which the Gibson Inquiry was conducted. She couldn't slug Gibson – not even the POP members, given as they were to occasional excesses, thought it was proper to go around baffing members of the Federal Court of Canada – so she baffed Nigel Dunn instead.

She, and most members of POP, hold that the inquiry into a second airport for the Toronto area was a farce. This is a grave misstatement. Farce has the element of comedy about it; it smacks of thrown custard pies, stepped-on banana peels, and water-squirting flowers. The inquiry had none of these; it was not a farce, but a travesty, which my dictionary defines as "Any grotesque or debased likeness or imitation." It was a travesty of justice.

There never was a time, from the beginning to the end of this sorry mess, when the inquiry could seriously consider the only two issues that mattered in connection with the proposed airport; whether it was needed, and whether Pickering was the proper site. It was not an inquiry in any real sense of the word; it was, instead, an act of Symbolic Reassurance. Such acts are common in Canada. The National Energy Board meets to consider an application from an oil company. Everyone in Canada knows, before the process begins, that most of whatever the oil company seeks will be given. But the hearing soothes the public psyche; it assures us that somebody is in charge, and looking after our interests. Bell Canada will come before the Canadian Radio-Television and Telecommunications Commission for yet another massive increase in its rates. Long before the hearings open, we know, Bell knows, that the company will get virtually everything it wants, that the appearance before the CRTC is a form of ceremony, nothing more. In the old days, priests used to slaughter a goat and examine its entrails, which always spelled out whatever it was the gang behind the altar had in mind anyway. I think we should go back to that; it's harder on goats but cheaper on taxpayers, and the results are the same.

You do not have to take my word for it that the inquiry was not the "free and open" affair promised by the government. If you want to peek once more into documents that you have no right to know about, you can see the Deputy Minister of Transport, O.G. Stoner, writing to the Minister, Jean Marchand, on January 15, 1973, in exactly these words: "In some ways the word 'Inquiry' is misleading because it is meant to be more of an effort to harmonize formally the plans of the Federal Government, the Provincial Government and the Toronto-Metro Region before initiating an airport." Indeed, a cabinet memo dated the same day noted "Construction work will be undertaken during the Board's deliberations."

That, of course, is not what was said publicly. It is worth while to examine exactly what was said publicly because what the record shows is that on a number of occasions two cabinet ministers told stories which, if fed into a lie-detector, would have blown every gasket in sight.

You will recall that, as far back as May 19, 1970, then Transport Minister Jamieson had said that he was prepared "To withhold the final decision until there had been adequate opportunity for all appropriate submissions to be received and considered thoroughly."

On September 22, 1972, Jamieson wired POP counsel J.J. Robinette that any inquiry "would be expected to examine the full range of issues" – a reference that obviously included site and need. The MOT later said that this telegram shouldn't be counted, because a week later the minister wired again, to say that "The government considers that neither need nor location are in question." But this same telegram contained a promise that he "would do nothing to tie the hands" of those who would be assigned to look into the issue; the inquiry would be expected to examine "the full range of transportation needs." So Jamieson made three public commitments to an examination that would be open to consider both site and need.

On January 30, 1973, Liberal MP Norman Cafik asked the new Transport Minister, Marchand, "Will the terms of reference for this independent Inquiry board be sufficiently broad to allow a full-scale consideration of the questions of airport need and location by that inquiry?"

Marchand replied, "We want the terms of reference to be broad enough to cover what the Honourable member has mentioned."

When Marchand made that reply, not only did he have Stoner's memo, dated fifteen days earlier, as to the real purpose of the inquiry, not only did he have the cabinet directive of June 29, 1972, which made it clear that need was not to be questioned, he had another memo, dated January 22, 1973, eight days before he got up in the House, that said that if the inquiry was allowed to consider either need or location, the expropriations that had already taken place might be rendered null and void.

The memo notes that "Certain Members of Parliament feel strongly that need should be included," but "The Department of Justice has advised that if the terms of reference of the independent body set up to study the Toronto II airport include a requirement that the body review the necessity for a second airport or the suitability of the Pickering site prior to confirmation of the expropriation, the result would be to render the expropriation invalid. Even if terms of reference such as that were announced following the confirmation of expropriation, it . . . would render inoperative the presumption of validity."

It could not have been put plainer than that; the inquiry must not consider site or need. However, given all the public commitments to date, which were thoughtfully researched, there was only one way out, as usual: fake it. "We recommend that the Terms of Reference of the Board cannot explicitly include need in the absolute sense. Recognizing Mr. Cafik's concern, however, you might consider incorporating some words of a broad nature similar to the telegram to Robinette, that do not explicitly exclude need and provide for general presentation and discussion of all points of view."

Note the timing. Cafik made his views known privately to the minister some time before January 22; the legal opinion was turned over that day and, eight days later, Cafik was on his feet, asking about the terms of reference. He was told that the government wanted site and need in the inquiry.

The POP group trekked down to Ottawa on March 12, for a meeting with Cafik and Marchand at which they were assured again, by both of them, that, in the words of the POP minutes, "There would be nothing in the Terms of Reference to prohibit discussion on need and location."

On April 16, NDP leader David Lewis asked Marchand again if the inquiry would be able to consider "the whole matter affecting the Pickering airport."

Marchand wobbled a bit in his reply, but came through in the end: "Mr. Speaker, the public will be able to make representations on the specific issue of type and timing of facilities and the transportation and planning context. The government has made it clear that decisions taken to date on need and location may be reconsidered in the light of new facts, new information on technology or travel habits which nullify the basis of these decisions. The Board will be authorized to inquire into all aspects of the question."

On May 8 and 9, Marchand appeared before the Standing Committee on Transportation and Communications, and said twice that the inquiry would be allowed to consider "the need for a new airport and alternative locations if these points are brought before it," and that "It is also free to make recommendations regarding these latter topics."

On June 21, Marchand was up in the House again, announcing general terms of reference for the inquiry, which would be "full and ample." The terms included the inquiry's right to "review all aspects of the regional air system" and to make "recommendations to the Minister of Transport respecting any or all aspects of the questions to be examined by it."

That broad sweep would obviously include location and need, but it didn't say so. Accordingly, the next day, Conservative MP Reg Stackhouse asked, "Will the Minister inform the House if the Board is being directed to study [airport need and location]," and Marchand replied, "Mr. Speaker, I think the terms of reference are clear on this. There is no doubt that the Board can receive evidence on need and location of the airport."

So, Jamieson had made three public statements and Marchand seven, all to the same effect: the inquiry would not be limited, it could consider need and location. None of the statements was true.

The Order-in-Council setting up the inquiry, passed on October 5, 1973, began with three flat statements: that Malton "will not be expanded," that "the Government has decided . . . that there be established another international airport," and that "the Government has chosen a site near Pickering, Ontario." To keep the betrayal from looking as flagrant as it was, the sneaky advice of the January 22 memo was adopted; the inquiry would be allowed to consider "any new evidence, if available" that would persuade the government to change its mind. New evidence was later defined by Mr. Justice Hugh Gibson, the Kingston, Ontario judge appointed to chair the inquiry, as "evidence of any relevant factor, the evidence of which has arisen since the 30th January, 1973," the day the expropriation was confirmed. "Arisen" meant "Something that was not in the mind of the Canadian government when it took, on the 30th of January, 1973, the policy decisions referred to." Gibson made no attempt to define "the mind of the Canadian government," which is probably just as well.

In short, the decisions had been made, but if those wiseacres who didn't like them could dig up anything new, they were welcome to try to lay it before the Airport Inquiry Commission. All the earlier material was out of bounds; the government arguments that had been destroyed before could not be destroyed again; they had been made whole by a laying on of hands. All that stuff was already "in the mind of the Canadian government."

Every attempt to attack the new, narrow terms of reference was turned back, with contempt. B.J. MacKinnon, the senior counsel for the Government of Canada at the inquiry (now a judge), listened to a lot of argybargy about this and then said, flatly, "If people don't like it, then the only solution is, presumably, to have another Order-in-Council of some kind." Marie Antoinette covered the same ground faster with "Let them eat cake."

POP members were predictably outraged by the terms which were made public on October 23, 1972. At first, they said they would boycott the inquiry, and POP's counsel, who was to have been Donald Wright, was dropped. He did, however, appear on behalf of the City of Toronto, and presented what was essentially POP's position. The protestors hadn't boycotted the proceedings, they had just worked out a way to winkle Toronto into paying part of the shot.

It was beginning to occur to POP members that the case was stacked against them. Just how stacked was made clear in the Report of the Commission, when eventually it came down. The assumptions set down by the inquiry as the basis for its decision implied that to interfere in any way with new airports would bring the entire nation to its knees.

Just to drive a nail in the coffin of anyone fool enough to question Revealed Truth, the commission adopted, as the official history of the project, a MOT document called the Written Summary. The report does not refer to the summary as such; instead, there are a whole series of statements beginning, "It was said," which, in sum, comprise the Ministry's version of history. (The "It was said" tipped off the legal folks that this wasn't evidence taken before the commission, but hearsay.) The trouble was that in this "history" the commission was led to a belief that Pickering was chosen, in an orderly and progressive way, by a series of elimination contests. It didn't know that the MOT plunged into Pickering only after failing to put its airport in three other locations. That was old evidence, anyway; even if the facts had been known, they were certainly material that was in the mind of the government on January 30, 1973.

The Written Summary dealt with the proposal to reconfigure Malton by saying that "The proposal was found to be unsatisfacto-

120

ry," and cited six reports in support of this claim, but these were written two years after the proposal, and long after the government was committed to a new course. The government document, however, gives, and must have been intended to give, quite a different impression.

There were a lot of people missing from the hearings. The Province of Ontario sent representatives every day, but none was ever called. Their explanation today is that they were waiting to be summoned; the federal government's that it was waiting for them to come forward. This strange shyness on both parts may have had something to do with the fact that Ontario was beginning to get a little nervous about the airport, and Ottawa knew it.

United States airport consultant Tom Sullivan was brought all the way from Dallas to talk about the wonderful new Dallas-Fort Worth airport, as it was then conceived to be. (In 1976, Richard de Neufville would write in *Airport Systems Planning* that this $800 million facility was built because of a massive error in forecasting, and describe it as "an embarrassingly inconvenient and expensive airport.") However, nobody thought to send to Montreal to ask experts from the International Air Transportation Association for their views – which would have been negative. No British expert was called to explain why his country had recently put back plans to build another London airport near Southend-on-Sea. Any such witness would have testified that the Maplin project, which sounded reasonable when it was first mooted, was coming apart because the forecasts on which it was based were not working out, and that the noise problems which had led to agitation for shifting some of London's air traffic were being brought under control. More negative thinking.

The government didn't call any of these witnesses, because it took the position that this was an adversary hearing. It was less like an inquiry than a divorce trial. If the other side, with few resources, and cut off from dealing with the main aspects of the case, could somehow dredge up an argument, so be it; otherwise, to hell with them.

One witness who was called, but under wraps, was Hugh Devitt, the manager of Malton airport. Devitt was asked a great many questions about the size of terminals, the spacing of runways, and road access, but he was never asked if he thought a second airport was necessary. Yet he would have been a logical person to ask; not only was he running Malton, he had been active in the planning stages of Mirabel, and was slated to become that airport's manager, until he asked for a transfer to Toronto. He asked for that transfer because he thought Mirabel was a disaster. He thought a second airport in Toronto would be a disaster, too, but he wasn't anxious to say so, publicly. So he wasn't asked.

Despite the gaps in testimony, and the pre-determined nature of its findings, there were some lively moments during the Gibson Inquiry hearings, which took place between February 21 and June 5, 1974. When the commission moved out to the Pickering area, Brenda Davies turned up with a doggerel denouncing the MOT, and several other POP members gave eloquent, if futile, testimony in defence of their homes. Aileen Adams burst into tears on the stand, but she faked it. "I had made up my mind that I was going to cry. I thought it would have a dramatic effect." Agronomist Ken Fallis pointed out that the government's figures on farmland were so confused that the acreage of the area kept on going up and down.

The inquiry, incredibly, was not supposed to deal with the question of costs, and when Clark Muirhead, the Uxbridge councillor, asked, "Could you tell me what this is going to cost, please?," Gibson cut him off roughly: "You are directing yourself to something we are not required to inquire into."

The commission listened to all kinds of complaints from the locals, but gave them no weight whatever; it was not required to, and it didn't; not a word of this evidence made it into the report. Instead, a good deal of time was given over to playing cute legal games and knocking down opponents of the airport.

These folks had only a few bright moments. One came when H.R. Stratford of de Havilland Aircraft waded into the argument about expanding Malton. De Havilland were not, of course, innocent bystanders in this melee; as makers of the Dash-7 aircraft they wanted to see Canada turn to STOL instead of conventional jets for short-haul trips, and they found a community of interest with POP, which was willing to back STOL, or almost anything else that would obviate the need for Pickering. Stratford pointed out that LaGuardia Airport in New York, "with two 7,000-foot runways and nothing else, can handle almost three times what Malton is handling." He said that if airports were looked at in terms of passengers handled per annum per acre of land, John F. Kennedy Airport in New York handled 5,000, Los Angeles close to 6,000, and Malton only 1,833. "The conclusion in regard to traffic density is that no need for a second airport can be established on this basis; we have the acres at Malton today; only their efficient utilization is needed."

Stratford was simply ignored; he was never cross-examined, and his evidence was discounted. The same technique was used, with similar success, against John Wylie, former Director of Aviation for the Port of New York Authority, and Robert Simpson, Director of the Flight Transportation Laboratory at the Massachusetts Institute of Technology. Both were flown in by de Havilland.

Wylie said that if a dual runway was put down beside Malton's 14/32, the airport would have a configuration remarkably similar to that at Newark, "which, however, has only 2,300 acres of capacity and a narrow gauge runway separation of only 950 feet."

This evidence was simply brushed off, a fact that still amazes Wylie. When I talked to him in late 1978, he could only remember "the adversary nature of the hearing. Nobody wanted to listen to what I had to say; they already had their minds made up. I was just a nuisance."

An even bigger nuisance was Robert Simpson, who said, "There seems to be a communications lag in the planning process between the planners here and what we are talking about in the United States . . . I think Pickering is a mistake, clearly a mistake, a very large mistake.

"We are going to quieten the fleet, the rest of the world is going to quieten the fleet, Canada, as a maverick, is diametrically opposed to that and seems to be following the opposite course; leave the fleet noisy and spend the money on land."

Dual runways at Malton would solve the problem, and the MOT's rejection of them on the basis that wake vortex swirls would prevent their safe use was simply not valid: "With dual runways, with high-speed turnoffs, you can get 64 operations per hour on one runway. What is more, vortex can only affect a plane in the air, not on the ground, so planes taking off don't need the same six-mile separation as those landing. The effect is that Malton could get 128 aircraft movements per hour out of dual runways."

Simpson went on, "I find it impossible to believe that Canadians are accepting the kind of information that is being put forward here that there is not capacity at Malton." Then he held up a chart of American airports. "You will see in this line, this is San Francisco airport. Essentially, there are two runways there, they are dual runways, they are something like 1,000 feet apart and that airport today is handling more operations per year than the projection for 1985 at Malton. That is not analysis or projection. That is fact." At Denver, too, at a smaller airport than Malton, "Operations are well above the projections that you have for the needs of Malton." At Los Angeles, "One airplane takes off ten seconds after the other one comes over the end of the runway and touches . . . . That exact procedure has been used for more than seven years at Los Angeles International Airport."

Simpson now thinks his evidence may have been discounted because he seemed to be belittling Canadians. He is a Canadian, and has worked as an airport consultant here – you will recall that he was involved with the Montreal airport decision – but he sounded as if he was putting the home side down. "I had seven examples of airports where duals have been used for years. I should have confined myself to that." As it was, he was cross-examined on the fact that he had not done any studies at Malton, and dismissed.

The question of aircraft movements, which so vexed Simpson, and appeared not to vex the commission at all, is a complex one. The commission eventually decided that Malton's capacity was limited to an Instrument Flight Rules peak of 59 movements per hour, and that dual runways would only increase the load by 10 per cent. I took the Malton layout down to experts in the Federal Aviation Administration in Washington, and I was told, repeatedly, that, based on that layout, a minimum of 99 movements per hour could be expected.

"Somebody has to be pulling your leg about these numbers" is the way Jack Bourne, an airport planning specialist with the FAA, put it. So I asked if differences in air traffic control procedures would squeeze down Malton's capacity. Bourne replied that he had had the FAA air traffic experts go over the rules after I first raised the issue and "For all intents and purposes, the rules are the same." At 99 movements per hour, Malton could handle 578,160 aircraft movements annually if the present sixteen-hour day is maintained. That is much more than the forecast for movements in the year 2000 accepted by the Gibson Commission, namely, 430,200.

Still, I wasn't satisfied. I went to see Barney Parrella, Vice President, Economics, of the Airport Operators Council in Washington. In a phrase that was becoming familiar, he said, "Somebody has to be kidding you on the question of capacity." There are dual runway systems operating with perfect safety and efficiency all over the world, and Parrella couldn't see why Malton was so inefficient.

However, dual runways were not in the game plan of the MOT, and the Gibson Commission took the MOT evidence on board, hook, line and sinker. There would be 61.9 million passengers in the year 2000 for Toronto, and 430,200 aircraft movements, and there was no way Malton would be able to handle the onslaught.

"The Commission, therefore, comes to the conclusion that while the demand which is forecasted is staggering by any dimension, nevertheless, by using some rather broad yardsticks, it has satisfied itself that the forecast is within reasonable probability."

The MOT had worked out some new numbers since the decision

was originally taken in 1972, and these tended to come down sharply. The 8.8 per cent growth predicted for each and every year had come out to less than 2 per cent in 1971-2, and since then, the Arab oil boycott had shot up fuel and ticket prices. Therefore, the forecasts had to be modified, and this time they came out to 11.6 million passengers at Malton in 1980 (instead of the 15.9 million predicted in 1972), 23 million in 1990 (instead of 32.5 million) and 41 million in 2000 (instead of 61.9 million). The decision had been made on the basis of 62 million; never mind, it would be okay even if 21 million of these were wiped out by a blip of the computer.

No, no, the Gibson Report said, you chaps were right in the first place. "Estimates of demand in the past for American airports have all, very substantially, underestimated the demand. This, the commission believes, is of vital importance." This was hooey, but it sounded nice. In fact, when the Port of New York Authority was pushing Kennedy airport, it projected 59 million passengers in the area for 1973, but only 43 million turned up. The figures the commission accepted were the original 1972 MOT numbers, which have since been abandoned. "Every time we do another forecast," one of MOT's new planners, Nick Mulder, told me in 1978, "the figures come out lower."

The commission decided that the Ministry was substantially correct, even though it was able to identify nine fundamental errors in the forecasting technique, ranging from the fact that the projections were based on too small a sample to the fact that the fuel price projections no longer made any sense. The commission acknowledged that most forecasts are wrong and "the further the forecast is projected into the future, the greater the error." As we have seen, the argument for a new airport did not depend on the saturation of Malton today; it was in the period after 1985, eleven years away, that problems arose, but the fact that these far-off projections were bound to be wrong cut no ice. The second airport should be built.

The commission ran into some problems with the noise argument. It did not think the NEF contours used to measure noise annoyance were very good. "These contours are rather broad lines and cannot be regarded as rigid fences driven into the surface of the ground that will prevent the passage of noise." If the NEF wavered a little, areas of Stouffville, Claremont, and Markham, as well as the proposed city of North Pickering (projected population, 200,000), would be affected. Since the whole idea of the exercise was to cut down on the number of people in noise lands, this didn't look so good. The solution was to extend the area of protection; instead of buying up just the land within the 30 NEF contour, the government should buy up all the lands out to 25 NEF.

Well, if 25 NEF were to be taken, thousands more people were within the noise lands of Pickering; nobody even knew how many, because no measure had been taken. The whole shaky edifice of comparison between Malton and Pickering began to tremble. But there was a worse problem; the commission confused the contours in making the measurements at Malton. You will remember that the noise contours start from the inside and work out. At the centre are people subject to 40 NEF and above, then 35 and above, then 30 and above, and so on out. To simplify matters, let's suppose there are ten people inside the 30 NEF line and fifteen inside the 28 NEF line. There are therefore a total of twenty-five people exposed to 28 NEF or above. It would be wrong to add to this the ten inside the 30 line to come up with thirty-five people affected by noise. That, however, is exactly what the Gibson Report did. It added the two zones up by double-counting those in the inner ring, and wound up with 131,000 people hurt by noise at Malton – more than lived there. The error, once adopted, was repeated twelve times as the commission sought to show how many more people were bothered at Malton than would be bothered in Pickering. This bungle did not entirely wreck the argument, but it didn't help any, either.

The argument held up, in any event, only as long as the NEF figures were taken seriously. No one had actually measured the noise at Malton, a fact that George Capern, Director of Operations for the Air Transport Association of Canada, can't get over. "It turned out there is no goddamn instrument for measuring the noise. Nothing. There is no fixed point on the ground with anybody taking readings. Incredible."

Well, who cares what ATAC says? They only represent the airlines who have to use the airports, and they say, repeatedly, that they think a second airport for Toronto is a bum idea. Instead of the blunt, crude actual measurements that ATAC seems to favour, Transport Canada has a sophisticated computer to play with. A computer can produce much more interesting results than merely listening to airplanes. For example, the NEF contour can be made to billow outwards simply by adding one more night flight to the mix; it can be drawn back in by assuming that more noisy jets will be replaced by quiet ones. One DC-8 with a Conway engine, flown at night, has as much impact on a computer read-out as 160 L10-11s flown during the daytime.

Many of the fancy results culled from the computer were put to the commission on MOT's behalf by Richard Edmiston, a consultant with Tracor Corporation of Austin, Texas, and they were accepted, as was most of the government case, as the gospel. What the commission didn't know was that there was a brutal wrangle about Edmiston's testimony inside the Ministry. On April 1, 1974, Larry T. Filotas, Senior Research Officer, Aviation Research for the department, wrote a devastating critique of the Tracor noise study as presented by Edmiston. He said that, "Two of the reports should not have been commissioned, let alone released." The conclusions drawn were "not supported by the references cited." Filotas wrote of "questionable assumptions" and "serious questions as to the report's objectivity . . . in many cases, the report's wording carefully weasels around actual falsehood." Another report was "very slanted and ill-conceived." What is more, the case being put by Tracor, that noise was bad and bound to get worse around airports, was in "direct contradiction" to the position then being taken by the MOT in Vancouver.

Filotas' memo was turned over to Larry Potvin for defusing. Potvin, in his reply, noted that the Tracor study came about as a result of a chance meeting with Edmiston at a convention, after which the American was asked to do a hurry-up report. If the study was flawed, well, that was only to be expected when it was produced under such time constraints. The Ministry had been fooling with noise studies since 1952, and with Malton noise since 1966; now it didn't have time to do a decent job. If the Ministry was telling one story in Vancouver and another in Toronto, Potvin wrote, then that was something the Ministry should clear up for itself; it had nothing to do with Edmiston. Besides – and here was the clincher – Edmiston had already appeared before the commission and "It is clear that Mr. Edmiston has projected the image of a forthright, knowledgable, and convincing witness."

If the image was right, who could ask for anything more?

Edmiston, who had first been hired on a contract for $5,000, including witness fees of $280 a day at the inquiry, got another $5,000 to make his contract $10,000. Filotas appeared at the inquiry, and didn't say a murmuring word about the concerns he had voiced in private – and the MOT went on churning out two stories in Vancouver and Toronto.

In January 1975, about the time the Gibson Commission was reporting, the Ministry published a pamphlet designed to prove that Vancouver International Airport could be expanded without increasing noise – the opposite to the tale it tells in Toronto. This little gem, titled "Sorry About the Noise – But We're Doing Something About It," noted proudly that "Industry has developed quieter aircraft," and included a whole page, headed "It's getting quieter all the time," which showed that changes in technology and flight procedures were bringing down noise. All the tricks that the inquiry was told wouldn't work, from retrofitting to changes in flight procedures, were held up as major advances that would lick the noise problem.

I later asked W.H. Huck, the former Air Administrator, about this two-faced approach, but he could see nothing wrong with it. The airport in Vancouver had to be expanded, because there was no place to put another airport there. In Toronto, the situation was different, he said. I guess that explains that.

The Gibson hearings ground to a halt on June 5, 1974, and anyone who doubted what the eventual report would say must have been out of the country. The Ministry kept in touch with the judge and learned that he intended to have his report complete before October.

The City of Toronto had put itself on the record as opposing the airport, but had not had time, it said, to prepare a thorough brief. By the time it got the work done, it was too late to appear before the inquiry. City council therefore passed a resolution requesting the commission to reconvene for purposes of receiving its study, which had been prepared by Diamond and Myers, Architects, and Jack B. Ellis and Associates. The study cost $30,000, or about one-eighth of what it cost MOT to count the gulls in Pickering. There was no legal reason for the commission to oblige the city, but, when copies of the study were given to Toronto's Executive Committee, Jack Ellis, the major consultant, said not only that the government forecasts were exaggerated, but that, in private, some of the government experts agreed with his own lower estimate of around 21 million passengers in the year 2000. This, as the commissioners noted in their report, suggested that the commission might have been misled. Accordingly, on August 21 and 22, the Toronto study was received and its authors, especially Jack Ellis, were cross-examined.

Ellis did not fare well. The "experts" who agreed with him appeared to be one man, our old pal Philip Beinhaker, who denied flatly that he had done any such thing. Ellis was no expert on airports, and it was not hard to show that he had done no previous work in either air travel forecasts or noise. "Yet," as the Gibson Report later thundered, "Professor Ellis and other authors of the study purported to criticize the opinions of others . . . under the circumstances, the Commission can give no credence to the unsupported opinion of Professor Ellis and his associates, in respect to (1) forecasts and (2) noise, and rejects them."

Despite this summary dismissal, Ellis did make two telling points before the commission; both dealt with statistics, with which he was familiar.

In the first place, he took apart the government's travel propensity model. In arriving at the ticket fares expected to affect this model, the government had assumed that fuel prices would remain stable. In 1991, jet fuel would probably cost about twenty-five cents a gallon, certainly no more than thirty-four cents. And yet, Ellis noted, the average fuel cost was "already forty-five cents a gallon." If the air fares' assumption was adjusted to take account of this one factor, it could change the year 2000 forecast by 10 million passengers.

Ellis's other main point was that the MOT forecast study was "like a little windup toy that you wind up and it produces the need for a new airport."

The travel propensity of foreign-born Canadians was shown, in the model, to be nearly three times that of native-born Canadians. Instead of assuming that the proportion of foreign born in the population would eventually come down, the MOT whizzes kept the proportion constant, and projected it forward, with the inevitable ballooning effect on the forecasts. They wound up with a scenario in which every Canadian would have to make six times as many international trips per capita as in 1971.

"At any given time in the summer of each year around 2000, some ten to twenty per cent of the entire population will be away on an international air trip." Even if Canadians had the money to take all the trips forced on them by the MOT projections, where would they get the time?

This argument, too, was dismissed, gone with Ellis's reputation into the maw of the commission's rage.

The Gibson Report was not turned in during October, thanks to the Toronto intervention. It didn't arrive in Ottawa until December 23, 1974. It accepted all the MOT forecasts, rejected virtually every attack on the department's experts, ignored the complaints from Pickering residents, and gave the government what it wanted, a rationale for the decision that had been made in 1972.

However, when the report was passed around inside the department, and circulated to other government departments, some cracks began to appear. The magnificent airport contemplated for Pickering, with as many as six runways, would not be built after all.

Chapter 11

The Incredible
Shrinking Airport

Gordon Ness, lawyer:
"The fight was a big boon for me, I worked for people who opposed the airport. Now all the people out there are gone, it's a desert. Some people did well, some poorly. One woman whose husband was killed in a car accident just before the takeover came, she was a wreck. Her doctor advised her to settle for whatever was offered and get out. She did. One farmer on the edge of the Century City development had been offered $390,000 for his farm in 1967. He accepted, but when Century City went down the tube they refused to pay on his offer. In December 1971, he decided to sell out and retire, but he said he was only going to sell to another farmer, he wasn't going to have anything to do with those bastards of developers. He got an offer of $100,000, in a deal to close in the fall of 1972, and accepted it verbally. Then the government arrived with expropriation papers. He said he would go through with the deal anyway, and sold it for $100,000. Then the new farmer turned around and was expropriated for $450,000. My man said, 'Well, a deal is a deal'; he wasn't going to welch. The people who were straightforward and honest got screwed. Those who kicked and bit and screamed did very well. It makes you wonder."

David Menzies, former property manager, North Pickering Project:
"If you're going to screw a few people, fine, as long as you treat them the same."

When copies of the Gibson Report began to circulate in Ottawa, the bureaucrats liked some, but not all, of what they read. The commissioners had found no New (always capitalized) evidence to suggest that there was anything wrong with the arguments on either need or location, and they ruled that Malton airport would never do to accommodate the expected traffic. The present facility's runway capacity could be increased to meet the demand until 1980, and perhaps even until 1985 – it depended on what was done – but runway space would run out in 1990. Malton's terminals could be made sufficient for 1990, but not for 2000. So, to meet a demand somewhere between 1990 and 2000, there was going to have to be another airport. So far, so good. This second airport should be started at once, but not opened until everything was in place – terminals, runways, access roads, the works. There should be no phasing-in; that meant that Malton must be expanded at once to take up the slack until the new facility was in full flight. And the way to expand Malton was with that perennial favourite, a parallel to runway 14/32.

Dagnabit. The report had taken the MOT's arguments on, all right, but it embraced them with such enthusiasm that the government was being pushed right back to a decision it had rejected in 1961, and kept rejecting at regular intervals ever since. Shakespeare fans among the MOT planning team may well have nodded to each other over copies of the Gibson Report and noted, "We have scotched the snake, not killed it." Damn snake was still winding around their legs.

Since it was departmental theology that dual runways wouldn't work, the new parallel would have to be a long way from the present one: "The Commission is of the opinion that a new runway parallel to runway 14/32 is probably required now at Malton, and that such a runway should be separated from existing runway 14/32 by a distance of 4,400 feet. Construction of such a runway must take place even if there is a decision to proceed with the Pickering Airport as, realistically, the earliest date that Pickering Airport can be in operation is 1982 or 1984. Without such a runway, there could be a transportation breakdown at Malton until the Pickering Airport is in operation."

With such a runway, of course, noise would be increased and extended, but "The residents of Malton will have to accept that until Pickering Airport is in operation there will be an increase in the noise level to which they are subjected and that additional people will be affected by noise."

The entire trembling structure of MOT logic would collapse if this runway was built. The confidential cabinet document, dated January 28, 1975, that dealt with the Gibson Report noted, "The recommendation to develop a fourth runway at Malton is directly contradictory to the commitment by the Government and present Minister of Transport that there would be no new runway construction at Malton." What is more, the document argued, this runway would have to be serviced by a new terminal on the west side of the airport, but access to such a terminal could not be provided because "The Ontario Ministry of Transportation and Communications has repeatedly stated that no connection can be made to Highway 401."

This last bit was another dash of flim-flam. The MOT had a fall-back position – that if anyone ever beat through the undergrowth of the other dim-witted arguments against Malton expansion, it could not be done, anyway, because Ontario would not allow a road connection. What Ontario had said, however, in a letter to the Ministry, was that no "direct" connection to 401 could be put in place, because the road system out Malton way already looks like a game of Snakes and Ladders. What it would allow, and what it was already moving to protect, was an indirect connection: "There is provision for either a roadway or rapid transit facility under Highway 401 to enter into the Malton area from the south of Highway 401. We are taking the necessary steps, that are within our jurisdiction, to protect for this option." What the feds did, repeatedly, was to ignore all this last part and cling to a phrase higher up in the letter, "There will be no direct connection at this point."

During the inquiry, airport planner Jack Vance was asked about the province's position, and admitted that "While these facilities could be provided, this would be very expensive and certainly in the view [of Ontario] would be disruptive to traffic on Highway 401 and if they did not allow that connection, it certainly would cast some serious doubt over the viability of providing adequate access." This mumbo-jumbo started out acknowledging that access would be provided and ended by assuming that it would not be. To clear up any doubts, all the government had to do was to call any provincial planner to the stand, but nobody wanted the doubt cleared away. It could then be argued that the expansion was impossible; the Gibson Report recommendation to expand could therefore be ignored.

Another problem was the commissioners' excessive zeal in adopting the government testimony about how annoying and unhealthy noise could be. This led to the recommendation that, instead of merely buying up the land within the 30 NEF contour, "It is the Commission's view that the airport project should include, as a minimum, the expropriation of all land within the 25 NEF contour." That could lead to the purchase of another 25,000 to 50,000 acres – the amount depended on the size of the airport put in place, which nobody knew – and would require buying up parts of Markham, Stouffville, Claremont, and the yet-to-be-born city, once yclept Cedarwood, but now North Pickering.

So, while the bureaucrats were generally pleased with the report there were those embarrassing bursts of over-enthusiasm, which would have to be smothered. That process was barely under way when other departments began to get into the act.

The Privy Council Office circulated the Gibson document to other ministries with an interest in the project – the Department of Finance, the Treasury Board, Urban Affairs, Environment, and Agriculture. Their confidential replies were soon winging back and, while the finance department folks were brief and friendly, everybody else had crushing things to say.

The Treasury Board thought that "Both the Airport Inquiry Commission and MOT seem to have succumbed to a form of 'technological determinism' – the assumption that potential demands in a subsidized market must be fulfilled and that the government must react passively, despite its priorities with respect to regional and demographic distribution. Even within this framework, the possibility of the alternative strategy of intensively exploiting Malton was rejected too soon. Furthermore, there are apparent weaknesses in the Report which lead to a loss of confidence in its conclusions."

The commission had swallowed MOT forecasts, "Which are, essentially, a 1972 prophecy of continuing exponential growth at 7-8% per year. Given the developments in energy costs, and federal policies on immigration, population distribution, and user charges, and our own work in the STOL evaluation, there is much to be said for revising these exponential projections downwards, at least in the short run."

The Treasury Board also caught the commission's technical errors: "It overestimated the effects of noise at Malton by misinterpreting the technical evidence – it double-counted people within noise contours, not realizing the cumulative value of the measure. It apparently misinterpreted the technical evidence on dual-runway systems, and their possible contribution to increasing capacity. It apparently overestimated the runway capacity required."

That was not all; by subjectively deciding that retrofitting of existing jet airplanes to make them quieter was not going to work, the commission acted too hastily. It would only cost $45 million to retrofit the entire Canadian passenger fleet and, "If all planes are retrofitted by 1980 and Pickering is not built, there will be fewer people affected by noise at Malton in 1980 than if retrofitting does not occur and traffic is transferred to Pickering as planned. This scenario wasn't considered by the AIC."

The urban affairs department pointed out that the recommendation to expropriate all land within the 25 NEF contour made nonsense of the whole notion of putting a new city down beside the airport, and would probably cost between $200-$400 million extra. In

133

addition, the whole premise of the report was at odds with stated government policy, because it assumed that "National demographic and urban concentration trends should or will continue unabated," that Toronto would continue to sprawl, that air traffic would continue to shoot up, and that government could do nothing about these trends. But the whole nub of government policy was to "confine urban sprawl and rationalize growth patterns." The airport was bound to "spread the urban sprawl to the east," the department said – indeed this was something that anyone with the brains of a bullfrog could see, and every source outside the MOT's stable of experts kept saying. The only thing to do was to shelve the whole project and study it some more.

The Department of the Environment weighed in with a snippy note that made it clear – in contrast to everything said publicly – "That the process was virtually complete and notice of expropriation had been given before Environment Canada became involved." The Ontario government had looked at Pickering and Beverly, but that work was "very hurriedly done," and "No other alternatives were considered." This ministry, too, wanted the whole project looked at again.

The Department of Agriculture agreed with the commission that 12,000 of the 18,000 acres of airport land could be continued to be used for farming. However, it pointed out, no one had looked at the effect of jamming access roads and other user facilities down on valuable land. "It is possible to see the continued availability of 12,000 acres of land for agriculture in the area, with a rapid loss of most other agricultural lands outside the airport."

These departmental rivals were dealt with in the usual way, by burying their reports, ignoring their comments and denying that there was anything wrong. The background document, with ten appendices, that was given to cabinet ministers before they were to make their decision on what to do with the Gibson Report, contains not a murmuring word about the reservations and condemnations expressed.

However, something would have to be done about the recommendations to buy all the land out to 25 NEF, to build a parallel runway, and to delay opening Pickering until the thing could be done properly, with at least two runways, terminal facilities and access roads all in place. These, after all, were contained in a public document, not hidden in a buried report.

The first point was met by the news that it would "require careful study" and that this study was already under way. Even if more land did have to be bought, the Cabinet was told, it could be resold later to recover most of the cost. One down. The parallel runway argument was met by the ingenious suggestion that it costs just as much, and takes just as long, to build a new runway as to build a whole new airport. There was all that land to buy – as long as the dual-runway concept was accepted and a 4,400-foot spacing required – and the government already owned land in Pickering. Two down. The feds did not want to build a big, new airport at Pickering all at once, anymore, as the commission insisted they should; instead, they wanted to go at the thing in phases, as at Montreal. Times were tough in early 1975, and despite all the earlier folderol about not having to finance the airport out of public dollars, the MOT knew that it stood a better chance if it could get going with a small version of Pickering; but here was the commission saying that would not do. The confidential cabinet document rose to the occasion. The report's objection to a phased opening was "Because of concern that a new airport, opened with temporary facilities . . . would result in adverse public reaction . . . . However, it is clear . . . that there will have to be temporary facilities until the first major phase is opened."

The commission was off its onion, that's all, and the thing to do was to start with a small airport and work up to something really worth while. Indeed, the document noted, "A development schedule has been prepared which indicates that it is possible to have the first major phase commissioned and operational for the peak season of 1981." This first phase would cost $542 million in 1974/75 dollars.

It was a nice try. But no sale. A number of cabinet ministers were getting leery of the whole deal, especially those whose departments were telling them that the MOT's work was suspect. The sceptics included Housing Minister Barney Danson and Treasury Board President Jean Chrétien. The non-sceptics included Norman Cafik, Liberal MP for the Pickering area, who made his contribution to the debate in a memo to cabinet on January 30, 1975. Cafik, who is nothing if not flexible, had some minor quibbles with the Gibson Report, but "My public position has always been that I would accept the decision of the Airport Inquiry Commission and I am prepared to do that." In fact, there was nothing Cafik was not prepared to do. If the government decided to press ahead with Pickering, "I am quite prepared to support the Government decision in this direction." If the government wanted to drop the project entirely, "I think that position could be justified, regardless of the Gibson Report." Or, finally, if the government wanted to postpone Pickering, "This solution could be defended – I would support it as well."

In short, the MP most involved took the position that he could best defend the interests of his constituents by stating forthrightly that he would put up with anything on their behalf. Although his public posture was that he would accept the Gibson Report, he was equally prepared to chuck it out the window; he would support building the airport, or not building it, or building it later. Whatever the government wanted was aces with him. Cafik was later elevated to the Cabinet, which shows the premium governments put on the sturdy independence of MPs.

However, there were others who were not quite so malleable; for the first time since the airport hassle began, the MOT was unable to slip one of its documents quietly through Cabinet. The Gibson Report was made public on January 31, 1975, and Cabinet argued about it in private that same day, but no decision was taken. Instead, the MOT was asked to come back later, with more options and a new recommendation.

This time, there would be no slip-ups. The document prepared to guide the ministers for their next meeting was written and signed by Michael Pitfield, Secretary to the Cabinet, and Prime Minister Trudeau's right-hand man for many years. His report, dated February 15, 1975, is titled, "An Evaluation by Officials of the Proposal to Construct a New Toronto International Airport at Pickering." In fourteen foolscap pages and seven annexes, Pitfield constructed an argument in which the only sensible course to pursue was to build a teeny-weeny airport at Pickering.

He acknowledged that "Questions have been raised by Ministers and others as to whether the Commission . . . took adequate account of (a) possible modification downward of demand projections in light of the new energy situation and continuing inflationary pressure and the prospect generally for world economic growth; and (b) the feasibility of expanding capacity at Malton and, concurrently, of achieving effective noise abatement, thus permitting expansion to proceed there without disrupting the life of surrounding communities."

Note that the real knocks on the report – that the commissioners made blunders and did not seem to understand government policy – were not mentioned; instead, lesser objections were raised, only to be dropped without explanation: "The forecasts of growth made by the Ministry of Transport and which, with few qualifications, were accepted by the Commission, may be taken as a convenient starting point for analysis of the problem."

All the negative thinking was dumped; instead, we would go back to the daft forecasts that began the whole process because, by cracky, whatever else you said about the Gibson Report, it accepted those forecasts. What better way to begin an analysis? And that analysis led, right where it always led, to acceptance of the government's wild guesses and the demand for a new airport. To expand Malton, Pitfield said, would cost $306 million, and there was no way of knowing if Ontario would provide the necessary road access (he backed off from the earlier flat statement that the province would not). He wound up, as clever mandarins do, by appearing to give the Cabinet ministers four options to choose from, but in fact giving them no choice at all.

"Option A: Proceed now with the full project at Pickering with no further expansion at Malton."

The problem with this was that it would cost $351 million immediately, according to Pitfield's figures, "and result in serious capacity problems at Malton."

"Option B: Proceed now on a phased basis at Pickering with no further expansion at Malton."

This would cost $383 million, but only $102 million of this would have to be spent at once. What's more, it would "provide flexibility for two years before any further decision was required. It should result in new capacity being in place in time to avoid serious disruption of service at Malton and would provide the earliest possible relief from disturbance from noise."

Anything that provides "flexibility" in a government document is the real McCoy; this was it – the answer. It was placed second on the list, so as not to seem pushy, but the game was over.

"Option C: Proceed now and simultaneously with construction of Pickering and expansion of capacity at Malton."

This would cost $657 million, "all of which would have to be committed now." The government did not have that kind of change hanging around loose, and, besides, "It would extend the area, number of people, and severity of noise disturbance at Malton to 1985 and beyond." Actually, Option C was, in essence, the Gibson Report option, but no one was to know that. In later arguments, the government would say that the second airport had been examined in detail and supported by the months of work and mounds of evidence drawn before the Gibson Inquiry; with the shyness that is characteristic of government, however, no one would point out that all that work and evidence was junked in a few pages in a memo written by a Cabinet official who was only slightly more qualified in airport planning than Jasper the Bear.

"Option D: Make more intensive use of Malton, including expansion of capacity to the extent necessary and, probably, mea-

137

sures to limit demand and direct traffic to other modes, meanwhile postponing a start on Pickering."

This option would cost $657 million, too, of which $306 million – the assumed cost of expanding Malton – would have to be spent at once, and it would "imply higher levels of congestion in the 1980s." There would also be "other serious problems associated with expropriation."

The Pitfield document, like all the other really important documents relating to Pickering, is a secret, and that is too bad; it should be required reading in political science courses. It would show Canadian students how in fact, as opposed to theory, cabinet decisions are made. Once the pronouncement has been handed down by a handful of people who have some vague notion of what is actually happening, a scenario is constructed, which only the most dogged investigation can unravel, and then a clutch of simple options are put before ministers, who merely have to read about 300 words to select the choice that obviously stands alone. The comforting thing about the Pitfield document was not its erudition – it is not erudite, nor even clear, and it leaves out far more than it tells – but its author. When the Secretary to the Cabinet gives you Option B, if you are a clever Cabinet minister, and upwardly mobile, you know that Option B is the only option in town.

Accordingly, on February 20, 1975, Transport Minister Jean Marchand announced that the government had at last made up its mind *in re* the Gibson Report. There would be an airport at Pickering, but it would not be a great big, vulgar one. It would be a "Minimum Airport," with only one runway, and it would cost $204 million. Remember that five days earlier this cost was given to Cabinet as $383 million.

The one-runway airport was nonsense. Even if the government's entire case were accepted, this facility was going to be built to meet a demand that would crop up somewhere between 1990 and the year 2000. But if the demand was real, one runway wouldn't do much good. It would have to be in the direction of one of the runways at Malton, since the prevailing winds are the same. That meant that whenever the Pickering runway was shut down because of contrary weather, Malton would be over-taxed, and then all the Pickering traffic would be dumped onto it. What was the point of building an airport like that?

The Canadian government had now been working away at airport planning in Toronto since 1966, and in 1975, nine years later, all it could come up with was a plan that no one, not even its air-happy consultants, could defend with anything like enthusiasm.

138

Everyone outside the Ministry of Transport who had looked at the problem had come to the conclusion that the expansion of Malton was feasible – even the Gibson Commission could see that – but the MOT clung to its game plan. To get the thing rolling, a one-runway airport would be put down; it was not an answer, and no one inside or outside the Ministry thought it was an answer, but at least it would get some money spent. The financial figures given were a hoax, and the minimum airport was a fraud. When that obvious truth began to penetrate to the provincial planners who were going to have to find tax dollars to support Ottawa's dreams of grandeur, the whole Pickering project began to come apart.

Chapter 12

The Brakes Go On

Heather Dinsmore, housewife/activist:
"Across the road was an older couple, and they said they were waiting for expropriation. 'That's their privilege,' I said, they had no mortgage and no kids to worry about. But people in the position we were in, the best thing to do we thought was to co-operate with the government. So we signed, and sold out, and we have been moving ever since. My son, Geoff, withdrew more and more into himself. He wouldn't go out, he would only sit in his room. One night I was going past his room late at night and he was crying. I said, 'Geoff, why are you crying?' And he screamed at me, he says, 'I hate the government, I hate you.' He said, 'Why were we so stupid that we sold out?' This had been building up in him; he'd lost his horse and heifer and animals and everything and now we were living in a strawberry box. I said we couldn't be so selfish; the Government of Ontario had to have our house for people from Toronto. At least we had a place to live, some people didn't have anything. I was so stupid I thought they were going to do something with the land they took. How could I explain to my children that you should always expect the government to cheat you?"

Minutes of a Meeting of Provincial Civil Servants, April 21, 1972:
"Staff were advised that speed was essential to ensure all the effective dates of the appraisal was [sic] as close together as possible. Furthermore, they were advised that we should be in a position to register final expropriation as early as possible, whether such an eventuality actually occurred or not. The danger in the present situation is that the market could react at any time."

All the time the Gibson Commission was being created, blossoming, withering and dying, that is to say, all during 1973 and 1974, the airport opponents were kicking up a stink back in Pickering. From time to time they grew lonely, and even desperate. Minutes of a POP executive meeting on April 25, 1973, note "Isobel felt we have been too quiet and should resort to violence." Another minute

140

reads, "Margaret willing to lead rebellion to pull out survey stakes and burn them if any willing to go to jail."

POP had lost the argument over the federal expropriation when that was confirmed after the Swackhamer hearings; now the second blow fell. You will remember that the province was trying to gather up the lands for its project by negotiation, and holding the threat of expropriation in the background. People like Heather Dinsmore were told that they would be better off if they gave in, and some, like Heather, did so; however, many more heeded the advice of POP, which was to stand their ground, sign nothing, and hope for the best. By January 10, 1974, the province had assembled less than half the acreage it needed for its dream city, so the Minister of Housing moved that day to expropriate the rest. The amended Housing Development Act would now come into play; under its broad powers, the province reached out and swept in all the necessary titles. The hearings of necessity were simply junked, by order of the provincial Cabinet. At least everyone in the area was now in the same boat; before, there had been two groups, those whose land had been seized because they happened to live on property the feds wanted for the airport, and those who were being pressured by land agents for the province. Now they were all being expropriated, and they were all kicking like steers about the prices being offered. Once the land seizures began at the federal level, and 35,000 acres of prime land was taken off the market, property prices all around began to shoot up, and the displaced Pickering residents could not afford to buy new homes for the amounts they were given for the old.

They quickly learned that, in the matter of expropriations, sweet reasonableness was the worst possible state of mind. Those who accepted their fate with grace, and took the government offers, were cheated; those who locked their doors, drove assessors off their property, refused to answer the telephone, and, in general, raised bloody hell, got whacking big prices for their property. Roy Bamborough, who owned twelve acres of land and a barn he had converted into a house, battled the provincial government for five years, turned down an offer of $225,000, and, in the end, had to be evicted. Heather and Terry Dinsmore accepted an offer of $45,000 for their five acres and home, moved several times, looking for decent property, and wound up in a cramped house on a lot 143 feet by 174 feet, for which they paid $58,000. Aileen Adams and Anne Wanstall gave up their fight against federal expropriators, when Aileen collapsed under the strain, and were given $89,000 for their 10.5-acre place, Melody Farm, with its lovely old house; then they had to pay $90,000 for an inferior house on one acre of land. Peter McCowan was offered $200,000 for his house and ten acres, sight unseen; he refused to allow assessors onto his land to check it out, and the estimate was raised, by men standing across the road and peering at his home, by $50,000. He cashed the cheque and is still fighting for more.

There was no equity in the pricing, only caprice. Because both governments were working so hastily, and so sloppily, some people were overpaid, many more were underpaid, and no one was satisfied. Conditions were especially difficult for those who had to deal with the Ontario land agents; they were under instructions to close deals as fast and as cheaply as possible, and some of the agents used harassment to get the job done, while others were fair and polite. The result was that Pickering residents, comparing notes, soon discovered that the last thing they could expect was even-handed treatment, and their resentment was compounded. One elderly couple were paid $26,000 for a one-acre lot with a comfortable split-level home; a mile to the east, the same government paid $24,000 for a shack on a smaller lot. One family had a twenty-acre plot with a six-room house, a garage, machine-shop and storage shed; they were offered $3,500 an acre. Another tract of about the same size in the same area went for $3,250 an acre, and it had no buildings whatever on it. It is not Ontario's fault if people are foolish enough to put up homes and businesses on the property they own.

The Ontario expropriations were examined by provincial Ombudsman Arthur Maloney, who noted that "the appraisal reports were often brief, incomplete, and poorly supported." He found that the land agents used harassment and pressure tactics, that many property owners were misled and that complaints were brushed aside.

The Ombudsman's report led to a series of legal and political squabbles; a royal commission was established to deal with some of the worst cases of hardship, but quickly bogged down. Three commissioners were appointed, with Mr. Justice J.F. Donnelly as chairman, and the judge insisted that he was not conducting an investigation, but a trial. As with the Gibson Commission, it was up to the knaves and rascals who dared to contest the conduct of the government to prove their case. One commissioner resigned in disgust, because he said it was obvious that "natural justice" could not be served in an adversarial hearing. The complaining landowners withdrew in a body after a series of rulings made it clear that they would never be able to put their case to the commission. Rulings of the commission were appealed to the Divisional Court and the landowners won, but by this time they had given up.

Finally, in March 1978, the commission reported, after hearing only the testimony of Ontario land agents, that it had come across no evidence that "the allegations of misconduct" cited in the Ombudsman's Report were justified. When Maloney resigned from the Ombudsman's Office in August 1978, he mentioned the frustrations of this commission, whose report he called "totally valueless." The cases that arose after Maloney began his investigation were dealt off to a separate hearing, which was supposed to report in early 1978, but has yet to be heard from. In a fine show of tit-for-tat, the land agents who gave the only testimony before Donnelly refused to appear at this hearing.

The upshot is that none of the dozens of families whose cases have been shown to be most urgently in need of correction, and who have been searching for justice for five years, has even been heard. These people have spent thousands of dollars of their own money in the bizarre belief that if only their cases can be brought to court, they will receive fair treatment. They are Flying Dutchmen, sailing mortgages instead of ships.

The effect of the bullying tactics of some – I repeat, not all, but some – of the land agents was double-edged in the Pickering area. Soon, all those who were willing to go, or could be forced to go, had gone, and those who remained behind were united in their rage against both federal and provincial governments, the courts, and all land agents.

POP, which was now scheduled to fold up its tents, according to the Ministry of Transport timetable, was instead growing stronger, and its members were learning to play on the media like a fine-tuned instrument. The protest marches, bazaars, dances and publicity stunts continued; so did the money-raising. When a CBC crew arrived in Pickering to film a television series – nothing to do with the airport – the protest group offered to feed the crew at POP headquarters, for a fee. The protestors cleared $1,000 out of the arrangement, and made a whole new batch of media converts to the cause.

The Gibson hearings not only produced their own spate of publicity, they drew all waverers into line. "After the hearings, I grew quite bitchy," says Isobel Thompson. "We realized we were up against something ruthless."

Growing bitchy, however satisfying, would not block the airport, and, towards the end of 1974, POP's spirits began to sag again. Then came the publication of the Gibson Report, with the blunders that were immediately pounced upon by POP's technical team. When that was followed by the Minimum Airport proposal, the protestors realized that they had been handed a club and a target too tempting to miss. The Metropolitan Toronto Airport Review Committee took the lead on the attack on this daffy proposal, because, as Pat McClennan noted, "People were beginning to get a bit bored with POP; it was time to use something else." MTARC approached the de Havilland Aircraft Company, which was still trying to push its STOL program, and de Havilland came through with research material with which to attack the MOT noise forecasts, and with $4,000-worth of booklets called "Pickering Minimum Airport – Why?," a slick but excitable document that attacked the federal studies hip and thigh. The pamphlet used the MOT's own computer program on NEF to show that Malton could be reconfigured without expanding the noise contours if a runway was built parallel to 14/32 close in. MTARC then argued that this should be done, or, as the Gibson Report had suggested, the parallel could be put at 4,400 feet, and restricted to the so-called "quiet" jets, "plus STOL and general aviation." This reference is all de Havilland got for its $4,000.

While this material was still in preparation, MTARC chairman Douglas Turner approached a lawyer he knew in the prestigious firm of Blaney, Pasternak, in downtown Toronto. The lawyer was William McMurtry, and his entry into the lists of battle was to prove decisive. McMurtry is a slender, intense, charming, highly intelligent, and enormously enthusiastic man. His desk is untidy, his dress immaculate, his looks boyish, and his credentials impeccable. His family has always been prominent in law, and he and his brother Roy, later Ontario's Attorney General, have always been up to their hips in politics. William worked on the drive to stop the Spadina Expressway. He also worked as an organizer, and then speech-writer, for William Davis during the latter's drive for the Tory leadership. No one was going to slam any doors in his face.

He recalls that when Turner first came to talk to him, "I didn't know much about the Pickering deal except that there had been arguments and a series of commissions. I felt that it was beyond my expertise. However, that first meeting whetted my appetite. They wanted a lawyer and lobbyist to get some sort of injunction, so I asked them to send me some material. They brought in the stuff and it was a pile three feet high. I never did read it all."

McMurtry was a little dubious about Turner and MTARC; after all, two governments had done an awful lot of work on the project; surely it was futile to question their expertise. Just to satisfy himself, he called a man who had been one of his teachers at Royal Military College, and who was now a senior official with the Ministry of Transport.

"I told him I was thinking of acting for a group called MTARC and he told me they were a bunch of nuts. But I put a couple of questions to him from the MTARC material and he seemed to have trouble answering them. So then I asked 'Are you willing to say you're satisfied that there is a need for a second airport?'

"He said, 'I never said that.'

"I said, 'Is it fair to say you're satisfied that they must go ahead at this time?'

"He said, 'There may be a need some day. But they weren't listening to me, anyway.'

"I said, 'You mean there isn't a need at this time?'

"He said, 'You said that, I didn't.'

"I went on to say that there seemed to be an attempt to mislead, because the government was saying one thing in Vancouver and another in Toronto, and he replied, 'I'm not saying there was misleading, you are.'

"So I said, 'Well, I'm giving you a chance to deny it.' He said he couldn't. That did it; I was convinced."

The man McMurtry called was not only a senior official in MOT, he had been one of the government witnesses before the Gibson Inquiry. If he was suggesting that there was something fishy about the government case, McMurtry was satisfied that it must be so. He went back to the MTARC documents and began to prepare his own case against the airport. It quickly struck him that, if the Malton problem was political, so was the Pickering problem. The protestors were trying to make a convincing technical argument, but no one would be persuaded that a bunch of amateurs who staged balloon ascents and mock hangings knew more about airports than the certified experts. The way to attack the airport then, was not on its technical failings, but through its weakest link – the fact that the province was going to have to co-operate.

"There were so many things that came under provincial jurisdiction – the roads, water and hydro, sewers – and they were going to get it in the neck from everybody from the Federation of Ontario Naturalists to the ratepayer groups. The feds could walk away when the airport was built and say, 'There, that's done, now you service it.' We had to show that, and we had to say to the province, 'You've been misled.' "

McMurtry didn't know it, but that was a good time to put such an argument to the province. His first meeting with MTARC was on April 7, 1975. About that time, William Miller, a civil servant, who had worked with the federal Ministry of Transport, and then moved to the Ontario transport department, had prepared a background paper for his new bosses which said just what McMurtry was saying: that the MOT was not to be trusted, and that Ontario should act to protect itself.

McMurtry met more of the protestors – "Charles Godfrey was terrific; he was totally objective" – and then swung into action, not as a lawyer, but as a lobbyist. He went to see his brother Roy, who responded with a brutal attack on the airport in a column he was then writing for the *Toronto Sun.* Roy was not yet a member of the Cabinet, and could afford non-conformist views. Next, William went to Clare Westcott, an old friend, and the premier's chief aide, received a sympathetic hearing, and set up a meeting with four Ontario Cabinet ministers. That meeting led to an invitation to appear with MTARC members before the Executive Committee of the Cabinet on April 24, 1975. McMurtry worked hard on his presentation for that meeting, and produced an impressive argument.

"It was a goddamn jury address," says McMurtry. "I began by telling the committee that they all had more expertise than I did – some of them didn't know the first thing about the airport, but they like to hear that – and all I was going to do was to put a fresh perspective on the thing. My job really was to say 'For Christ's sake, listen.' I knew if I could get their attention, I had them. I went into my talk and I was about seven minutes in when I departed from the text and said, 'Gentlemen, you've bought a pig in a poke.' One of the ministers looked up and said, 'We've bought a bag of shit.' I knew I had their attention."

McMurtry's argument, essentially, was that the proposed airport was a monstrous affair, which would cost an amount that had never been determined, and create enormous social and economic problems for which the province would be blamed. He pointed out that Malton Airport covered 4,200 acres, LaGuardia Airport in New York handled more traffic on 640 acres, and Pickering would take, with its facilities, noiselands, and access roads, "105,000 acres, or more than two-thirds the size of Metropolitan Toronto." Air traffic was not rising as the MOT had said it would, noise relief was being provided by technological improvements, and if the province did not pull back, it would be stuck for incalculable costs. Ontario had been reckoning on a bill of somewhere around $80 million, but that was only for the first stage of the airport; to do what the feds were hoping to do at Pickering, McMurtry said, would cost "in excess of $275 million," for access alone.

The Executive Committee did not commit itself at that meeting, but its members came away looking thoughtful. Later, McMurtry spoke to Transport Minister John Rhodes, and suggested that it might be a good idea to have another chat with Transport Minister

Jean Marchand in Ottawa. Rhodes thought so too, and, with a senior aide in tow, raised some of the issues McMurtry had laid before the Executive Committee, before his Ottawa counterpart. The senior aide now recalls, "Marchand told us to trust him. He could not answer our concerns, but he told us to trust him anyway. We were not impressed."

Construction of the new airport was now imminent, and on April 30, POP, with as shrewd an eye as ever on the media, held a Bulldozer Tea, to round up the signatures of those who would be willing to lie down in front of construction equipment when the time came. More than 2,000 signatures were gathered, but the sincerity of the signees was never put to the test. Soon after, MTARC's minutes noted, "There would not be any need for people to lie down in front of tractors on June 1, because there was obviously going to be a delay."

So there was. On Tuesday, May 27, Premier Davis met with Transport Minister Marchand, Housing Minister Barney Danson, and Science Minister Bud Drury, in Ottawa. He said his government was concerned that "The Minimum Airport, without guarantee of further development, represented an insufficiently secure basis for Ontario to take the kind of infrastructural investment decisions that will be required."

That was cutely put. Ontario was not, at least not yet, ducking out of the deal made away back in March 1972. Davis was simply suggesting that the Minimum Airport, which had little to do with the deal made at that time, didn't look like the kind of operation he should hang several hundred million dollars of infrastructure on.

Marchand wanted to reassure Davis, but ended up trying to bully him. He said the federal government would be putting in "well in excess of $200 million" at the Pickering site. He was now stuck with his announced figure of $204 million, so he made that "well in excess of $200 million," and argued that this showed that Ottawa was making "a very major and permanent commitment." It was time for the province to throw something into the pot. "We consider that commitments to infrastructure should be made now to support this major initial development."

Davis is not easy to bully, and that didn't go down well; nor did the argument that the feds were going to go ahead, no matter what Ontario said. "We are finalizing the acquisition of the site," Marchand said, "and pushing ahead with the possible development of all these lands for appropriate airport uses."

The premier refused to commit Ontario to provide the roads and sewers, and when Marchand pressed him again, in a letter dated

June 12, 1975, Davis replied shortly: "You will receive a more detailed response in the near future."

The Transport minister would not like that response. POP was already hearing from its provincial contacts, once so hostile, now so friendly, that its members should "cool it" and take no drastic action. Isobel Thompson recalls, "John Rowsome in the Premier's office would phone up and ask if there was going to be any violence. I would say 'We're holding them in check, but only just.' I was lying in my teeth. I was using Rowsome, just as he was using me. He could go back and say"POP is going to get violent,' and that would help us both."

When Johnny Lombardi, a Toronto radio station owner and entrepreneur, held his annual Dominion Day picnic on Toronto Island, Premier Davis went along, and William McMurtry met him there. "He gave me a clear understanding that the airport would not be built," McMurtry says. "But he didn't want it used in the election campaign that had just started. He thought it was too important to become a partisan issue."

On July 10, Ontario Transport Minister John Rhodes sent a telegram to Marchand containing the "more detailed response" Davis had referred to. It was a pretty sneaky telegram. Ontario was still not backing away from the commitment of 1972, but, on the other hand, it was. "We accept the fact that, under the Canadian Constitution a decision regarding the location of a major international airport rests clearly with the federal government." However, "If effective government is to be maintained in this country, each level of government must be left to determine its own priorities," and Ontario's priorities did not, "at this time," include another airport. Rhodes asked that construction be held up until a federal-provincial meeting could be held in Ottawa.

That meeting took place on July 29, and the province could not be made to change its mind, even though the feds tried to sweeten the deal by holding out the possibility of more cost-sharing money. There would be no funds forthcoming for roads "at this time," and Ottawa was urged to hold off its bulldozers at least until after the Ontario election was over.

On July 31, Marchand wired Rhodes to say that no start was likely on construction, "until, at the earliest, mid-September, or perhaps beyond."

Less than two weeks later, on August 13, bulldozers rolled onto the airport site and began knocking houses down. Rhodes wired Marchand on August 15 to complain. "It is difficult to understand why the federal Government should wish to proceed at this time, when there is no agreement with Ontario as to roads, sewers, and other support services, and when arrangements have been made for officials of our two governments to meet on this very matter early in September." He therefore requested a halt to "all demolition and construction" immediately.

It took Marchand five days to respond, with an explanation that what was going on at Pickering wasn't really serious, it was just knocking down houses. "Rough grading," however, would not be started until after Ontario and Ottawa made a deal. The next day, when reactions to that high-handedness were beginning to raise dust in Ottawa, Marchand sent his aide Normand Begin out to announce that the work was being halted after all, temporarily, at the request of Ontario. That took some of the heat off, but the feds were only funning again. There were sixty-two houses involved in the contract to clear a space for a runway; nine of these houses had been bought, and moved, by former owners; thirty-seven others were sold to wrecking contractors for private demolition, and that left sixteen to be knocked down under government contract. Twelve of these had already been smashed when the work was halted, so when Marchand called off the bulldozers, he was calling them off precisely four houses. Destruction of the remainder went on, under private auspices, as before, but fences were put up to keep out the protestors.

Not surprisingly, this double-dealing had the POP troops up in arms again. Chairman Charles Godfrey was running in the Durham West riding in the provincial election; if the bulldozers could be stopped until after the voting, and if Godfrey won, chances were that the airport could be blocked. So there were demonstrations, marches, shoving matches, and confrontations all over the airport property, while television cameras rolled and the perfidy, or stupidity – it had to be one or the other – of the federal officials was exposed to public comment.

On Sunday, September 15, POP put on a party at the home of Ernie Carruthers, a grizzled sixty-six-year-old farmer whose lovely, century-old farmhouse was next in line to be demolished. While the party was at its height, three POP members were slipped into the house, with food, bedding, and other supplies. If the feds wanted to knock down Ernie's place, they could do so on top of this trio, who were chosen with POP's keen eye to public relations: a grandmother, Brenda Davies; a judge's wife, Fran Moore; and a pretty young writer, Anne Howes.

For the two older women, the decision was a brutal one. Moore, a cheerful, comely woman, explains:

"We had got in touch with Ontario people and got the message back, don't do anything until after the election, something will happen after the election, and we just sort of subsided. Then there were the wreckings. Then one day we had a phone call. We had people out driving the roads looking for activity and somebody had seen a bulldozer on the 22nd sideroad. We held a meeting right away. I was so furious I wanted to do something. I had no family at home anymore, and I said I wanted to go into Ernie's house. The houses were coming down in a row, this was in line, and if we could stop them there they really couldn't go ahead with the runway. If we could just stall them long enough for the province to react, that would be enough. Then Anne said she would go. Brenda had just got her radio operator's licence, and I thought that would be useful, because we expected to be completely cut off. I phoned her, and she said no. It was against her religion. She was Bahai and she said Bahai followers are not supposed to do anything against the law. I said, 'Neither is anybody else.'

"She said maybe her husband, Brent, would go; he didn't feel quite so strongly about it. Then she phoned back and said she and Brent had talked it over and she would go. It wouldn't look right if Brent was cooped up in that house with two women. People might make something of it.

"Terry, my husband, was dreadfully upset. He was sure we would be hassled and hauled out and mishandled. We would be hurt by it, probably our passports would be marked. We had a meeting one night and he presented all the legal arguments to us, and told us all the things that could happen to us. But it was just so apparent that what they were doing was wrong that you got to the point where you either put up or shut up. We hadn't fought for all those years to give up at the end."

Not for the first time in human history, the menfolk stood around talking about fine points of law, and the women got on with the job. In the middle of a noisy, hilarious, and publicity-drenched party on Sunday afternoon, the three women climbed through a window into the boarded-up Carruthers house, called the CBC to make sure their stunt made the evening news, and settled down for a siege.

It was a daffy situation. It must have been clear to federal officials long before this that Ontario would not co-operate on the airport, that whatever it had said earlier, the province was putting on the brakes. However, the juggernaut was in motion, the Carruthers family had been turfed out and now the house was going to come down, even though it was an historic landmark. (A committee to preserve such landmarks had been established, but somehow missed the Carruthers place until it was too late.)

When the destruction started, there were going to be three people in the rubble and a battalion of reporters and photographers on hand, and they weren't going to like the results, all those smart folks who had set this chain of events in motion. So the bulldozers huffed and puffed, but they did not blow the house down. The women inside were not, in fact, cut off. If anything, they had too many visitors. Brenda Davies complains, "You could never get a moment to yourself." The "No Trespassing" signs set up by the Department of Public Works were simply ignored, and a constant stream of visitors – supporters, curiosity seekers and newsmen – poured onto the property. POP had organized the Pickering Cavalry, a group of local riders who were prepared to gallop across the countryside with supplies. They were never needed. A long cord had been strung from the back door of the house through the fields so support parties could find their way in after dark, but that wasn't needed, either. The women nestled down to read and write and knit and receive visitors, and to wait for the provincial election on September 18.

The morning of the eighteenth, one of the security guards told Brenda Davies that the siege would soon be over; he knew the women would want to vote for POP Chairman Charles Godfrey, and when they went out to the polls, they would find they couldn't get back in. They had him there, though; they had voted in the advance poll.

When the votes were counted that evening, the Davis Conservatives still held power in Ontario, but with a minority government. Charles Godfrey was elected, handily, in Durham West. The message was plain; the airport was not a popular item for the Tories, and, in a minority position, they couldn't afford to push it, even if they wanted to. But they didn't want to. The federal government has since concocted a story that the only reason the province discarded the airport was because of its minority position, but, as we have already seen, Davis had given his word to POP that help was on the way once the election was over, however it went.

On September 24, the Ontario Cabinet met and voted formally, for the first time, to withdraw from its earlier agreement to provide infrastructure for the airport. A telegram was dispatched to Marchand, asking him to stop all work on the project until a meeting could be held between the two governments. Explaining Ontario's position to the press, Premier Davis said, for the first time, publicly, that the need for a second airport was not clear. There had been "Negative information concerning traffic and energy problems associated with air travel."

Davis also noted that no agreement on cost-sharing had ever been reached between the province and Ottawa, and indicated that Ontario wasn't pleased by the federal action in starting to knock down houses before such a deal could be struck.

The next day, September 25, an angry Jean Marchand emerged from a federal cabinet meeting to announce that work on the airport had been suspended for "at least two or three years," in light of Ontario's refusal to co-operate. But the province was going to be sorry.

"The people of Toronto will not now receive the service they deserve," he said, his voice shaking with rage. "Toronto will be ten years behind Montreal." The airport was still needed and, "It is very imprudent to wait until Malton is congested before beginning plans to relieve it."

Prime Minister Trudeau was also sore as a boil. "They [the Ontario government] signed a formal agreement in 1972 . . . . The question now is how many other agreements are they going to back down on?" However, he would be happy to spend "the $400 million slated for Pickering" elsewhere in the country. This was vintage Trudeau; ripe, pungent, and totally misleading. Ontario's agreement in 1972 was based on an understanding that the cost-sharing would be successfully negotiated, and that had never come to pass. On the cost question, it is clear that the Prime Minister, like just about everyone else by this time, was confused. If the Minimum Airport was to cost $204 million, the figure Marchand had been using, then the only way it could get to $400 million was either to add in the province's $196 million, which was not available for Ottawa to spend, or to include some of the costs, such as land, which had already been poured in and glossed over by the Ministry of Transport – but this money, too, was beyond recovery. There was no $400 million to spend elsewhere.

In any event, the airport was suspended, at least for the moment. POP held a celebration party at the Carruthers place, and the three women came out to join the festivities. At Melody Farm, the 1837 rebellion bell was rung, and all across Pickering, there was a momentary surge of jubilation. It did not last long. Marchand had said that the airport would be postponed until Ontario changed its mind again; it was not cancelled. He announced, firmly, that Malton would not be expanded, and, although he was shuffled out of his cabinet portfolio the very next day, his replacement, Otto Lang, stuck to the same line. Gates had been put across a number of roads on the airport site; they were probably illegal, since no agreement had been reached with the township on price for the land under the roads, but they were in place anyway. They went down, and the heavy machinery moved off the Carruthers property, but no one was fool enough to think that meant the battle was over.

Carruthers did not, of course, get to keep his place. He was given $400,000 for his farm, and he moved to a small town north of Pickering, where he retired. Junk from the federal wreckers was piled in the fields next to his home, heaped in grotesque mounds of rotting refuse. There were old chairs, broken beds, a baby carriage, smashed walls, and scattered garbage. It is still there today, the debris of a dozen homes, scattered across what was once a cornfield; the handsome Carruthers place has been turned into a mess.

So, while the airport had been stymied, everyone involved in the struggle knew that there was no happy ending. In fact, there was no ending at all. Within days of the September 25 announcement the Ministry of Transport planners were hard at work again, trying to revive the scheme.

Chapter 13

The Beat Goes On

Bill Leach, homeowner:

"One morning a reporter turned up at my place; he had read in the Oshawa paper that the sheriff was going to have us out of there by any means. I hadn't even read it. The sheriff phoned about eleven o'clock and said he had been putting it off hoping something could be worked out. He said he didn't want to have to do this, but he reminded me that he had evicted Roy Bamborough and I said, 'Well, I guess you've got to do your job.' I said, 'You can put me off, but how are you going to keep me off?' He said that they would charge me with trespassing, and I said, 'At what point do you put a man in jail for trespassing on his own home?' and he said, 'Oh, Jesus, you're making life difficult.' "

Philip Beinhaker, consultant:

"Get your land so you're protected – land of course never goes down in value, it sits there as an investment . . . . Wait and see what happens with the growth of traffic, and if the traffic doesn't grow, then you're fine, you've just got the land. If the traffic does grow, then you've got the flexibility. That's a very flexible plan."

My tour of Transport Canada's regional headquarters in Toronto was going splendidly when I spotted a model, about four feet square, of the proposed Pickering airport. It was a topographical model standing on its own table, under a clear plastic dome. All the hills and valleys were moulded in green, and there were little yellow buildings and, right in the middle, the scar where the airport runways were once laid. The runways, also in yellow plastic, had been lifted to one side and lay there, under the dome, but off the grass. This was three years after the airport had been officially shelved, and the model still held a place of honour outside the office of the regional director, Robert Moffatt. I told the gent assigned to shepherd me around the place that I was touched; I said that pathetic model reminded me of the stories you read about the loving parent, whose child has been struck down in an auto accident, maintaining his room as a sort of shrine, with the little pyjamas folded on the bed, and the socks tucked lovingly in their drawer. My escort glowered. "This child," he said, "is not dead."

I believe him. Pickering Airport is merely sleeping, waiting for some bureaucratic prince to come along and kiss it back to life again. The people who made all the original decisions, or their heirs and assigns, are still in there pitching. Larry Potvin, Director-General of air planning, says, "I suggest to you that in 1987-88 we will be talking about the same kinds of issues. What the government has done is to acquire the land-bank for a new airport." He and his fellows have no apologies to make whatever for all the blunders and cruelties committed in the name of planning: "Even now, they should get on with Pickering."

Murray McLeod, who moved from the consulting firm of Peat, Marwick, to take up Potvin's job in the Toronto planning team, says, "It's going ahead, but in stages."

Robert Moffatt, Regional Director for Toronto, told a radio interviewer, "The airport is not necessarily dead, but it's not necessarily alive, either," which is one of my favourite quotes of all time.

Philip Beinhaker, still the government's chief consultant on air transport, thinks that the only thing that went wrong at either Pickering or Mirabel is that "Any process which takes such a long time is subject to changing values in society." The pendulum has swung away, but it will swing back again. "I am satisfied that additional major airport facilities will be required," and Pickering is a "good site." Dr. Josef Kates, another principal consultant, says, "Even if the federal government doesn't build, Pickering is still a suitable place." That is, the government was smart to grab the land; anyway, who can tell what it might be needed for? "If technological changes come, you give back the land."

The strange thing about this near-unanimity among the Canadian aviation planners is that it is not shared anywhere else. Robert Joerger, Director of Aviation Studies for Peat, Marwick, Mitchell, the American version of the old Kates-Beinhaker firm, told me "The chance of a new airport being built anywhere in the United States any time soon is remote. I just don't believe either the environmentalists or the financial people will go for it. In case after case, where second airports were contemplated, they have been killed, and we're making do." Joerger approves: "We're constantly harassed by the build-more-and-bigger-and-better syndrome, but people won't accept it any more."

Barney Parrella, Vice President, Economics, of the Airport Operators Council in Washington, D.C., says, "The feeling is that instead of building anything new we should make the most of what we have."

Jack Bourne, an airport planner with the U.S. Federal Aviation Administration, says, "I don't think there will be any major airports built from scratch for the next few years; it's just not in the cards."

In Britain, where a third airport for the London area was cancelled, the sentiment is much the same. A spokesman for the British Airports Authority told me, "There was a time when you could get away with these billion-pound wonders, but no longer."

Sir Henry Marking, Chairman of the British Tourist Authority, told me, "I can't see anyone putting up with another airport; the environmentalists simply won't allow it."

In Japan, the second Tokyo airport, at Narita, has turned into a bloody battleground, with full-scale riots, fires, shootings, bomb-threats and the effective crippling of the new facility by enraged, sometimes deranged, opponents.

Everywhere, it seems, the lesson is sinking in; new airports are not wanted, not needed, not allowed. Everywhere, that is, but in Canada. Here, the pressure to revive the stricken airport began within days of its suspension on September 25, 1975, and continues unabated.

That pressure has taken three forms. The first has been a constant stream of reports, advice, studies, and warnings, all pointing to the same conclusion – if we don't have another airport, civilization will topple. The second has been the pressure to make both the present Toronto airport and Montreal's Dorval facility unworkable, to justify Mirabel and Pickering. The third has been the drive to force out those foolish enough to try to hold onto their lands in Pickering.

Of these three pressures, the one with the most tragic human consequences has been the federal government's war on the holdouts in the Pickering area. When the airport was suspended, these people believed, somehow, that they would get their homes back. As I write this, houses are still being bulldozed, government negotiators are still beating down the demands of area residents for decent prices for their homes, and the courts are still being used as a club against the holdouts. On the rare occasions when someone does win a case against the government, it is promptly thrown into appeal. Steve and Maria Gerencer, expropriated in 1973, with an offer of $100,000 for their home and twenty acres, won double that in a legal action in 1976; the federal government appealed, lost again, and has now appealed to the Supreme Court of Canada. God knows when the case will be straightened out, but the government has all the time in the world.

Consider the case of Willard James Leach. Leach, in his mid-forties, works for a Toronto investment house. He is a square-built man of medium height, with a strong face, a stubborn jaw, and a tenacious grip. He was once an RCMP officer, and still carries himself like one; he is neat, polite, self-assured, and assertive. He moved to Pickering on June 25, 1967, with his wife and three children. They had always wanted to live in the country, and had been shopping around for more than a year when they found ten acres on Sideroad 26-27 in Pickering Township, just north of Highway 7. Leach built his own house, bought horses, put up a stable, put in a well and trees, and landscaped the property. Then came the decision of March 2, 1972. Leach recalls:

"I was confused. The idea of an airport didn't upset me. What upset me was that after working for six years, all of a sudden everything came to a stop. Everything was frozen. It was the little things that really burned. For example, we had signed a contract to put in a swimming pool. Then all building permits were cancelled, and I didn't own my own land any more, and that was the end of the pool.

"I couldn't believe they were serious about the airport. You've got Markham, Stouffville, all these towns, and the TCR plan. To fit an airport around all that, it just couldn't be done, so we didn't take it seriously at first. It was about this time that we began to realize that Mirabel was a problem. True Canadians. Up to that time, we didn't care what was going on in our own backyard; then, as we got more interested, we found out more, and it seemed more and more bizarre. We were so sure it was a nightmare that we felt all we had to do was to show the government it was a mistake and that would be the end of it. Then came the Swackhamer hearing, and they kept saying we would get a chance to state our side. We did, but they obviously weren't listening. The hearing made it clear that the need for the airport didn't exist, and Swackhamer almost said as much. We felt confident.

"Then came the real shocker, when they confirmed the expropriation. It began to occur to us that we were in real trouble. We started to look at the [Federal Expropriation] Act, and talked to some lawyers, but we couldn't get any lawyer who was willing to fight. I looked at the Act myself and discovered that, the way it read, they could expropriate, decide later not to build the airport and they still didn't have to give the land back. It made my blood run cold.

"A federal appraiser came to the house and looked around and, on April 25, 1973, we received an offer of $76,000 for the land and house. There was no way we could buy anything like our place at that price, so I wrote and asked for particulars of how they arrived at the price. A while later I got a call from a man named Reddick. He said, 'I hear you're having some problems with your offer, and I'm here to answer your questions.' I said I would rather have the answers in writing. He got tough, then he started to tell me I was looking for enough to retire on, and if I accepted now I'd get more than if I held out. I told him that was intimidation, and the call wasn't very friendly after that. He said, 'Well, we'll see how big your lawyers are.'

"I wrote to the Department of Public Works, since they handled the land acquisitions, to complain, and they sent around a Mr. Frank Wolfe. He came down to my office and we talked about everything but my property. He smiled and said, 'I hear you've been having some problems,' and I said I didn't see what was funny about it, so he stopped smiling. We got talking about property values and he said he could get lots for $18,000 not far from my place, so I asked him to get me three lots right away. He didn't know what the hell he was talking about, and he left.

"The offer they made, for $76,000, was supposedly without prejudice. You could accept that much money and it wouldn't interfere with your right to bargain for more. I was nervous about this, and we had some talks and correspondence, but finally they came up with a letter saying that if I accepted that much money it would not in any way prejudice my right to appeal. I did accept it and it did prejudice my case. After that, they always said, 'Well, you accepted, didn't you?' Even the judge said that.

"We still figured this was our property. Even after the Gibson Inquiry was such a screwup we still figured that. After all, they did shelve the airport. We thought it was over then. We were dreaming.

"In 1975, they came around to demand physical possession of the property and I said, 'Well, when am I going to get some more money?' They did make an awful lot of adjustments as time went on. They raised the prices ten per cent for everybody, and gave us $3,000 more for moving costs. Then the Land Compensation Board went over the cases and made improvements. In my case, it went up by $1,800. And on May 30, 1975, they made a final offer based on a final study of area prices, and boosted the price by about forty-five per cent. If they had offered those kinds of prices in the first place, everybody would have accepted and gone.

"Instead of being satisfied, I was more and more convinced that something was dreadfully wrong. If they could pay that kind of price now, why couldn't they do it before? And even if the price was fair now, it was completely arbitrary, and I wouldn't go along with it.

"We were getting to know more about the Act, and the Act said that when they bought you out, you had to be able to get 'reasonably equivalent' premises for the same price. That was not possible. The project had taken so much land, there wasn't any market anymore. We went as far away as Owen Sound, looking for an equivalent property. We could get property all right for the price, but not within commuting distance of Toronto. The whole thing was ridiculous. Their figures still didn't make any sense. Their offer of May 1975 was final, they said, but they still did improve it later. They just kept going on and on. The lawyers' fees and appraisers' fees were piling up. The patronage was terrific. And we still couldn't get a lawyer who would stand up to them."

Finally, Leach did find such a lawyer. Most of the local legal talent was either already on the books of the government, drawing down sizable fees to advise clients to accept whatever was offered, or unwilling to take on a long, bruising battle against authority. However, MTARC Chairman Douglas Turner introduced Leach to David Estrin, a young, intense specialist in environmental law. Under Leach's leadership, and with POP's help, eighty-nine families banded together to fight for their homes, and pooled their resources to carry on the legal battle. One by one, as time went by, the families dropped out. In some cases, the reasons were medical – the strain was simply too much – in others, they were emotional. Some were frightened, some – a few – were satisfied that the government's newest offers were fair, but most were simply fed up with the uncertainty and tension of the long struggle. In the end, Estrin went to court on behalf of three clients, all that were left of the original eighty-nine: Verla and Willard Leach, Anita and Edgar Fisher, and Margaret Persutti.

Estrin's argument on their behalf was that, since the government had announced the shelving of the airport in 1975, the reason for expropriating the land had evaporated; therefore, the owners were entitled to retain possession. This reasonable proposition was never accepted; indeed, Estrin was never even able to argue in court.

All of the key cases were heard before Mr. Justice Patrick Mahoney, a former Liberal MP who was translated into a judge after his defeat in Calgary South, in the 1972 federal election. He was named a *persona designata* to hear the evidence under the Expropriation Act. Here is David Estrin's recollection of what happened:

"My argument was that if the government didn't need the land, it had no right to it. If they weren't going to put it to use for the purpose declared, they weren't entitled to it legally or morally. In effect, they were sterilizing this huge area, and to me that was an environmental issue.

"Then there was the constitutional angle. It's quite clear that the federal government can use its powers of expropriation only for purposes within the federal jurisdiction. If they were allowed to purport to expropriate for one purpose and then divert to another purpose, then they could expropriate anything in Canada for whatever reason. If they tried that in Quebec, there would be hell to pay. It was obviously an invasion of rights.

"We tried to attack the expropriation procedure at the point where it had not been completed and the government had changed its mind. Once the government has gone through the procedures of announcing an intention to expropriate, holding a hearing, then confirming the expropriation, the title to the property becomes vested in the government. My clients no longer owned their property. But we said that the government had yet to obtain possession. That step hadn't been completed when the airport was dropped, and we said they lost their right when it was dropped. They could get possession in any of a number of ways, including eviction. Obviously, if we signed a lease, that would indicate possession. That's what the government was after. My clients said they wouldn't sign unless the government would promise to return the land if the airport was not built. The government refused that.

"The corps of people attacking the government was whittled down. The government used various techniques; they bullied, they intimidated, and scared people into signing leases. In June 1976, there was a newspaper story saying that the government had obtained warrants of possession for the properties. That meant eviction. The story was totally false. There was no way they could obtain warrants at that stage. The government had to give notice of possession and then move for eviction when people refused to vacate their premises. However, the effect of the story was to terrify the people into signing. They assumed the sheriff would be out the next day to evict them, and they caved."

With his small band of remaining clients, Estrin persisted. He not only battled the government's attempts to obtain warrants, he launched his own suit to knock down the expropriation procedure. It was all a waste of time and money. The government lawyer was Thomas Dunne, who had served as associate counsel before the Gibson Inquiry. He was a law partner of Joe Potts, who was campaign manager for Liberal Finance Minister Donald Macdonald. Dunne was a well-connected fellow, at least as tough as Estrin, and

160

he had a much more sympathetic audience in Mr. Justice Maho-ney. Mahoney ruled, on August 16, 1976, that the reasons for the government's original expropriation were not to be brought before him. Once the feds had decided to take the land, what it did with it didn't matter. In Mahoney's own words, "The effect of the ruling was to exclude evidence, and argument based on evidence, of any change, postponement, or abandonment of the intention to use the land to build an airport, formed after January 30, 1973." January 30, 1973, you will remember, was the day the federal cabinet con-firmed the expropriation. Mahoney's decision meant that if the gov-ernment decided to put a string of brothels on the seized land, he didn't care, and he didn't want to be told about it.

Then the judge used his own ruling to beat off every attempt to put the case before him. Mahoney's doctrine was laid down in one of the preliminary jousts that make the law so interesting and ex-pensive, not in the main legal action. So Estrin tried to get around him; he argued that since the judge had already declared himself on the substantive issue, he should step aside and let someone else handle the trial. Mahoney would have no part of this, and in his reasons for refusing, he cited Estrin's "offensive efforts to bootleg argument based on irrelevant and unproved facts into the proceed-ings." The irrelevant fact Estrin wanted to bootleg into the proceed-ings was the shelving of the airport, and the reason it was unproved was because Mahoney wouldn't allow any evidence on the point.

Estrin says now, "My clients were more or less beaten down by the hostility of the judge. They just couldn't believe they were being treated this way and, frankly, I found it hard to believe, too."

During one preliminary skirmish, which took place without a stenographer, Estrin tried to mention the shelving of the airport, and Mahoney cut him off abruptly: "Mr. Estrin, your meter is run-ning." Estrin says, "I replied, 'My lord, I didn't know there was a meter on justice.' After that, I got in a court reporter."

At another hearing, when Estrin was out of town, Douglas Turner took up the gloves for Leach et al, and got into a bitter wrangle with Mahoney. Crown witnesses were refusing to answer questions that Turner deemed relevant (like Estrin, he kept trying to bootleg the airport shelving onto the record), so, in pique, he in-structed his clients to refuse to answer any of the government's questions. The hearing became a farce, and Mahoney was so in-censed that he levied the costs of it against David Estrin personally, as the lawyer of record.

Estrin tried to appeal from Mahoney to the Federal Court of Ap-peal, but that body held that, since the judge was sitting as a *persona designata*, and not as a judge, it had no jurisdiction. So Estrin went to the Supreme Court and "The judge said we appeared to have the right to appeal, but there was a gap in the rules. Nobody knew who had the jurisdiction to hear the appeal to which we had a right."

That exercise cost thousands of dollars, and the case wound up right back in front of Mahoney. His judgment, on March 30, 1977, came as no surprise. The government got its warrants of possession, and all the costs were levied against Estrin's clients, except those in the Turner incident.

"We lost," says Estrin, "and every time we tried to do something else we lost. My own view is that I'd never go before any branch of the Federal Court if I could avoid it. I finally advised my clients to get another lawyer, because the Federal Court didn't like me."

The new lawyer had some old advice for Leach et al: Give up. Finally, they did. In the spring of 1978, thousands of dollars poorer, Bill Leach signed a lease to rent his own home from the government. "We knew it didn't matter what we did, we didn't stand a chance. It was just a waste of time. The game was over."

Constitutional lawyer Eugene LaBrie says of the Leach case, "I don't have the words to describe the court's action in assessing the costs against the lawyer. It was completely unjustified and so oppressive that it should be taken up by the International Commission of Jurists. You are in the area of political law, and no matter what argument you pull out of your hat, the government is going to win. We've got the machinery of justice, but in practice, we're about at the level of some African states. Tanzania has the machinery of justice. It all comes from British justice. But the question is, what use do you make of the machinery?"

Now that the government has possession of all the properties in the originally expropriated area, what does it propose to do with them? It proposes to knock them down, in due course, and build an airport. The evidence lies not only in the vigour with which the holdouts were pursued, but in the welter of reports and statements that have been oozing out of Transport Canada since September 25, 1975.

Within a week of the decision to postpone the airport, on October 1, six senior members of the Ministry, with the faithful Philip Beinhaker in attendance, met to discuss strategy. Minutes of the meeting show that the first decision taken was that there would be no more foolishness about forgetting the airport and getting on with some other solution: "It appears that Cabinet in its recent decision wishes to retain the Pickering option, and that as a result, planning work to date should be put in some form of 'cocoon,' i.e., packaged in such a way that the Pickering option should be revised."

The emphasis would be on briefing the new Transport Minister, Otto Lang, on how to fight the good fight when he met his provincial counterpart later in October. Accordingly, Lang was briefed on October 10, 1975, and the background papers for that meeting show that he was instructed how to "Seek provincial recognition that in light of its particular responsibilities and its conviction that Pickering is required by 1979, the Federal Government should continue with contingency planning for Pickering, while joint studies of other transportation alternatives proceed."

The minister was also told, "There is no doubt that certain of the facilities at Malton will be completely saturated by 1979." It would therefore be necessary to divert traffic to Mirabel, to refuse any new flights to Toronto, and to encourage the by-passing of Toronto in flights between such communities as Regina and Quebec City. That is, to get to Quebec, flights should be routed through Mirabel instead of Toronto.

Lang bought the package so enthusiastically that, two days later, on October 12, he was solemnly telling Pat McNenly of the *Toronto Star* that if Toronto continued to oppose Pickering, Ontarians would soon have to fly to Montreal to get to Vancouver, and that there would be serious congestion at Malton, no matter what was done.

Like all his predecessors, Lang was massaged into a belief that Chaos and the Long Night would descend on the world if Pickering wasn't put into motion at once, and he held doggedly to that position for three more years. In late 1978 he began to waver, and in private conversations with some airline executives he suggested that there might be something in their argument that the airport was not needed. However, he added, it was too late to change his position, because, "That would be one hundred and eighty degrees from where my officials stand."

Just the same, Lang was not dim enough to buy the package his Ministry tried to slip past him in an October 17, 1975 position paper entitled "Pickering Go It Alone Option," which argued that the feds could build their own airport, and to hell with Ontario. The Aeronautics Act could be used to control building around the airport, noise lands could be controlled by expropriating more property, wells could be drilled on the site to provide water, and sewage could be processed. If Ontario Hydro refused to provide power, that could be fixed, too, with a Total Energy Plant, not otherwise described, which would cost a mere $4 million. Getting to the airport might not be much fun if the province balked but, "In the event of 'a go it alone decision' consideration should be given to taking legal action to force Ontario to meet its obligations with respect to highways as defined in the BNA Act."

Sue the bastards. This inspired lunacy died aborning, which is a pity. A vision of the feds hunkered down in an airport bunker outside Toronto, digging wells, burying sewage, turning windmills and firing off writs, while the Ontario Cabinet galloped around outside, howling with rage, might have provided many rich hours of entertainment over the years. Instead, we got the Chinese water treatment, an endless series of interviews with Lang, with senior government officials, with aviation experts attached to Transport Canada, all saying the same thing: build another airport.

The joint federal-provincial study referred to in the October 10 minutes came into being. Its chief officers were Gerry Johnston, Executive Director of the Planning Division of the Ontario Department of Transport, and Nick Mulder, strategy planner for Transport Canada. Johnston was one of the provincial officials who became convinced that Ontario was being conned by Ottawa, and his role in the three years he served on the committee (he was replaced in 1978 by another career civil servant, Ian Oliver) was to keep a wary eye on federal reports. In fact, the province hired Washington consultant Secor Brown to go over the federal work every time it comes in to make sure the conning has stopped.

Nick Mulder worked as a provincial civil servant in Nova Scotia and New Brunswick before joining Transport Canada just about the time the airport was shelved, and he brought a brand new approach to the Ministry. He believes in joint planning. "After all, my background is provincial. The last time, the communication stupidities helped Ontario to pull out."

He also believes there may be other solutions than a second airport. "Suppose you can reconfigure Malton . . . it may be possible to put in a short runway and keep Malton going forever, or use that time to examine alternatives. It's obvious we can make the current system last a good deal longer. How much bigness do we really need? All the forecasts were wrong, so you have to do them again. You were looking at a $600 million project and it appeared you didn't know what you were doing."

Finally, Mulder believes that the planet will continue to rotate, even if businessmen suffer an occasional delay in air transportation. "If they have to wait half an hour before they get on or off an airplane, so what?"

It is easy to see that Mulder is heretical; it is harder to tell whether his heresies will ever be heard. When I first spoke to him, in March of 1978, he was expecting the federal-provincial committee to come out, soon, with a series of alternative plans for Toronto. A year later, there is no sign of such a report, and virtually everyone else on the planning team holds to the ancient faith: build another airport. The federal-provincial study has now been going on for nearly four years, without visible result. Instead, we have had a long string of headlines:

"No Major Plans for Malton; Ottawa Still Wants Second Airport," and "Toronto Needs A Second Airport, Otto Lang Says," and "Airport Not Dead – Ottawa," and "Ottawa Still Sees Airport for Pickering."

The Toronto Area Airports Project team was held together until the fall of 1978, although it declined in size from 146 members in 1975 to a mere dozen at the end. The key functionaries are still in place, however, in the federal government's splendid new building at the corner of Yonge and Sheppard in Toronto. Also on hand are the usual consultants, whose work is so intermingled with that of the Ministry that, on one occasion, a consultant had a departmental secretary fill out and type up his application for a government contract – which was, needless to say, approved. On another occasion, a $35-an-hour consultant spent his time arranging a Christmas party for yet another consultant. All the Transport Canada chaps were invited. It's what you might call a chummy arrangement.

When they are on the premises, the consultants work in the same office with the bureaucrats; while I was using the facilities for a period of two weeks, the desks around me were mainly occupied by consultants, busy churning out study papers and talking about how the results of their work could be seen to conform with the departmental line. When a senior officer came in and realized that I was making notes on the conversation, he had me whisked the hell out of there. Then I got to sit in a public relations office and heard a departmental official tell a junior PR person how to fake a press release to cover up the fact that the department's estimates had been off so badly. It was very instructive, and I guess I won't be invited back.

The most impressive of the consultant studies to emerge after the decision to shelve Pickering was a two-volume Contingency Plan produced on June 10, 1977. Phil Beinhaker, as always, was a major contributor to this study, but others were in on the act. The plan was based on a notion beginning to be grasped, dimly, around Transport Canada, that a second Toronto airport was not going to be built right away, and something should be done to cope with things until the kissing prince turned up. The report's main conclusion was, and was intended to be, blood-chilling: "The single most far-reaching conclusion resulting from this Study is that no amount of traffic management, within reason, will be able to resolve capacity deficiencies before new facilities can physically be put into service in the Toronto area."

The damage was already done, and there was no point in whining to Transport Canada when the Dark Ages began to descend; all the boys could suggest was action to block any new air carriers coming into Toronto, the diversion of traffic to other airports, and such air traffic control techniques as "slot-timing." In slot-timing, arriving aircraft are required to reach a given point in the airport airspace within a five-minute limit, or they lose their place in line for landing, and have to circle, sometimes for hours.

These drastic steps would help to offset some of the damage, but life was still going to hell. By 1980, no matter what was done, "When the single runway 14/32 is in operation, the annual average per hour delay for air carrier traffic will be 10-12 minutes."

Egad! What this fierce-sounding stuff meant was that if the feds had their facts right for once (and that plan carried a special note that every effort was made to "maximize the quality of input data"), there would be times when air travellers would have to wait an average twelve minutes.

American air carriers don't even begin to count themselves late unless the delay is more than fifteen minutes. But for the boys at Transport Canada, there is a sterner test. Any delay over two minutes is bad business, and by cranking all its forecasts through the old computer, the Ministry was able to show "shortfalls," "critical overloads," and "serious levels of congestion," which are bound to "get progressively worse by 1985."

"Something must be done to relieve the airport system as a whole before that time," the plan trumpets, or air transport at Malton faces a "breakdown condition." In less excitable language, unless we spend a few billion dollars on the airport planners' dreams, there is a fair chance that air travellers will face the same kinds of crowding, delays, and generally bum service that are routine for the peasants who travel by train or bus.

The Contingency Plan produced a burst of news reports telling us that we were going to hell in a handbasket, and, predictably, strengthened the resolve of Transport Canada to get on with the second airport before the moon turned to blood.

If Malton was becoming unusable, as the plan suggested, at least part of the blame could be laid at the feet of the Ministry itself. At a meeting between federal and provincial officials and airport consultants on June 8, 1976, Hugh Devitt, General Manager of the Toronto airport, charged that Ottawa was "determined to revive Pickering by refusing to develop any facility which will help to relieve pressures at Malton."

Devitt was about to retire from government service, and before he went he unloaded his grievances, which were put into a memo by Gerry Johnston of the Ontario Transport Department to his bosses. Johnston's memo, dated June 11, 1976, set down Devitt's argument in the following points:

"If Malton is fully developed and run really efficiently, it can probably meet the needs until 1985-1990.

"Another airport, not necessarily to major international standards, may be required at a later date.

"A really honest, factual, non-emotional explanation should be given to political leaders and the public of what can be done at Malton.

"The present terminals, processing arrangements, handling of ground vehicles, etc., are at the root of the problem, and all phases of ground operations could be greatly improved based on the best practices and procedures in use at airports which are efficiently operated. The Toronto Area Airports Project team does not hold these views, and consistently plays back the well-known refrain, 'the main constraint is the limited capacity of the single runway 14/32 under IFR conditions.'

"Construction of a third terminal, for which the site is already chosen, would permit the efficient handling of a substantially increased volume of traffic.

"There is enormous room in Air Traffic Control procedures which could result in increased capability to handle larger numbers of aircraft movements, patterned on efficient procedures at major U.S. airports, some of which handle two to four times the traffic at Malton."

The memo also noted that when Devitt raised the obvious suggestion of building a new terminal with his bosses, he was told "Just forget it."

I went to see Devitt about this memo, and he refused to comment, except to make it clear that everything he said in June 1976 still holds, including the practicability of expanding Malton and the federal government's determination not to do so.

Another who claims that Ottawa is, to put it mildly, not doing its best to foster efficiency at Malton is Paul Davoud, the crusty former Chairman of the Air Transport Board. Davoud says that at an

Ottawa meeting, where he advocated the use of STOL aircraft to relieve some of the pressure in Toronto, William Huck, the Air Administrator, told him, "There is no way we are going to accommodate any more flights in Toronto, I don't care what they are." (Huck's recollection is somewhat different. He claims he said only that he would never agree to the mixture of slow-moving STOL craft with 747 jets, although that isn't what the STOL advocates are pushing; they want to use Toronto Island airport for their craft.) As he was leaving the meeting, Davoud contends, another federal official said to him, " 'The party line is to let Ontario wither and die on the vine until they come to us and beg for Pickering.' "

It's going to be a long wait. The province has little confidence in either the competence or the motives of Transport Canada. The next time a new airport is up for discussion, one of the provincial experts told me, "We'll do things differently. There will be open debate, open discussion, and we will see all the numbers before we sign anything. We're going to be damn hard to convince."

At the federal level, however, the beat goes on. Devitt's successor as Malton manager, David MacAree, believes that the level of service in Toronto is "bound to deteriorate" and that the choice is to "fall behind" or "build a second airport." He told Andrew Weiner, in an article for *Quest* magazine, "I hope that we will get a decision as to when a second airport will be built so that we can decide on interim measures."

However, MacAree still believed that the provision of a fourth major runway, parallel to 14/32, was essential, and the department launched yet another study into that possibility. It came to a halt abruptly when, on November 28, 1978, Transport Minister Lang told the House of Commons, "I have today directed the studies with regard to the fourth runway to be stopped immediately." He explained that the studies had only been launched "in order to have the information against any argument that we should have a fourth runway." Since every inquiry in that direction, including even the Gibson Commission, had replied, "Yes, you should," the government wasn't taking any more chances.

If there is no parallel runway, all the experts agree, then Malton won't do. There will have to be another airport. Here we go again.

Here we go even though Otto Lang was defeated in the May 1979 election, and the Liberals are no longer in power in Ottawa. While the federal Conservatives will certainly block a second Toronto airport in the short run, unless they speedily develop a coherent transport policy – and they had none during the campaign – they will be backed into taking action by Transport Canada.

Chapter 14

Getting Back on the Rails

Hugh Miller, farmer:
"They destroyed the community. Take the village of Brougham. A lot of decent people lived there. They moved away, went to other jobs, other communities. What was left was mostly vagabonds and drifters. All the organizations in the community disappeared. They had a championship baseball team, a good hockey team, a community centre, two lodges and a citizen's league that ran the fire department. They all disappeared, every one of them. And the farming has certainly deteriorated. Down the Eighth Concession there were a lot of dairy farms, more milk per mile than anywhere else in Ontario. Now there are only two left."

Eric Krohn, property management:
"There was a lot of vandalism, that is true. I remember one property was an awful mess and I set out to fix it up to rent it, spent a whole lot of money to fix it up and then one Saturday morning at five A.M. we got a call. Four young lads had gotten in and did $7,000-worth of damage in less than an hour, smashed doors and windows, shit on the rug, wrecked the walls. It was an awful mess. That was the attitude, 'If I can't have it, by God, I'm going to leave a mess!' It was always the kids who gave us a hard time. I can tell you of cases where people sold out and got out of there as fast as they could. They were happy too, just to get their kids out of there. The place was in trouble, but we put the lid on it. We finished it off for them."

Canada has a transportation problem. Not an air transport problem, not an airport problem, but a problem in moving the increasing numbers of people and the increasing tonnage of freight that must be moved from place to place around this large land. The most apparent congestion is in our airports, because more people are flying, and the trend, after a brief pause, is steadily upwards. Competition in air fares has sprung up at the international level, and it is now cheaper to fly overseas than ever before. We all want to do that, usually at the same time. The effect is to crowd air terminals. Government policy, from the beginning, has been to meet this surge by building more and larger airports. The demand is there, all the official reports say, and must be met. This response parallels that of a mother sparrow spotting the open beaks of her brood. It is not policy, but instinct; instinct demands that the appetite be assuaged, the chirping stopped, and the bureaucrats hop off in search of worms. The worms, in this case, cost a billion dollars a crack, and must be pried loose from the claws of the taxpayer, but that is no problem; the government has never run out of taxpayers.

This mothering instinct on the part of Transport Canada is touching, but is it wise? Richard de Neufville, author of *Airport Systems Planning*, thinks not. He points out, "As regards the assumption that the existence of congestion requires that society do something about it, we must recognize that this is not so."

We are smarter than sparrows. The world will not come to an end if all the businessmen who travel on expense accounts have to wait to board an aircraft. Society will continue to function if passengers are put onto airplanes in less opulent surroundings than the costly palaces we use for airports today. The new Calgary terminal, which started out at an estimated $21.3 million and blossomed to $75.7 million, is a lovely place to visit, but Calgarians still managed to get away, somehow, before all that money was spent. International travellers, happily cashing in on Sir Freddy Laker's come-as-you-are transatlantic flights, wait for hours, sometimes days, to catch a plane; they make do with minimal services, and they all survive. People who travel by train are faced with sketchy and inconvenient schedules and begin their journeys in dirty, windy, crumbling stations, or cavernous and crowded ones. Bus travellers, at the very bottom of the totem pole, fight their way on board vehicles from stations that are usually a public disgrace and often a public menace. I asked Transport Canada's Larry Potvin why taxpayers should shell out millions for the few who travel regularly by air, and nothing for those who go by bus. His reply was succinct: "People who travel by bus don't complain."

Actually, they do, but nobody cares. Their complaints are made to the next guy in line, or the harassed ticket-seller. Bus passengers are not the kind of people whose engraved letterheads rivet the attention of Transport underlings. When businessmen yowl because they are delayed on a commercial flight, they carry political weight. The Ministry's attitude towards less affluent travellers can be summed up in two words: tough titty.

However, the fact is that the overwhelming percentage of travel in this country is by automobile. Four out of every five inter-city trips are made by car; bus travel accounts for 7.6 per cent of all such trips; air, 6.8 per cent; and trains, 4.2 per cent. In terms of passenger-miles travelled, the car accounts for 85 per cent of all mileage, while air accounts for 7 per cent, buses for 5 per cent, and rail just under 3 per cent. Even on business trips, the car dominates; again, about 85 per cent of all inter-city business trips are made by car, with the rest divided among the other three modes.

I mention these figures not because I think we should be putting more money into roads – I don't – but to bring some sense of perspective to this issue. Car travellers have gradually learned that, even if they scream, a new expressway will not be built every time there is a traffic jam. If that logic applies to the car, why not to the plane? Where is it written that we have to do anything at all about congestion at Malton airport, or any airport in the country? I fly a good deal; I prefer to fly quickly, without hassles, and I prefer spacious, attractive terminals. However, I won't stay home, and I won't die, if the terminals are crowded or the flights delayed, and I certainly haven't the nerve to demand that my expense-paid flights be made more comfortable, while some poor bugger who buys his own bus ticket helps me out by paying higher taxes to smooth my way.

It is a revolutionary thought, but as Canada addresses itself once more to the wearying problem of air transport, the best solution may be to do nothing. Looking back to the beginnings of the Pickering disaster, you may recall that the trouble started because residents of Malton objected to the prospect of more noise. For the money that was scheduled to be spent to relieve that problem, we could have moved the whole damn community to Tuktoyaktuk. Surely, in this day of long faces and short dollars, the time has come to call a halt to this berserk logic. Leave the airports alone, and if travellers don't like it, let them go by train.

There is little chance that this brutal but sensible advice will be taken, so I turn myself, dutifully, to other solutions.

To meet the kind of congestion that appears to have our experts totally baffled, airports around the world are applying literally dozens of cures. Air traffic control is being improved. A new system called JETS – Joint Enroute Terminal System – tracks an aircraft all along its route, instead of merely when it enters or leaves an airport control zone. This allows better runway use, since controllers are in a better position to anticipate traffic. New and more sophisticated radar will allow aircraft to take off and land, in perfect safety, with smaller separations than ever before. The International Civil Aviation Organization, at its April 1978 meeting in Montreal, approved a new system called Interscan, to replace the Instrument Landing System in use today. ILS only allows a pilot to choose one approach in difficult conditions; Interscan will permit him to choose from a number of approaches, and the result will be greater capacity for airports. This relief should come to Canada by 1983. It will cost money to re-equip our airports with JETS and Interscan, but not a patch on what it costs to build new airports.

General aviation is ·a major problem at international airports, and accounts for twenty per cent of all aircraft movements at Malton. Elsewhere, private aircraft are discouraged by high landing fees, but not in Canada. At Mirabel, you can park your single-engine aircraft as cheaply as you can park your car. At LaGuardia airport in New York, general aviation fees were raised from a minimum $5 to $25, and private traffic dropped from 52 per cent of all LaGuardia landings to 18 per cent; the result was an immediate improvement in conditions for scheduled airplanes. Why don't we take the hint?

To meet the noise problems posed by increasing air traffic, not much now remains to be done. New regulations have given us quieter aircraft, and by 1985, airlines that fail to meet strict standards will be barred. At the same time, work continues on reconditioning noisy engines to make them quieter. Just the same, there is no such thing as a noiseless jet, and the problems on the ground have yet to be met, at least in Canada. However, at Seattle, Washington, the locals have come up with an answer that appears tailor-made for any airport area, and I draw it to the attention of anyone who wants to raise it with Transport Canada. (I have done so, several times, and drew nothing but blank stares.)

In 1973, when the international airport between Seattle and Tacoma proposed an ambitious expansion program, it found itself sued down to its socks by residents who had put up with enough jet noise, and were not going to stand any more. In all, 300 court actions were levelled against the airport. Sea-Tac, like most U.S. airports, is owned by a port authority, King County, and run by elected commissioners. It occurred to these commissioners that it might be a smart idea to consult with the dissidents before launching the expansion program. Accordingly, King County, Sea-Tac, and the citizens joined in a tri-partite study, funded by the Federal Aviation Administration, into all the problems of noise and pollution posed by the airport. The citizen group was led by Mrs. Jean Pihlman, Chairman of the Zone Three Committee, as the dissidents were called (Zone Three because the organization sprang out of the third-tier noise zone – i.e., loud). The meetings of citizens, bureaucrats, and planners were often noisy, sometimes rancorous, and seldom dull. Ed Parks, Sea-Tac's director of planning, says, "We all paid a price for working together, but the result was worth it."

Mrs. Pihlman agrees. "We have had our problems, and we still feel we have to watch them, but the important point is that we were listened to. We have never asked for a piece of information and had it denied; we have never been misled, lied to, or treated with contempt. And we have made an impact."

So they have. The Sea-Tac Community Plan, a massive document that emerged from the three-year process, laid down the ground rules and shared out the responsibilities for the airport expansion. It is a marvellous plan, and covers everything from the allocation of parks to the treatment of oil spills. (During one study of the effect of the airport on two nearby streams, volunteers discovered a 30,000-barrel oil spill that had gone unreported.)

Sea-Tac's approach to noise relief involves four levels of action. Homes in the area closest to the ends of the two runways were expropriated and levelled. The land was turned over to community and park use. There were some complaints, but the prices paid were fair, appeals were easy, and the Zone Three committee threw its weight behind anyone who thought he was not being fairly dealt with. Most important, however, the overwhelming consensus of the citizens agreed that some expropriation was necessary. "We knew from the beginning that the airport was here to stay," says Mrs. Pihlman, "and that meant that some of us have to be moved."

Next, owners in the heaviest remaining noise zone were given the right to sell their homes at a guaranteed price. That is, these people know that the noise is not going to get any better in their area, and if they want to move, their homes are appraised by independent evaluators. If no buyer can be found at the evaluated price, the airport must make up the difference.

Then, those in the third noisiest area are given a grant, covering 75 per cent of the cost of soundproofing their homes, up to a maximum of $5,000 per house.

Finally, those in the fourth noise zone receive 50 per cent – again up to a maximum of $5,000 – for soundproofing. In addition, the airport is spending $3.6 million to soundproof all area schools.

The Sea-Tac program is, in Ed Parks' words, a "pay up and shut up proposition." No one is required to join the program, but those who want to move are helped to do so, those who stay can get help to stay in comfort, and everyone is involved in setting the rules and monitoring the progress of the program.

The Sea-Tac plan has received the unstinting praise of the American League of Women Voters – no gentle critic – among other groups, and the approach could be applied, with good effect, around every major airport in this country. Again, it would cost money – Sea-Tac will spend more than $65 million in its housing program – but only a fraction of what it would cost to build a new airport.

STOL aircraft can be used to take some of the pressure off crowded airports, as well. Current projections indicate that, by the year 2000, 59 per cent of all air traffic movements will be less than 500 miles, the outer limit for STOL. If these craft were to absorb even a fraction of the traffic from, say, Toronto to Montreal, the need for another airport would disappear.

In short, on the airside, the difficulty is not to find solutions to obviate the need for building giant new complexes, but to choose between the multitude of available options. At Malton, the possibilities run from building a parallel to runway 14/32, to removing all general aviation, to implementing a Sea-Tac-type solution.

To meet the groundside problems – crowded terminals, limited access, jammed baggage facilities – takes more money and more ingenuity than Canadian planners have produced to date, but the task is not impossible. One reason Heathrow airport outside London can handle twice Malton's load in less area is that the British discourage meeters and greeters. At Malton, there are two to three times as many well-wishers as passengers on the premises at any given time. Heathrow provides scant and expensive parking facilities, and lays on off-terminal check-in services, so that travellers can bid their farewells downtown, and, once at the airport, simply walk through the terminal to the aircraft. In addition, a new subway link from London to Heathrow encourages travellers, greeters, and workers to leave their autos at home. Heathrow is not a lovely airport, but it certainly is efficient. So is Gatwick, London's other airport, which is served directly by train.

It is possible to design a terminal that is both functional and flexible. The Americans have done it at Tampa, Florida, where a series of satellite terminals ring the main passenger complex. Airplanes and service vehicles are clustered at the satellites, instead of competing for space in parking lots, gawkers and the baggage-smashing machinery, as at Malton. The system is expandable – simply add more satellites – and efficient. Passengers arrive at the main terminal and are whisked by train to the appropriate satellite, baggage is streamed separately, meeters and greeters are left behind, and the football scrum that takes place in every Canadian airport on every long weekend is avoided.

To contend, as our experts have been doing for years now, that Canadians are too stupid to learn from the examples of others is not merely insulting, but ignorant. U.S. aviation authorities Marjorie Brink and Robert K. Joerger noted in *Management Controls* magazine, "No longer can the industry hold with a planning philosophy that relies solely on expansion of physical facilities to accommodate aviation demand. The environment won't stand for it, the airports, the airlines, and the public cannot afford to pay for it . . . The airport industry must figure a way to make do with what it has."

If our planners still can't find that way, I have another suggestion for them; it is big, made of metal, runs on tracks, and goes *blaaat*. It used to go *toot-toot*, but, alas, no longer. The train is the normal mode of inter-city travel in Europe and in the U.K. Trains are cheaper, cleaner, safer than airplanes, and infinitely superior in terms of saving energy and preserving the environment.

For every gallon of fuel consumed, a jet aircraft provides seventy seat-miles. (I like "seat-miles," it has a ring to it. Actually, to obtain this figure, the computer-wielders simply take the number of people moved a given distance by any transport mode, and divide it by the fuel consumed.) The private car is about twice that efficient – 140 seat-miles per gallon. The bus is more than seven times better than the plane, at 500 seat-miles per gallon, and the train is twice as efficient as the bus, at 1,000. Like all figures, these must be treated with caution; an empty train doesn't compare so favourably with a full aircraft; the ratios only apply to "comparable load factors" – the proportion of passengers to seats. Whatever measure is used, however, trains are much more efficient than any other form of transport.

They can also be just about as fast. The train is not the speediest way to get from Montreal to Vancouver, and never will be; but to get from Ottawa to Montreal, or Toronto to Ottawa, or Windsor to London, it is the ideal solution. At least, it should be. The fact is that we have allowed our railway system to get into such appalling shape that our trains are dirty, old, and unreliable. I have ridden on Paris-bound transcontinental trains that hit 200 mph; I have gone from Cardiff, Wales, to London in seventy-five minutes; I have eaten a sumptuous breakfast while skimming from Newcastle to Edinburgh at 125 mph; and I have sat on a siding between Montreal and Ottawa for four hours, wondering why I hadn't hitchhiked instead.

In Canada, until recently, trains have been something you run through slums and into the red. The average age of our passenger rolling stock is twenty-five years. While the Japanese can run trains at 300 mph and the West Germans are linked by speedy express trains, Canadians still struggle along with rickety coaches, wobbly tracks, intermittent timetables, and dismal service. Even so, the obvious cost advantage of trains is so great that when Canadian National, in a burst of whimsy, actually began to promote its passenger service, ridership shot up. CN, naturally, stopped that foolishness at once, cut down the service, and jacked up the fares.

This is not western Europe, but we do have, in the heart of this country, the stretch from Quebec City to Windsor, Ontario, a corridor ideally suited for train operations. There are other ideal train routes within Canada, as well – Calgary-Edmonton, Regina-Saskatoon, Halifax-Saint John-Moncton – all they need is decent service.

It may be on the way. When Via Rail, the crown corporation born out of wedlock to CN and CP, took over its parents' passenger services on April 1, 1978, we entered a new era. God knows how we will come out. Via has been stuck with poor equipment, little money, and much ill will. The company president, Frank Roberts, is a robust, energetic, fast-talking, arm-waving man who thinks that rail "has been getting the shaft for years." He is quite right.

"We have to move into the twentieth century. You have to look at the mix that suits you best. You can't just go on saying we need more planes and airports. Right now there are twenty-three flights a day from Montreal to Toronto, all moving at a loss. To break even, for Christ's sake, the airlines would have to show load factors of 110-115 per cent. It can't be done. So what's the point of putting in more planes if you can do it more economically and better by rail? Instead of planning a system with rail and bus and car and air, there hasn't been any planning. There has just been a call for more roads and more airports.

"Between Edmonton and Calgary, you have twenty-two buses a day, sixteen flights a day, and four lousy dayliners with half a dozen people in them. All they generate is complaints, because the service is so lousy. What do you do when the highway fills up? Build another highway? Why not put in a first-class rail service instead, as an alternative. You can't beat rail at that distance – 150 miles.

"We are the last country in the world, the last 'have' country, that is starting to do something about rail passenger service. Even the Americans are seven or eight years ahead of us.

"What you've got here now is a whole bloody bunch of people in a lobby for air and air exclusively. They're going to say, 'How many flights a day do you need from Toronto to Montreal?,' instead of 'How many people do you want to move, and what's the best way to do it?' In the air branch of Transport Canada you have about

176

500 guys running around selling airplanes; for rail you have maybe twenty-five people who are not well loved. That's the nub."

In Roberts' corner are a handful of stalwarts in Transport 2000, a rag-tag mob of academics, eco-freaks, train-nuts, and public-spirited citizens. They are marshalled by a part-time Executive Director, Michael Jackson, of Regina, with an annual budget that probably doesn't match the take from the gum machines in Canada's airports. The group hopes to raise $64,000 during 1979, to offset some of the millions spent on air transport.

Under-financed, under-manned, and out-gunned, Transport 2000 has, nonetheless, been able to massacre government experts at transport hearings all across the country. For example, in mid-1977, a group of consultants, including Neil Irwin, Beinhaker's partner in IBI, appeared before the Canadian Transportation Commission in Fredericton with a study purporting to prove that the government should sink its money in air transport facilities in the Atlantic region, leaving a little left over for buses. The reason was that the use of rail was on the decline, and bound to decline further, because rail was so inefficient. Roy Ellis, a Saskatchewan civil servant who does volunteer work for Transport 2000, bobbed up to ask a few pertinent questions, and was able to show that one reason rail looked so bad in the consultant report was that the study carried rail deficits, but no figures for other travel modes. What is more, and worse, is that the study showed rail's share of passenger services dropping compared to other modes without ever acknowledging that two of the four Atlantic provinces – PEI and Newfoundland – have no rail passenger service. The Commissioner, D.H. Jones, told the consultants, "You have the railway passenger train set up like a golf ball on a tee and it is there for everybody to take a whack at, but when you go looking for the other mode it's lost in the rough somewhere." In the end, the commission rejected the consultants' work, and came down with a recommendation that more money be put into rail, which is not declining, but growing apace in those areas of the Atlantic region where it has not been closed down. Transport 2000 was certainly instrumental in that decision.

The group has also been effective in helping to block a Transport Canada scheme to shift Regina's downtown rail terminal out to the boondocks. The department had already shifted terminals in Ottawa and Quebec City, making rail travel much more inconvenient; this led, naturally, to an argument that rail doesn't amount to much, because people don't use it. Transport 2000 was able to prove that the studies purporting to show the advantages to Regina of shifting the terminal were faulty, and instead, a multi-modal facility should be developed where it's needed, downtown. In addition, Transport 2000 volunteers have participated in half a dozen campaigns to preserve or improve rail service from Vancouver Island to Halifax. If the federal government wants a real analysis of what is going on in transport, instead of just another consultant report that says, "You're doing fine, boss," it might drop a few bucks on Transport 2000, and watch what happens.

Rail does make sense, more sense than STOL, which will whisk a passenger from Ottawa to Toronto more quickly than a good train service would, but at much greater expense to both the passenger and the environment. Rail also makes more sense than burying the country in asphalt, or dotting it with airports. However, it is hard to tell if trains will ever be given a chance to prove themselves in this country. (Pardon me, prove themselves again. Frank Roberts says, "This country was put together with a band of steel and, by God, it's going to be held together by a band of steel.")

Via will be allowed to buy some new equipment – $90 million-worth of new trains to be delivered in 1980 – or a total of ten train sets, which will be able to go 125 mph if they can find stretches of track straight enough and long enough to get up speed. That sum, just to put it in perspective, represents less than the government is planning to use to expand a single airport, Mount Hope, outside Hamilton, less than the cost of two 747 jets, about one-fourth of the admitted expenditures on Pickering to date, and it could be covered, with millions to spare, out of the Mirabel deficits. Air Canada's bill for new airplanes for 1979 alone comes to $249.5 million, or two-and-a-half times the allowed capital expenditure on trains until God knows when. No major re-tracking program is on the books, and, while the artifacts Via calls its rolling stock will be refurbished, the new cushions won't make much difference if there is no comparable improvement in the road-bed.

British Rail made a profit in 1977 of about $140 million; Canadian rail passenger service that year dropped $260 million. Admittedly, it is easier to run trains in the small, crowded British Isles, but another factor, at least as important, is that the British believe in passenger trains. After a brief, unhappy fling at trying to do it all by air in the 1960s, the British government has put money, expertise, and planning skill into rail. Canada has been steadily downgrading our own. In 1954, CN and CP operated 234 trains over 6,805 miles of track; by 1978, they were running 110 trains on 2,968 miles of track. It is Via's job to turn those figures around again, but whether the task can be accomplished, I don't know. I do know that the alternative is more Mirabels, more Pickerings, more waste, and more disasters.

In sum, if we are looking for solutions, mine come in three steps: first, to hell with airports, let the pampered passengers get on the best they can; second, if that is not acceptable, there are many ways to solve the press of air traffic without building new airports, from rearranging flight schedules to taking a look at STOL; third, whatever else we do, Canada should be looking at rail passenger services as they are run elsewhere in the world.

Put a little money into Via, and take it out of Transport Canada.

Epilogue

It is easy to see that something has gone dreadfully wrong in Canada's transportation planning; Mirabel, the world's largest white elephant, and Pickering, a 35,000-acre wasteland, provide ample evidence. It is much harder to fix the blame.

Certainly, Transport Canada bears much of the responsibility. An Ottawa friend who worked for that department before decamping, rapidly, to the Public Service Commission, maintains that, "I only met three kinds of people in Transport: the incompetent, the indifferent, and the restless." The Ministry's planning process was a disaster from the beginning; the forecasts were muddled, the logic weak, the conclusions ludicrous. Knowing that, however, is cold comfort for the displaced burghers of Pickering or the ravaged taxpayers of Canada. Years ago, Jean Marchand said the department was a mess. Now we know; he had the right goods.

However, the department's besetting sin was the most common failure of every bureaucracy in the world, and that was the refusal to admit, ever, that an error had been made. It seems clear that the plans to expand Malton and Dorval airports were never reconsidered seriously, once a decision was made to build second airports instead. Whatever energy and skill the Ministry possessed was bound up in defending an increasingly untenable position, and the investment in that defence made retreat impossible.

Nor is there much to be gained by knocking the consultants. They reply that they did only what they were paid to do. For example, Phil Beinhaker would be paid whether he recommended building new airports, expanding old ones, or doing nothing. In theory, consultants work under the direct control of the Ministry. In fact, as we have seen, their roles are so intermingled that it is well-nigh impossible to tell the planners apart, to know who did what.

This is where our system of government is beginning to come apart. The essence of democracy lies in the ability of voters, the ultimate wielders of power, to fix responsibility, to allot praise and blame. It cannot be done, however, unless we know who made the decisions, but we have so ordered our system that the process of decision-making is buried under the cloak of confidentiality. The ultimate Catch 22.

The titular responsibility for the decision not to expand Malton came from Paul Hellyer, the Transport Minister, in 1968. In fact, he was merely acting on the (bum) advice of his staff, and in response to pressures from Ontario. The decision to locate an airport at Pickering belongs, in principle, to Hellyer's successor, Donald Jamieson, but the record shows that Jamieson had only a marginal grasp of what was happening when the decision was made, and that he, too, responded to Ontario's ultimatum.

The decision to press on with Pickering long after the arguments for it had been exploded belongs, in theory, to Jean Marchand, who took over from Jamieson, but Marchand's grasp of events was even more uncertain than his predecessor's; he simply assumed that his advisers knew what they were doing, and loaned them his rubber stamp on necessary occasions.

The story is the same at the provincial level. Two governments, representing two different parties, helped to create the mess at Mirabel, and neither of them is any longer close to the levers of power. How do we reward or punish them? Ontario rushed eight different Cabinet ministers through the North Pickering project in a period of forty-three months. The longest held office for a year exactly, the shortest held office for three months and nineteen days. (That was Robert Welch, probably the ablest of them all, but the man handed the noisesome task of ordering the expropriation.) None of these could possibly know what he was doing; each one, in the end, simply passed the buck to his civil service while agreeing, as we all agree, that only politicians can make political decisions.

In the end, a system that was supposed to allot responsibility became a system for avoiding it. To get around this problem, we are told by an increasingly clamorous chorus all we have to do is to get rid of Big Government. Oh, fudge. We have big government because we need it, to deliver the services, from highways to hospitals, that a modern society demands. The trick is to obtain the benefits of size without being crushed by the grossness of the organization, and we haven't worked that one out yet. The current demand to dismantle government agencies and departments is mean-spirited, because it is made on behalf of the well-to-do at the expense of the less affluent. Bank presidents call for the closing of hospitals to save tax dollars; stock-brokers applaud the slashing of unemployment benefits; corporation executives denounce government regulations, for exactly the same reasons that sharks dislike nets.

Planning documents are paid for by the public. Why should the public not be allowed to see what they pay for, every time? Governments argue that, much as they would like to tell us what is going on behind closed doors, they cannot. Decision-making would become impossible. Why? In Sweden, any government body that wants to keep a secret must be able to prove its case to sceptical and hostile courts. In the United States, a citizen refused information to which he believes he is entitled may sue, and usually the threat of a suit is enough to bring forth the information. Canadians can sometimes find out more about what is going on inside their own country in Washington than they can in Ottawa. In this nation, secrecy is a national fetish, cabinet solidarity is a moral imperative, and the right of bureaucrats and consultants to lie and conceal a canon of faith.

Mirabel airport could not have been built if the background papers had been made public at the time – if Canadians had known of the Dixon Speas' finding that no new airport was needed, or of the federal government's preference for another site, or of the grave reservations Ben Higgins had about the hasty acceptance of his rushed report. If the Province of Quebec had known that the reasons for dismissing their favourite site were manufactured, Mirabel would never have lifted its massive white trunk.

Pickering could never have been started if the public had known how the forecasts were compiled, how the site was chosen, and what the planners, consultants, and politicians were saying to each other in private papers. All of these matters are locked away in papers marked "Secret" and "Confidential" and "For Minister's Eyes Only" and "This Document is the Property of the Government of Canada." The official reason for all these secrets is that to reveal them would impair efficiency, but the real reason is that it would cause embarrassment.

I don't know whether Pickering Airport will ever be built. I do know, however, that the twisted, secret, disastrous process that led to Mirabel and Pickering must be revised and exposed. What this country needs is fewer airports and more information. If opening up the process slows down government, so be it; decisions that cannot withstand public scrutiny are not worth making.

A change in the law, requiring any government body that wants to keep planning documents secret to prove to the satisfaction of an independent arbitrator that there is just cause for secrecy, would do the trick. What we need is a Freedom of Information Act with teeth in it. Knowledge is our right, not a privilege, in any matters touching the public purse or the public weal. If we do not act soon to gain that knowledge, we can look forward to a long litany of Pickerings, and a whole platoon of paper juggernauts.

Chapter References

I don't like footnotes, and have tried to make sources clear in the text, where I could do so without intruding. Then, too, in a book like this, some sources must be kept confidential. Just the same some may want some guidance in order to check my statements against the public documents that are available, and some bureaucrats may want to know where to look in their own files. What follows, therefore, are some signposts.

Chapter One

p. 9: The agricultural produce figures are from K.B. Fallis, in a booklet called *Farming and the Environment*, 1972. Fallis, an agronomist, lives in Pickering.

p. 9: The $204 million figure was the one used by Transport Minister Jean Marchand, when announcing the Pickering Minimum Airport on February 20, 1975. The $383 million was cited in a Memorandum to the Federal Cabinet, February 15, 1975, Annex F, page 4, the $542 million in a Memo to Cabinet, January 28, 1975, page 11, the $2 billion to $3.3 billion figure is cited in the Swackhamer Report, page 21. Actually, Don Jamieson used $300 million when he was Transport Minister, and the high bid on the project was $5 billion, but these are enough wild guesses to be going on with.

p. 10: The 198 million passenger figure is from the Bureau of Management Consulting, Report to the Department of Transport, Project 3-79, 1969. The 96.4 million estimate is from the Department of Transport, December 1969, quoted in Gerald Hodge, Report to the Regional Government branch, Province of Ontario, March 1970. The 66.4 million is from a DOT report of September, 1970; 61.9 million, Ministry of Transport (same folks) document 2.13, Volume II, January 1972; 46 million, 33.9 million and 60.7 million figures are all from MOT Document B 55, March 1974. Each and every one of these figures was taken seriously at one time or another.

p. 10: The "not saleable" crack is from Philip Beinhaker, Report 1:14, to the Department of Transport, September 30, 1970, page 13.

p. 10: The $408 million figure has never been made public; officially, we never knew what this masterpiece would set the taxpayer back. However, the figure is used in a Memorandum to the Federal Cabinet, undated, but filed in September 1976, Appendix E, page 6. The memo says that this is the figure Ontario is now using.

p. 11: The acreage figures given here are from the statement to the Ontario Legislature by the Hon. Robert Welch on January 10, 1974, and from the Airport Information Special Supplement produced by the government of Ontario in March 1972.

p. 11: The $500 million figure is not certified; it is my own. The federal government has admitted, in a statement by then Transport Minister Jean Marchand to the House of Commons on April 21, 1976, that it spent $119,230,000 in capital costs up until March 31, 1976. Government Estimates for the Department of Transport in the three years since then show an expenditure of $46,255,000, for a total of $165,485,000. However, these are capital costs, and don't show most of the administration expenses, nor any interest charges since 1976, nor any of the costs that could be off-loaded onto other departments, such as the Department of Public Works, when court actions took up more funds. The federal costs are, therefore, well over $200 million. The province is now showing the cost of land holdings alone at $258 million up to March 31, 1978, according to the Annual Report of the Ontario Land Corporation, quoted in the *Toronto Star* on May 5, 1979. To this must be added millions in legal and administrative costs, consultant reports, and all of the province's own studies. My $500 million figure is conservative to the point of absurdity.

p. 13: The Ombudsman's Report was filed in June 1976. We will meet it again.

p. 13: The Housing Development Act amendment we will meet again, too. It is set forth in the Legislature of Ontario Debates, June 29, 1972, page 4638 ff.

p. 13: The elimination of a public hearing is detailed in a statement by the Hon. Robert Welch on January 10, 1974, page 5. The statement is called "A New Approach to Pickering." It was that. Welch assured us, as politicians always do, that the gag was being applied for the greater public good. When I find a politician who says he is applying a gag because not to do so would expose him to embarrassment, I plan to give the chap a cigar.

p. 15: The elimination of Pickering as a site is contained in a confidential Document "Memos on Site Evaluation of 79 Sites," a collection that begins on November 26, 1968, and runs to June 23, 1970.

Chapter Two

p. 16: Ben Higgins, at the time of his appointment, had taught at McGill, Massachusetts Institute of Technology, the University of Melbourne, and the University of Texas. He had undertaken several United Nations missions, and had worked for the Pearson government's Commission on Bilingualism, and as a consultant for the Quebec government. Paul Michaud, in *Le Devoir,* May 9, 1969, described him as *"Un des rares Canadiens à avoir atteint une stature internationale dans le domaine du développement régional."*

p. 17: The air passengers are from the *Canada Year Book,* 1957-58 page 875, 1968, page 853, 1970-71, page 815.

p. 18: The 1975 Malton air movements figure of 238,197 is from "Statistics Canada's Aircraft Movements," 1976 Annual, Vol. 9, No. 3, February 1977. The other figures are all from the cited report.

p. 19: To get Malton down to 34 movements per hour, when a single runway could handle 40 movements away back in 1961, and the combination of runways could handle 60, the Ministry had to argue that "When only the 14/32 runway can be used, capacity drops to that of a one-runway airport," and that "The acceptance rate of a single runway operation . . . [is] about 34 movements/hour." This guff is contained in "Fact Sheet, Toronto Area Airports Project," Transport Canada, July 1976, page 7.

p. 26: The confidential KPM report of April 1, 1968, is entitled "Final Report, Kates Peat Marwick, for the Department of Transport, Ottawa." It is marked "Confidential Document." This report does, briefly, mention the possibility of expanding Dorval, but only to knock it on the head.

p. 28: The Quebec government's puzzlement over the unwillingness of the Americans to amend the airspace treaty is set forth in Annexe IV, "Supplement du document de travail" of the Quebec Technical Committee on the airport, which wondered sensibly, on page 6, if airspace control was subject to an international accord, why couldn't a new airport be accompanied by a new agreement?

p. 29: The Higgins Report is titled "Répercussions économique concernant les diverse emplacements du projet d'Aéroport International de Montréal." Which is a mouthful.

p. 29: The McWhinney quote is from the *Montreal Gazette,* January 28, 1970. Higgins, who is not entirely happy with his own role in the Mirabel mess, gave me this clipping, in which he had underlined the complaint. I guess it stung.

p. 30: The $290 million cost for Mirabel, and its breakdown, are from Transport figures released in the *Montreal Gazette*, April 1, 1969.

p. 30: The cost of the transit line, $438 million, and much of the detail on the design of Mirabel, and its Plane-Mates, are from a special magazine, *Mirabel*, put out by the *Financial Times of Canada*, September 29, 1975.

p. 31: The text of Bertrand's telegram to Trudeau was carried in the *Montreal Star* on April 1, 1969. The "off his rocker" crack is from the *Montreal Gazette*, April 2, 1969. In the end, of course, the site had to be acceptable to Quebec, because the matter is wholly within federal jurisdiction, and Bertrand's cabinet agreed, with ill grace, to work with the feds in a cabinet meeting held April 9, 1969.

p. 31: The $20 million estimate of land costs given by KPM is from its April 1, 1968, report at page 9. The actual cost, $152,280,603, is as reported in Hansard, November 29, 1976, page 148.

p. 34: Trudeau's "on their knees" crack at the Mirabel opening is as reported in the *Toronto Star*, October 7, 1975.

p. 34: The figures on the cost of the opening are from the *Globe and Mail*, November 14, 1975.

p. 34: The reasons for the second delay are set forth in the *Montreal Gazette*, October 31, 1975.

p. 34: The forecasts and actual passengers at Mirabel are from the *Globe and Mail*, February 10, 1977.

p. 34: The $32- vs $7-a-head figure for handling passengers is from *Canadian Travel* magazine, December 8, 1977.

p. 34: Air Canada's extra cost is from *Maclean's*, November 29, 1976, page 76.

p. 34: The $35 cab rides are reported in a feature *The New York Times* did on Mirabel on August 3, 1978. The *Times* didn't think much of the place, either.

p. 34: The Logan Airport ads on Mirabel really hurt. In December 1978, Transport Canada brought out a promotional pamphlet on its new airport which reads as if it was written by the folks who do toothpaste commercials. It features this cute elephant, named Mirabel, talking right to the reader, and setting "the record straight." The airport was getting a bum rap, this elephant says, because, "A few travellers had a misfortune during a trip and told discouraging stories about Mirabel. There was even another airport that was old and congested and feared losing overseas passengers, so they printed stories about me." This animal gives Mirabel's future business as 50 million passengers a year, and, of course, there is no mention of any of the serious criticisms of the airport. The elephant forgot.

p. 35: The drop in airline usage is reported in the *Maclean's* article cited above, along with William Turner's comment.

p. 35: Material from the travel agents' survey was provided by its sponsors, the Metropolitan Toronto Airport Review Committee.

p. 35: The drop in Dorval's profit was reported in the *Globe and Mail*, February 18, 1978.

p. 35: The de-icing melt-down was reported by the *Toronto Star*, May 4, 1976, and the mice in Mirabel's basement by the *Montreal Gazette*, March 24, 1976.

p. 35: The scandals connected to Mirabel were first reported in the *Montreal Star*, November 6, 1975. The trials are still pending for some of those involved. The results to date were supplied to me in a letter from the RCMP's civil fraud squad.

p. 35: The $4 million spent on the industrial park is from *The New York Times* feature.

p. 35: The $115 million Mirabel deficit is from Hansard, February 28, 1978, page 3291.

Chapter Four

p. 38: The figures on Malton's growth and future expectations are from "Memorandum to the Cabinet," July 11, 1968. The figure on Malton's 1970 traffic load is from Transport Canada Fact Sheet, July 1976, and the 1980 prediction is from Transport Canada's "Contingency Plan Study," Volume 2, page 2.6, June 10, 1977.

p. 38: The quote is from "Master Plan Report, Toronto International Airport," by John B. Parkin Associates, November 9, 1967, Synopsis.

p. 38: The July 11 decision is from the Cabinet document of that date.

p. 39: The fact that house prices in Malton did not decline is documented in *Transportation Economics and Public Policy: With Urban Extensions*, by Alan Abouchar, Toronto: John Wiley and Sons, 1977, page 233. Abouchar's book is not exactly sprightly, but it does look at the Pickering decision, among others, with devastating care.

p. 41: The series of predictions for the year 2000 are from the Hodge Report, page 84, and from the Ministry of Transport, "Summary of Evidence" for the Gibson Commission, page 15.

p. 42: The major source for the outline of the site selection process is the series of documents already referred to, "Site Selection Process of 79 Sites." There are, however, three public documents that set forth some of the steps taken; two are from Transport Canada; a September 8, 1969 report, "Toronto Airport II Site Selection" and the Ministry's Summary of Evidence for the Gibson Commission. The third is an undated provincial item called "The Prospect of an Airport," written after Pickering was picked, and full of flannel.

p. 44: The Robarts quote is from the *Globe and Mail*, December 2, 1968. He was right, of course; the Ontario boys were going along with an estimated outlay of $70 million, but that was only for the first stage of the airport; when they later found out that the bill would be in the hundreds of millions, they nearly fainted.

p. 45-6: The gloomy analysis of the four sites is from a memo prepared for W.H. Huck, the Air Administrator, dated April 1971, and summarizing earlier work.

p. 46: The Bales affair. An excellent account appears in an excellent book, *The Power and the Tories*, by Jonathan Manthorpe, Toronto: Macmillan, 1974, page 247 ff.

p. 48: The deleting of Hodge's negative thoughts can be seen at its finest in the "Summary of Evidence" for the Gibson Commission, which is supposed to be an official history of the decision-making process, and which, naturally, refers to Hodge, but of his forecast analysis contains not a sniff.

Chapter Five

p. 49: Formation of the advisory committee: letter, Beinhaker to Hemming, January 13, 1971. This is the letter referred to in the text. It was a document to explain what the consultants had been doing for all their money, and much of what follows in this chapter, including the fees paid, is drawn from this document.

p. 51: The Planning Team Report referred to is called "Position Paper, Toronto Airport Planning, May, 1970." The "Planning Team" is a purposely vague byline; some papers produced under this designation were done by a few members of the civil service, some embraced a broad array of consultants, and sometimes, one planning team report directly contradicted another. No names, no pack drill.

p. 53: The quote from the Airport Inquiry Commission is from "The Report of the Airport Inquiry Commission," Information Canada, Ottawa, 1974, page 142. This is usually called the Gibson Report.

p. 53: The San Francisco and Los Angeles figures are from the 1977 Annual Reports of the two airports; the Malton figures are from the annual report of the British Airports Authority.

p. 54: Transport Canada's attitude to the 1970 studies shows at its clearest in a document called "Response to Synopsis Report of the Hearing Officer," Transport Canada, January 1975, at page 12. (This was the government response to the report of J.W. Swackhamer into the expropriations.) It claims that in "sharp contrast" to the August 1970 report, "All of thirty-three technical reports produced from August 1970 by the Federal Government challenge the conclusions of this report." Not so. The Beinhaker reports, produced in September, specifically embraced the Malton expansion as the best solution technically, and the other reports referred to were justifications of the decision taken, not independent studies. The department did claim that the August report contained errors, particularly in dealing with costs, but its conclusion, that the expansion of Malton was the best technical solution, was not "challenged," except by Blumenfeld. And the boys didn't like him, either.

p. 56: The Blumenfeld study I wanted to lay on Huck was called "The Relation of Airport Planning to Community Planning and Development." It was dated July 5, 1968, and submitted to the Higgins Commission. At page 17, Blumenfeld came down with "A Suggested New Concept," to locate airports "about ten to fifteen miles beyond the urban perimeter anticipated for the end of this century." The authorities should cut their losses at old airports, and move out of town, now: "The situation calls for bold thinking, far-sighted planned and decisive actions." Since this advice was not taken, Blumenfeld was able to recycle it for Toronto.

p. 59: The crucial sentence, beginning, "It was generally agreed . . ." is from Beinhaker's letter-report dated September 30, 1970, an elaboration of the Design for Aviation concept. The quote appears on page 13.

p. 60: In suddenly springing the curfew as a major block on the expansion of Malton, the cabinet document was simply ignoring what had been said in the August Position Paper: "The curfew is a problem of no major significance."

p. 60: The cabinet decisions referred to here are from Cabinet Document 1224/70 and the Record of Cabinet Decision, Meeting of October 27, signed by D.J. Leach, Supervisor of Cabinet Documents, on November 5, 1970.

p. 61: The fees paid to PM&P are in Beinhaker's letter to Hemming. The $2,147,077.92 paid to KPM is contained in the written answer to an Order Paper question by Ron Huntingdon, MP for Capilano, October 14, 1975. The $1,494,113 figure was tabled in answer to a question by Elmer MacKay, MP for Central Nova, October 14, 1978.

Chapter Six

Virtually everything of import in this chapter is from secret, confidential, and private documents; I see no point in laying down citations that cannot be followed, and have instead tried to indicate in the text the main sources used.

Chapter Seven

p. 82: The historic house Wanstall and Adams called Melody Farm was the Barclay homestead. It was George Barclay who was involved in the 1837 Rebellion, but a lot of the neighbours were in on it, too. An account appears in Robert T. Miller's delightful *The Ontario Village of Brougham*, privately published by the author, a local businessman, historian, and softball pitcher, in 1973.

p. 84: Cafik's shifting allegiances were described by journalist Barry Conn Hughes as "artful mugwumpery," which I think is a nice phrase. (Cafik was defeated in the federal election of May 22, 1979.) Hughes was a member of POP, and wrote a moving article about the organization, "Up Against Ottawa," in the April 19, 1975, edition of *Canadian Magazine*. I have drawn on this article, as well as on a book, *People Or Planes*, by Hector Massey and Charles Godfrey, Copp Clark, 1975, and on contemporary newspapers. Chiefly, however, I have relied on the minutes of POP and MTARC for details of the inner workings of the protest organizations. The POP minutes are available at the group offices in Cedarwood.

p. 86: The twenty-one cells represented: Atha, Altona, Bethesda, Brooklin, Brougham, Cherrywood, Claremont, Dixon Hill, Don Mills, Goodwood, Green River, Greenwood, Locust Hill, Markham, Pickering, Scarborough, Stouffville, Unionville, Uxbridge, Whitby, and Whitevale.

p. 87: Three others who were heavily involved with publicity were Al Graham, Monte Dennis and Bill Lishman, while Arthur Horne provided an endless stream of excellent photographs for the protestors. It was the women, however, who made a full-time job of teaching the bureaucrats that they were not put on earth for pleasure alone.

p. 89: Godfrey's crack about Adam and Eve was carried in the *Whitby Advertiser*, April 3, 1974.

Chapter Eight

p. 97: The April 10 leak by POP of the September 1970 study appeared in the *Toronto Star*, April 10, 1972, and the *Globe and Mail* of April 11.

p. 97: The April 14 POP communiqué was also covered by both papers.

p. 98: The April 15 leak of the ecological study was carried in the *Globe and Mail* of April 15. This same issue carried a page-one story which showed the early manoeuvres of Ontario politicos in the process of trying to shift all the blame for Pickering off onto the feds, with interviews with Premier Davis and McKeough, both busily exhorting the press not to look at them, boys, they just took Ottawa's word for these things.

p. 98: James Auld's waffling answer on the environment was covered in the *Globe*, April 18. It should be said in Auld's defence that he couldn't say yes or no, because the province really didn't know – it had done so little study of the site. However, this was not something the boys wanted to boast about, at least not yet.

p. 98: The Ottawa meeting with Jamieson. The Transport minutes show Jamieson giving the cost of the airport as "300 million including land – another 200 million – second phase beyond 1995," which seems to indicate that the minister either had no idea of the figures being used in the background papers, or chose deliberately to misrepresent them.

p. 100: The later meeting with Macdonald was set up because Douglas Turner, the Toronto lawyer and chairman of MTARC, had worked on Macdonald's campaign. The quote is from the recollection of Lorne Almack, who attended with Turner and Clark Muirhead. This meeting took place May 10, 1975.

p. 100: The Gillian Thompson incident led to a flurry of letters among Mrs. Thompson, John Fairchild, and Pierre Berton. Fairchild's letter to Berton is a little sick-making. It winds up, "I am a person who four years ago back-packed his way through fifteen of the underdeveloped countries of the world, until I nearly died during the Bangladesh war from illness, in order to appreciate the problems of the third world." This apparently proved that he hadn't bullied Gillian. The quotes are from notes made of the meeting.

p. 100: The key documents released by McKeough on June 6, 1972, were twelve reports, called Documents I through XII, which included the Hodge Report, Document IV. Some of them were only a few pages long.

p. 100: The POP meeting with McKeough. J.A. Coates, one of the lawyers on POP's legal committee, wrote to McKeough on June 9, enclosing a copy of the group's written questions and the Minister's reply, and I have quoted from these. The timing sequence is important. On February 17, 1972, there was a meeting between members of the TAAP team and Ontario planners, which included a legal adviser to the province. Expropriation was discussed in some detail, and D.A. Crosbie, Assistant Deputy Minister of Transport, said the province planned to proceed with expropriation under the Public Works Act. There was no barrier to doing so, at least in the minds of those present. Then came the meeting with POP, then the Housing Development Act amendment, which was explained in a letter from Larry Forster, Ontario's Project Director, to George Coleman, Assistant Managing Director of the Ontario Housing Corporation, dated September 28, 1972: "With respect to expropriation, it was initially anticipated that the future expropriation would be done under the Public Works Act. Legal advice subsequently suggested that this authority was not adequate and subsequently a decision [was] made ostensibly by the Ministry of Justice to amend the Housing Development Act to permit acquisition of lands by expropriation for large Community Development Projects such as this one."

p. 101: The amendment and the debate are from the Legislature of Ontario Debates, June 29, 1972, page 4638 ff.

Chapter Nine

p. 103: The Cabinet decision taken June 29. The quotes are from Memorandum to the Cabinet, New Toronto Airport, January 15, 1973. What was said out loud is something we will meet in detail in Chapter Ten.

p. 105: Although Swackhamer was not empowered to make any recommendations, his report, officially "Report of J.W. Swackhamer, Q.C., Hearing Officer, Site for Toronto II Airport, The Expropriation Act, Revised Statutes of Canada, 1970 Chapter 16, December 29, 1972," did make one. Swackhamer thought that because POP was engaged in such an unequal battle, its witnesses before him should be given some extra payment. The law would only allow payment of $600 – $150 a day – of Robinette's $7,500 fee, for example, and the expert witnesses could get only $35 a day. Swackhamer called these amounts "totally inadequate," and wanted them fattened; if his recommendation had been followed, POP and MTARC proposed to put the arm on the witnesses for their extra money, and would have added close to $10,000 to the war chest. The request was refused.

p. 107: The provincial concern for its water and sewer commitment is made clear in the letter from Ken Foley of December 16, 1971, cited on page 143. This commitment actually began with decisions made by the Ontario Water Resources Commission back in 1965. A detailed survey of Ontario's increasing involvement appears in the transcript of the "Royal Commission in the Matter of The Public Enquiries Act Into The Acquisition by the Ministry of Housing of Certain Lands in the Community of North Pickering," January 24, 1977, Volume I.

p. 107: Julius Caesar banning chariot traffic. *The Politics of Airport Noise*, by Gordon McKay Stevenson, Jr., Belmont, Calif.: Duxbury, 1972, page 1.

p. 107: The various noise measuring systems are listed in the Report of The Aircraft Inquiry Commission, *op. cit.*, page 55, and the description of projected reactions is from the transcript of evidence.

p. 108: The material on the development of modern noise legislation in the U.S. is from the "Report of the Committee on Public Works and Transportation of the U.S. House of Representatives," December 13, 1977, Airport and Aircraft Noise Reduction Act.

p. 109: The California study on airport noise effects is from an Associated Press report carried in the *Globe and Mail*, August 28, 1978.

p. 109: The Etobicoke development in a noise zone is taken from the *Toronto Star*, October 18, 1978.

Chapter Ten

p. 117: The department's claim that the September 22 telegram to Robinette should be discounted is contained in the memo referred to in the text: "New Toronto Airport, Public Board of Examination," dated January 22, 1973. The date, almost a month after Swackhamer reported, makes it clear that it was the inquiry that was up for discussion, not the hearing.

p. 120: MacKinnon's crack about getting another order-in-council was made at the February 21, 1974, organizational meeting of the Inquiry Commission, page 145 of the transcript. I don't propose to give the transcript or report page numbers here; they are of no use to general readers, and anyone who wants to check the transcript or report will find both fully indexed.

p. 120: POP's threat to boycott the commission was covered in the *Toronto Star*, February 24, 1974.

p. 120: The commission's assumptions are from the report, under the heading "General Comments on Air Transportation Industry." They include the remark that allows present travel habits are "irreversible."

p. 121: Ontario's non-appearance at the Gibson Inquiry was the result of a lot of background manoeuvring, and the exchange of numerous memos and letters between the province and the feds. A Confidential Memo of May 11, 1973, from W.H. Huck to Deputy Minister Stoner, makes it clear that Ontario did not want to be called, for fear of losing "flexibility," always a no-no. And the feds didn't want them in on the action because "If the Provincial Government is only indirectly involved as an ex-officio participant, the decisions as to the membership of the Board and the scope of the Board's activities would rest directly with the Federal Government."

p. 125: The forecast error at Kennedy Airport is from Richard de Neufville, *Airport Systems Planning*, Cambridge: MIT Press, 1976, page 46.

p. 126: The fact that one DC-8 can equal 160 L10-11s in a noise contour was turned up in the de Havilland study cited, and used in MTARC's excitable document, "Is The Minimum Airport Needed? New Evidence!" based on that study and published, undated, in 1975 (page 6). (The "new evidence" line was a crack at Gibson.)

Chapter Eleven

No notes.

Chapter Twelve

p. 141: Ontario's problems with land assembly. Statement by Robert Welch, Minister of Housing, January 10, 1974, page 4. Welch gave the figure as 49 per cent of the acreage.

p. 141: The hearings of necessity were junked – *ibid.* The way Welch put it was cute: "The Lieutenant-Governor in Council, under Section 6 (3) of the Expropriations Act, has considered it necessary in the public interest to direct that expropriation proceed without an enquiry procedure" (page 5).

p. 141: Prices began to shoot up. A detailed study of what happened to the land is contained in The Report of the Ontario Ombudsman, June 7, 1976, and many of the examples that follow are drawn from that document.

p. 142: The Ombudsman's battle with Ontario naturally drew the attention of the press. Two good roundup stories written later on were Michael Moore's May 6, 1978, article in the *Globe and Mail*, and Jonathan Manthorpe's column "No end in sight to Pickering war of words," *Toronto Star*, March 11, 1978.

p. 142-3: The Royal Commission hassle. There is a transcript available, which I have already cited, "Royal Commission in the Matter of the Public Enquiries Act," which I commend to anyone who wants to put his teeth on edge. The commission report is summarized in the *Toronto Star*, March 9, 1978. Another roundup story, on Maloney's resignation, was carried in the *Globe and Mail*, August 16, 1978, and I have quoted from this.

p. 149: The battle of the telegrams between Rhodes and Marchand was front-page stuff at the time, in both the *Toronto Star* and the *Globe and Mail*, and copies of the telegrams were released. The best roundup story was Michael Moore's "Wrecking of Pickering homes continues after halt pledged," in the *Globe* on August 23, 1975. Begin's role as front-man in the incident is set out in the *Toronto Star* of August 22.

p. 149: Stories of the Carruthers caper appeared in every Toronto newspaper, naturally, with items from September 15 through 28, 1975. A fine look-back piece was carried by *Maclean's*, and written by Angela Ferrante, May 17, 1976.

p. 152: Marchand's shaking-with-anger reaction on September 25, was reported by Hugh Winsor in the *Globe and Mail*, September 26, 1975. The Trudeau quote is from the same report.

p. 152: The claim that the road-closings were illegal is made in a statement by Douglas Turner, counsel for MTARC, to The Air Law Section of the Canadian Bar Association, Quebec City, August 26, 1975. Turner points out that the feds had been unable to make a deal with the township over a price for the land, so simply expropriated, but did not even bother to obtain "demolition permits as required by the Municipal by-laws." POP actually got a handful of warrants sworn out, and was prepared to have senior officers of Transport arrested when the airport was shelved.

Chapter Thirteen

p. 156: Steve and Maria Gerencer. This case was reported in the *Toronto Star*, May 1, 1978.

p. 159: The crucial decision in the Leach incident is JDP-6-76, dated March 30, 1977. The case was in the name of Her Majesty the Queen and Edgar Lloyd Fisher and Anita Inis Fisher (they come earlier in the alphabet than Leach) and it was a decision by Mahoney to issue a warrant of possession. The quotes on page 161 are from this decision.

p. 161: The levying of costs against Estrin was also part of this judgment. The incident took place on August 17 and 18, 1976, and Mahoney heard argument on the issue on March 24, 1977, then bundled his dicta all into the same judgment. It is fascinating to see how the judge dealt with the airport shelving, and his ruling that it was irrelevant: "At the opening of this hearing . . . counsel for the Respondent took the preliminary objection that, having already decided that I would not hear that evidence and argument, I had prejudged the application and ought to disqualify myself. I declined." He went on to say that his ruling came in an interlocutory proceeding, and that if it appeared to amount to less than justice, that "is to be measured against the patent injustice of permitting a lawyer, whatever his motives and instructions, but always at his client's and never at his own expense, to pursue matters that have nothing whatever to do with the issue to be decided." And who decided what was fit to be decided? The judge, of course. Same fella.

p. 164: The Chinese water torture. A quick flip through my files shows reports in a single paper, the *Toronto Star*, all quoting Lang or other senior officials laying down the argument that a second airport must be built, on September 25 and 26, 1975; October 13, 1975; May 8, 1976; May 22, 1976; May 25, 1976; August 26, 1976; September 15, 1976; October 3, 1976; October 15, 1976; February 3, 1977; and September 28, 1977.

p. 164: Secor Brown. In Washington, I asked Brown if it was his job to tell Ontario when Ottawa was lying. He replied that he would not describe it in "exactly those words," but that, yes, that was the nub.

p. 165: The slow decline in TAAP's staff caught the attention of the *Globe and Mail*'s Michael Moore, and he did a piece on June 19, 1976, which showed that, nine months after the airport shelving, the lads were still using up $334,000-worth of office space a year to percolate another dream. At that time, the staff was 96.

p. 165: Beinhaker is such a prominent figure in Transport Canada that one of the questions asked clerks bucking for promotion is to identify him. One correct answer I saw was "He is a consultant and

196

writes reports for us." This same applicant had identified Swack-hamer as "Our lawyer for the second set of hearings and he died."

p. 168: The *Quest* article cited appeared in May 1978.

Chapter Fourteen

p. 170: The figures on the Calgary terminal are from the 100th Annual Report of the Auditor General, Ministry of Supply and Services, 1978, page 507.

p. 171: The percentages are from An Interim Report on Inter-City Passenger Movement In Canada, Information Canada, Ottawa, 1976.

p. 171: JETS has been around for some time, and was discussed, briefly, before the Gibson Commission, but did not make it into the report. Some aviation experts don't believe it will make much difference in traffic-handling capabilities.

p. 172: Interscan. Reports on the new system, and the battle over its adoption, were carried in the *Manchester Guardian*, Overseas Edition, April 2, 1978, the *Toronto Star*, April 20, 1978, and the *Globe*, April 21, 1978.

p. 172: The startling effect of raising fees for general aviation is discussed in de Neufville, *op. cit.*, page 141.

p. 172: The Sea-Tac solution has been the subject of many articles and booklets, including a small cloud of pamphlets put out by the airport and King County. The U.S. Federal Aviation Administration brought out a booklet, "The Sea-Tac Success Story," in April 1978, and the League of Women Voters of King County South produced a more objective, but highly favourable study called "Sea-Tac and Its Neighbours," which is undated.

p. 174: The numbers of greeters at Malton are set down in the *Toronto Star* of September 27, 1977, as "2.5" for every passenger. I don't see how you can have 2.5 greeters, so I made it between two and three, which may not help much, but makes me feel better.

p. 174: I have called Gatwick efficient because, in 1976-77, according to the annual report of the British Airports Authority, it handled 16 million passengers on a single runway, or many more than Malton handles on three. It does not make money, although Heathrow makes it in heapfuls. That year, according to the same source, Heathrow cleared £21.9 million.

p. 175: The "Management Control" article cited is from the magazine's Volume 24, No. 4, July-August 1977.

p. 175: The seat-miles figures were supplied by Via Rail's research department. The British Advisory Council on Energy Conservation uses a more general figure: "In general, road travel uses two-and-a-half times more energy than rail per passenger miles, and air uses five times more." This is per mile travelled, and is probably a better figure, but it applies to Britain, and would not translate exactly for Canada.

p. 175: The average age of rolling stock is as given to me by Roberts, the Via president.

p. 176: The launching of Via Rail. A trenchant piece on the new crown corporation was written by Michael Jackson for the September 1978 issue of *The Canadian Forum*. Jackson has since told me that he feels much more positive about Via than he did when he wrote the article, but it remains the best piece I have seen.

p. 177: The debunking of the consultants over their Atlantic studies is from the Transcript of the Canadian Transportation Commission hearings in Case No. 3 3(e), 1977, Volume I.

p. 178: The problems with STOL. In April 1978, Transport Minister Lang announced a plan to foist STOL services off onto Toronto Island, and the city did a study, which reported on June 9, 1978, and concluded that STOL should be kept off the airport. That study was accepted by the Toronto Executive Committee, and remains municipal policy, although the *Globe* of January 3, 1979, reported that a Montreal firm, Canavia Transit, Inc., still lusts after the service, and has Transport Canada's blessing.

p. 178: Via's new trains are described in a feature article in the *Toronto Star* of February 25, 1978. The Mount Hope expansion was announced January 31, 1978, and the Air Canada purchases are from the *Globe*, January 5, 1979.

p. 178: British Rail's profit is from the *Guardian*, May 14, 1978, and the rail loss figures here are as supplied by Frank Roberts.

p. 178: The drop in trackage and trains is from the *Globe* of April 28, 1978.

Appendix
A Chronology

1961

Undated report examines need for a second airport in Toronto, and concludes none is required.

1966

Second internal study of need, same conclusion.

1967

Nov. 9   Master Plan for Malton suggests expansion by purchase of 3,000 additional acres, to provide capacity to the twenty-first century.

Dec. 19   Master Plan for Dorval suggests a second airport required. Subcontractor R. Dixon Speas argues that no new facility is needed, and Dorval should be expanded, instead. This advice rejected.

1968

April 1   KPM reports on site selection for second Montreal airport, suggests location west of city.

July 11   Federal Cabinet approves Malton expansion in twenty-year plan to cost $250 million.

Aug. 2   Malton expansion made public.

Sept.   Federal government decides to build second airport for Toronto; Transport staff have site search under way.

Sept. 10   Federal-provincial committee established with Quebec to resolve disagreement over site for second Montreal airport. Quebec wants it southeast of city, feds want it west.

Nov. 26   C.A. Appleton reports to Transport that an extensive search has been made of sites for a second Toronto airport; the potential sites have been sifted down to fifteen, then five "preferred" sites. Suggests detailed study of these.

Nov. 29   Stalemate between Quebec and Ottawa on choice of site for second Montreal airport.

Dec. 11   Professor Ben Higgins appointed to study Montreal area sites from point of view of regional planning.

Dec. 20 Transport Minister Paul Hellyer announces that, because of
local opposition, Malton will not be expanded. Instead, a second airport will be built, and a search for sites will commence.

1969

Jan. 17 Higgins Commission reports best site for a Montreal second
airport in regional development terms is one near Ste-Scholastique, provided bridges and rapid transit are built at once.

Feb. 17 Federal-provincial committee formed with Ontario to select
site for second Toronto airport.

March 27 Hellyer announces selection of Ste-Scholastique for Montreal
airport. Higgins is surprised, Quebec is furious. Cost is given
as $400 million, and the airport will open in 1974.

April 9 Still protesting, Quebec cabinet accepts Ste-Scholastique site.

May 5 Hellyer resigns, Donald Jamieson becomes Minister of
Transport.

May Ontario begins study of Toronto-Centred Region.

June Site search continues in Toronto area. Four locations are now
in serious contention, near Orangeville, Sutton, Port Perry,
and Guelph.

July 2 A preliminary look is taken at three sites closer to Toronto.
One of these is near Pickering, which had been eliminated before as unsuitable. It is eliminated again.

Sept. Ontario objects to Sutton site as interfering with holiday
traffic.

Sept. 19 Dalton Bales, then Attorney General of Ontario, and two
friends buy parcel of land in Pickering.

Oct. 1 Planning memo from Transport to Ontario says expansion of
Malton is "out of the question."

Oct. 27 Planning memo shows new Toronto airport will cover 80,000
acres, and contain at least six runways.

Nov. 26 TCR plan study group looks at the four sites, draws no conclusion.

1970

March Professor Gerald Hodge reports to Ontario on four sites, favours either Orangeville or Port Perry. In an appendix, he
warns that the forecasts, on which the need for an airport is
based, may be wrong.

April Second provincial report on four sites strongly favours Port
Perry.

April 22	Consultant Philip Beinhaker, who worked on Montreal airport, is given Toronto planning papers.
May 11	Beinhaker reports, suggests government should either expand Malton or build a series of airports. The same day, Toronto Transport planning team reports that none of the Toronto sites works well, but Malton expansion would solve the problem. The team is to explore this further.
Aug.	Position Paper from Toronto Planning team suggests Malton be "reconfigured" within present boundaries. This will be cheaper and work better than a second airport.
Aug. 17	Urbanologist Hans Blumenfeld says, in a letter, he has studied the Malton expansion program and argues that it cannot be done. The government should instead close Malton and build a new airport at Guelph.
Sept. 8	Consultant Beinhaker reports that the expansion of Malton is the "best and least costly" solution, but provides no "fallback" position. To maintain flexibility, the government should consider more options, including regional airports. This approach is called Design for Aviation.
Mid-Sept.	Toronto team reports again, sums up all earlier reports, and concludes that the government should build a six-runway airport near Guelph. It will cost $5 billion.
Sept. 18	Beinhaker briefs Jamieson on Design for Aviation, and the Minister agrees that "Malton alone is not saleable."
Sept. 30	Ontario accepts Design for Aviation.
Oct. 15	Beinhaker appears before Cabinet committee in Ottawa, outlines Design for Aviation with flashcards. It is accepted.
Oct. 26	Negotiations begin between Ontario and Ottawa over cost-sharing for the airport. They will never be concluded.
Oct. 27	Federal Cabinet approves Design for Aviation.
Dec. 11	The concept is presented to Ontario Premier John Robarts. He accepts in principle, but says he may want to put off final site selection for as much as a year.
Dec. 16-29	Federal-provincial meetings discuss noise zones.

1971

Feb. 12	William Davis succeeds Robarts as Ontario premier.
Mar. 16	Deputy Transport Minister O.G. Stoner prepares memo for a meeting between Davis and Jamieson. Memo suggests how Davis can be pushed into accepting any one of three sites: Guelph, Orangeville, or Port Perry. Transport prefers Guelph. Jamieson prefers Orangeville, and a fourteen-page memo is attached, warning of problems with that site. Stoner suggests a site decision should be announced April 12.

March 18	Davis and Jamieson meet. Jamieson pushes for Orangeville. Davis does not commit himself, but will not oppose the site publicly if announced.
April 21	Cabinet document is prepared to approve Orangeville. Transport withdraws all objection, and now agrees this is the best site. About the same time, a weather study on Orangeville arrives, ruling out the site.
April 27	Another internal study suggests no decision should be made at this time, as STOL development may solve Malton congestion.
May 5	Toronto-Centred Region plan made public, argues that airport should go east of Toronto.
May	Federal planners tell their provincial colleagues that none of the four previous sites will work, but they have two new sites instead, one at Pickering, one near Peter's Corners in Beverly Township. Beinhaker prepares "A Revised Approach" to airport strategy. There will now be five airports for Toronto, and instead of a six-runway site, planners will now settle for two 5,000-10,000-acre sites. Beverly and Pickering fit the bill, one west, one east of Toronto.
June 21	The two new sites are toured by planners, and Beverly is favoured.
July 8	Second tour of Pickering site shows that it could be used for a two-runway airport, nothing larger.
July 23	Jamieson meets Ontario Treasurer Charles MacNaughton, tries to get agreement to Beverly site, offers to buy land for a site east of Toronto for an airport to be developed there later. MacNaughton stalls.
Aug. 9	MacNaughton writes Jamieson to complain about the "extremely brief" evaluation of sites, and asks that Pickering be looked at again.
Aug. 21	Ontario releases a Status Report on the TCR plan, confirming boundaries and suggesting new airport should be built in accord with concept – east of Toronto. This same day, the TCR plan and Pickering site are compared by planners. The airport will wipe out two towns, violate a provincial reserve for agriculture and recreation.
Aug. 23	Preliminary airspace survey shows that Beverly works well with Malton, but Pickering presents "major conflict."
Sept. 17	Jamieson replies to MacNaughton's August 9 letter, agrees to reconsider Pickering.
Oct. 21	Davis wins Ontario election. Cabinet Committee on Government Operations in Ottawa endorses three-airport policy.

Oct.	Planner Peter Oehm reports to Ontario that Pickering conforms to TCR concept better than Beverly.
Oct. 27	Full federal Cabinet accepts new policy, one airport west of Toronto, one east, with more to follow.
Oct. 28	Provincial planner Ken Foley writes to feds that both Beverly and Pickering present "substantial disadvantages," but the province prefers Pickering.
December	Toronto Area Airport Project team reports that earlier favourites are now all "unacceptable"; only acceptable airports are at Beverly and Pickering, and Beverly is best. If only one airport built, it should be at Beverly.
Dec. 16	Province is told an airport will be built at Beverly and another, later, at Pickering. Planner Foley replies that Ontario is already committed to infrastructure east of Toronto and can't afford to service an airport at Beverly.
Dec. 22	Jamieson and MacNaughton meet. Jamieson agrees to build at Pickering first. After this, there is no reference to any third airport.
Dec. 29	A new study shows that "major conflict" in airspace between Pickering and Malton no longer exists.

1972

January	A rushed study of Pickering environment is done in seventy-two hours, in the snow. It will later be described as "important."
Jan. 28	TAAP briefs Ottawa on new plan – an airport at Pickering and expansion of regional airports.
Feb. 1	Cabinet Committee on Government Operations accepts new plan.
Feb. 7	Full Cabinet accepts new plan.
Feb. 10-17	Federal-provincial meetings re-draw TCR boundaries to ease conflict with Pickering.
March 1	Federal-provincial agreement signed on Pickering.
March 2	Pickering and Cedarwood city announced jointly by Ottawa and Ontario. The site is described as "ideal," and presented as the logical choice after elimination from a list of fifty-nine possibilities.
March 3	Protestors meet at Melody Farm. POP is born.
March 6	Pickering Township passes resolution protesting site.
April 10	POP produces leaked report showing Pickering was not in the list of 59 sites referred to on March 2.
April 26	POP members trek to Ottawa to meet Jamieson, get promise of release of more papers.
June 6	Ontario Treasurer Darcy McKeough releases Ontario study

papers, which show that little work was done on site before selection.

June 8   McKeough meets POP, is told province may not have right to expropriate land for Cedarwood.

June 29   In late-night session, Ontario amends Housing Development Act. Province now has power to expropriate, but purpose of amendment is concealed. Same day, the federal Cabinet confirms need for a second airport, but promises a full Public Inquiry as well as Hearings under Expropriation Act.

Aug. 4   Dalton Bales' Pickering land-holdings emerge. He resigns.

Sept. 6   Darcy McKeough, accused of conflict of interest, resigns.

September Expropriation notices go out to Pickering residents on federal lands. Province begins to negotiate to purchase lands for Cedarwood; will expropriate only if necessary.

Nov. 23   Swackhamer Hearings begin.

Nov. 27   Jean Marchand new Minister of Transport.

Dec. 29   Swackhamer Report to federal Cabinet, lambastes both decision to build airport and its location.

1973

Jan. 22   Federal Cabinet is told that promised inquiry into airport may not consider either site or need, or expropriations may be invalid.

Jan. 30   Marchand says in House of Commons that inquiry will be able to consider site and need. Swackhamer Report is released, and expropriation is confirmed.

March 12 POP meeting with Marchand and MP Norman Cafik; protestors are assured inquiry will consider need and location of airport.

April 16 Marchand tells House again that inquiry will be able to consider all aspects.

May 8-9   Marchand tells parliamentary committee, twice, that inquiry will be free to consider site and need and make recommendations on both.

June 13   POP protestors stage mock hanging in Brougham.

June 21   Terms of reference for a "full" public inquiry are released.

June 22   Asked about inquiry, Marchand reaffirms "there is no doubt" it can receive evidence on need and location.

Oct. 5   Order-in-Council establishes Gibson Inquiry.

Oct. 23   New terms of reference released; inquiry will not be allowed to consider need or location of airport.

1974

Jan. 10   Ontario, able to obtain only 49 per cent of needed land, expropriates in Pickering.

March 13   Charles de Gaulle Airport opens outside Paris. Hailed as ex-
            ample of multi-airport systems, it is a disaster.
March 18   First public hearings of Gibson Commission.
June 5   Gibson Hearings end.
June 18   Report commissioned for City of Toronto condemns Picker-
            ing airport. City asks Gibson Commission to reopen to accept
            its brief.
Aug. 20   Authors of city study cross-examined for two days; dis-
            missed.
Dec. 23   Gibson Report to Privy Council Office.

1975
Jan. 31   Gibson Report public. Federal Cabinet considers it, shelves
            action, requests review.
Feb. 15   Michael Pitfield paper to Cabinet suggests phased develop-
            ment of Pickering Airport.
Feb. 20   Transport Minister Marchand announces a one-runway
            "Minimum Airport" for Pickering, gives cost as $204 million.
April 24   MTARC meets with Ontario cabinet committee; lawyer Wil-
            liam McMurtry argues that province has been misled.
April 30   POP holds Bulldozer Tea to recruit members to block con-
            struction equipment.
May 10   POP members meet Finance Minister Donald Macdonald in
            Ottawa. He tells them he can't accept their arguments be-
            cause they go against what is said by bureaucrats.
May 25   Article in *Toronto Sun* by Roy McMurtry, soon to be Attor-
            ney General, attacks airport.
May 27   Marchand and Premier Davis meet in Ottawa, Davis ex-
            presses concern about airport.
June 12   Marchand, in letter to Davis, acknowledges Ontario concern,
            but says airport will go ahead, anyway. He presses for com-
            mitment on provision of roads and sewers, doesn't get it.
July 1   At political picnic, Davis tells William McMurtry airport will
            be dropped.
July 6   Barrage ball on party at Lorne Almack's farm.
July 10   Ontario Transport Minister John Rhodes announces that the
            province will not provide airport infrastructure "at this time,"
            asks delay in building.
July 29   Ontario federal cabinet ministers meet in Ottawa, and the
            province again refuses to start infrastructure.
July 31   Marchand wires that construction not expected to begin on
            airport until after mid-September.
Aug. 13   Demolition of houses on site begins.
Aug. 15   Rhodes wires Marchand to complain, demands end of demo-
            lition.

Aug. 20	Marchand replies that "rough grading" won't start yet, but current work is only demolition.
Aug. 21	Under pressure, Marchand aide announces work will stop. Instead, fences and barricades are erected to keep demonstrators from protesting.
Aug. 22	Government explains that construction halt only applied to four houses.
Sept. 15	POP party at home of Ernie Carruthers. Three women leave party, take up residence in boarded-up house, defy bulldozers.
Sept. 18	Ontario election returns minority Conservative government. POP Chairman Charles Godfrey elected in Durham West.
Sept. 24	Ontario Cabinet meets, rejects airport, asks all work on site be stopped.
Sept. 25	Federal Cabinet shelves airport. Marchand and Trudeau are enraged.
Sept. 26	Otto Lang replaces Marchand as Transport Minister.
Oct. 1	Transport officials meet, agree to "cocoon" plans for Pickering until later.
Oct. 5	Official opening of Mirabel, late, and at double budget. Planes can't be received yet. At official opening, Trudeau says Torontonians will be "on their knees" begging for a second airport.
Oct. 10	Lang is briefed on Pickering.
Oct. 12	Lang announces that, because of the shelving of Pickering, Ontarians will soon have to fly through Montreal to get to Vancouver.
Oct. 17	"Go It Alone" option paper shows how feds could build Pickering without provincial co-operation.
Oct. 26	Mirabel opening postponed again.
Oct. 27	RCMP launches investigation into fraud in Mirabel contracts.
Nov. 30	Mirabel opens.

1976

May 7	Lang announces that, because of shelving of Pickering, air traffic will be diverted to Mirabel, overflying Toronto.
May 21	Lang announces no new air carriers will be allowed at Toronto until at least 1981.
June 8	Hugh Devitt, retiring General Manager at Malton, complains that Transport officials are stalling on improvements to make Ontario reverse Pickering decision.
July 7	Ontario Ombudsman Arthur Maloney reports that Pickering area residents were cheated and misled by government land agents.

July 26   TAAP reports a Malton expansion would cost $365 million, more than figure being publicly used for a second airport.

Aug. 12   Survey of Ontario travel agents show they avoid Mirabel "like the plague."

Aug. 25   TAAP press conference says Toronto must have a second airport.

Oct. 1   A Royal Commission will be established to deal with mistreatment of Pickering landowners.

Oct. 12   Lang says Toronto must have a second airport.

1977
Feb. 10   Mirabel reports first year passenger load much less than expected.

March 30 Ottawa announces Mirabel industrial land unused, will be made into a park instead.

April 21 Logan Airport in Boston begins ad campaign thanking Mirabel for lousy service, suggests flying overseas via Logan.

June 10   Transport Canada releases Contingency Plan, says Toronto faces fierce congestion, action must be taken at once.

1978
Jan. 12   Pickering landowners get better terms from federal government.

Feb. 16   Ontario changes land freeze order around Pickering to make it conform to other airport sites.

Feb. 28   Mirabel losses in first two years reported at $115 million. Lang says airport is a "great investment."

April 1   Via rail takes over passenger services from CN and CP Rail.

May   David MacAree, new Malton manager, hopes new airport will be started soon.

Nov. 8   Lang assures House of Commons no expansion will be allowed at Malton.

Nov. 28   Lang tells House that a study into the possibility of a fourth runway at Malton has been halted.

1979
Jan. 3   Montreal firm reports that STOL service, turned down by Toronto in June 1978, and supported by Transport Canada, is being planned for Montreal-Toronto run.

May 22   Conservatives form new federal government, but have no coherent transport policy.